mecanoo

francine houben

herbert wright

mecanoo
people   place   purpose   poetry

nai010 publishers

Contents

1 From Purpose to Poetry 6

2 Fitting In 8

12 Museum Kaap Skil
Texel, the Netherlands

18 Whistling Rock Golf Clubhouse
Chuncheon, Republic of Korea

24 Taekwang Country Club Café
Gyeonggi-do, Republic of Korea

28 Eurojust
The Hague, the Netherlands

34 Palace of Justice
Córdoba, Spain

44 De Nederlandsche Bank
Amsterdam, the Netherlands

52 Museum Boijmans Van Beuningen
Rotterdam, the Netherlands

58 Natural History Museum Abu Dhabi
Abu Dhabi, United Arab Emirates

3 Home Sweet Home 64

68 Kampus
Manchester, United Kingdom

76 Villa Industria
Hilversum, the Netherlands

82 Key Worker Housing, University of Cambridge
Cambridge, United Kingdom

88 Lawson Center for Sustainability, Trinity College
Toronto, Canada

92 Glass Villa on the Lake
Lechlade, United Kingdom

98 Villa Vught
Vught, the Netherlands

4 The Big Picture 106

110 A New Perspective for Rotterdam South
Rotterdam, the Netherlands

120 Dordrecht Railway Zone
Dordrecht, the Netherlands

128 Nieuw Land National Park
Flevoland, the Netherlands

5 Wisdom and Wizardry 134

140 Library Delft University of Technology
Delft, the Netherlands

148 LocHal Library
Tilburg, the Netherlands

158 Library of Birmingham
Birmingham, United Kingdom

168 Tainan Public Library
Tainan, Taiwan

178 Martin Luther King Jr. Memorial Library
Washington DC, United States of America

192 The New York Public Library, Stephen A. Schwarzman Building
New York, United States of America

214 The New York Public Library, Stavros Niarchos Foundation Library
New York, United States of America

6 Come Together 230

234 Longgang Cultural Centre
Shenzhen, China

242 Heerlen City Hall and Municipal Offices
Heerlen, the Netherlands

258 Unilever Benelux Headquarters
Rotterdam, the Netherlands

264 Amsterdam University College
Amsterdam, the Netherlands

272 Manchester Engineering Campus Development
Manchester, United Kingdom

7 Touch Me, Feel Me 284

288
Netherlands Open Air Museum
Arnhem, the Netherlands

296
Bruce C. Bolling Municipal Building
Boston, United States of America

304
St. Gerlach Pavilion & Manor Farm
Valkenburg, the Netherlands

312
Nelson Mandela Park
Amsterdam, the Netherlands

318
Westergasfabriek Terrain
Amsterdam, the Netherlands

326
Keukenhof
Lisse, the Netherlands

332
Mekel Park, Delft University
of Technology
Delft, the Netherlands

340
Delfland Water Authority
Delft, the Netherlands

8 Things are Looking Up 346

350
Montevideo
Rotterdam, the Netherlands

358
Icoon
Frankfurt, Germany

364
Kaohsiung Social Housing
Kaohsiung, Taiwan

370
Brink Tower
Amsterdam, the Netherlands

374
Heungkuk Tower Namdaemun
Seoul, South Korea

378
Heungkuk Tower Busan
Busan, South Korea

380
Shenzhen North Station
Urban Design,
Shenzhen, China

9 On the Move 386

390
St. Mary of the Angels Chapel
Rotterdam, the Netherlands

398
Hilton Amsterdam
Airport Schiphol
Schiphol, the Netherlands

404
Delft Railway Station
and City Hall
Delft, the Netherlands

416
Kaohsiung Station
Kaohsiung, Taiwan

427
Taichung Green Corridor
Taichung, Taiwan

10 Dear Audience 432

436
Trust Theater
Amsterdam, the Netherlands

440
National Kaohsiung Center
for the Arts
Kaohsiung, Taiwan

460
HOME Arts Centre
Manchester, United Kingdom

466
La Llotja de Lleida
Lérida, Spain

476
Kunsthal Art Shows
Rotterdam, the Netherlands

486
De Nieuwe Schuur
Herpt, the Netherlands

11 Forward to Basics 494

498
Beginnings

500
Leadership

502
Four Decades of Mecanoo

518
Project Data

523
Awards

526
Four Decades, 1500 people

528
Credits

1

From
Purpose
to Poetry

There's an expression for something that just doesn't make sense — it has 'no rhyme or reason'. What about the opposite? Something with 'reason' follows some logic, it has a purpose and it suggests that it is there by design. Clearly, architecture has this sort of reason. But what about 'rhyme'? The word usually applies to poetry. A poem is a composition that can resonate deep in our mind, generate emotion, conjure up magic, and evoke memories, either personal or collective. These are elusive things. They don't come from instructions in a design manual, but our intuition senses and finds them. If we can add rhyme to reason in architecture, it becomes poetic, and it is great architecture. That is what we find with the work of Mecanoo.

What Is the Path Mecanoo Has Taken To Poetry?

The practice was founded in the Netherlands in 1984 by a group of student architects including Francine Houben. She is now its principal and creative director, and its base remains in the historical city of Delft. Nowadays, Mecanoo is a global practice, with projects in four continents. Wherever their work is, what has always made it special has been a humanistic approach. That means that it recognizes the individual as someone unique, with innate dignity and goodness, capable of emotional fulfilment that can be encouraged by the right conditions. Architecture can be a benevolent agent, with a mission to help deliver the potential we all have, individually and collectively. Mecanoo's designs are progressive and social, because they are rooted in an intimate concern and sensitivity for people. Every design considers what people do in real life and makes it better — it creates space you want to be in, in which you feel human, and when it brings people together, it gives you social relevance.

Mecanoo also designs with a passion for place. Each space is crafted according to its location, and aims to make it even better without making it somewhere else, or (as with so much architecture) nowhere in particular. Every site for which a project is designed has certain elements that should make it unique. A project can draw on and enhance the assets of a location, for example its history, architecture, landscape or lifestyle. It can also address the deficits of a location, for example by bringing facilities or identity where they are lacking. A Mecanoo project creates a new place with its own presence, but it is defined by, and unique to, the place that is already there.

Every architectural commission has a purpose, or function, to deliver. That may be to house people, host cultural activity, create a workplace or deliver a transport link. Formulaic design can produce solutions to serve each purpose, but if the concerns of the users are at the core of the design and it is contextual to its location, the purpose itself is enhanced.

A Fresh Look

In 2015, Houben assessed her practice's philosophy and history in a book called after these three key considerations — People Place Purpose. It was Hubert-Jan Henket, the founder of DOCOMO (an international organization dedicated to modernist buildings) who once suggested that Mecanoo's 'three Ps should actually be four'. The fourth he referred to is poetry. Mecanoo forges a trail through people, place and purpose to that poetry.

This new book is not just an update on the last one. We offer a completely fresh look at Mecanoo's work, and it's structured differently. It will group projects that have things in common, such as typology (their function and form) or a particular attribute (for example, it moves or is tall). It's a good time for this new appraisal, for three reasons.

First, things have moved on since 2015. Mecanoo is prolific as well as progressive, and nowadays, it is more productive than ever before. Unlike many practices, Mecanoo has never had a 'visual signature style', so there is a surprisingly diverse range of new Mecanoo designs, from a futuristic arts centre with the largest roof of any in the world (see p. 440) to a small chapel in a cemetery (see p. 390). We will show them with the help of some great photography, sketches and drawings.

Second, it is now almost twenty years since Mecanoo completed the design for their first project beyond the Netherlands, a concert hall and conference centre called La Llotja de Lleida (see p. 466). What has been learnt since then? Projects in the pipeline now may take years to be realized, but they have already boarded the train to the future. That future is changing. The world is in flux, swept up in climate change, ceaseless urbanization, the digitization of systems, knowledge and life, and global shifts in power, population and wealth. What will these forces demand of architecture? How will Mecanoo respond to them, after another twenty years on the international stage? The Netherlands has always been challenged by the world around it — a sea that, if left unchecked, would have long ago submerged its population, and a land so confined to work with that it has had to be re-engineered. The Dutch know how to build from disaster. But the answers to tomorrow's challenges must also lie in Mecanoo's constant, consistent concerns of people, place and purpose. How do people find an identity in this changing world? How is the sense of place preserved when the context is transformed?

Third, we can take our fresh view with that idea of poetry in mind. It's more crucial than ever. We need that elusive, emotional dimension beyond just purpose that can be sensed in a really special building.

2
Fitting In

In a globalized world, there is a clear trend towards architecture that looks the same everywhere. Too often, it is stripped of any reference to local history or geography, and ignores vernacular styles that made the built environment of a city, region or country distinctive. This is nothing new. The Romans, for example, spread the architectural language of columns, colonnades and other classical elements throughout their empire, and had in any case taken these ideas from the Greeks before them. A Roman temple built in Britain would be much the same as one in North Africa. Similarly, the beautiful sixteenth-century Italian villas that Andrea Palladio built inspired an architectural style that in just two centuries would spread from St Petersburg to Massachusetts.

But every place is different. Each has a local dialect not just in spoken language, but in the way the landscape, the cityscape and each vernacular building speak of its unique identity. Contemporary buildings can join in the conversation, expressing themselves in this local dialect but saying something new. It's like architects asking the place, 'may we join you?'

Mecanoo's architecture has always responded to its location, from the very first built work, the Kruisplein affordable, flexible housing project for young people in Rotterdam. The city is dominated by post-war modernism, much of it bland, but Kruisplein is distinctive with its balconies and touches of colour, it has a style which echoes great social housing projects by le Corbusier, and one of its two blocks is not afraid to curve elegantly to follow the street. Although completed in 1985, the heyday of postmodernist architecture (which mixed historical architectural features and styles), this is no post-modern pastiche. It's more like a poem in the language of modernism, written just for the street it stands on.

Jagged Roofline

A fishing village on a Dutch island called Texel is the very different setting of **Museum Kaap Skil** (2011). Two things strike you as you approach it — its jagged roofline, like a wild graph plot, and its skin of thin vertical wooden slats, closely and regularly separated, allowing light through the gaps. Probably the only other museum with a flat facade and zig-zag roofline is Zaha Hadid's contemporaneous Transport Museum in Glasgow, but that doesn't reference its location. Kaap Skil's zig-zag peaks, however, echo the steep pitched roofs of the village, and the slats are all cut from re-used Dutch canal hardwood sheet-piling. That gives the building a wonderful wind- and water-weathered texture. The main museum gallery upstairs, under a white jagged ceiling, is full of light, yet most of it is filtered by dark wood. The ground floor café and shop receive light from both sides, between the brick floor and slatted wood ceiling. In the basement no daylight is needed for the special exhibitions that are on display. Kaap Skil resonates with the sea, and incorporates elements from it, from the wide light of its open sky to the weathered woods the sea washes up on the shore.

Belvedere

Wood plays a different role in the facades of the **Whistling Rock Golf Clubhouse** (2012) in the hilly countryside around the Korean town of Chuncheon. Spaced vertical beams of laminated wood seem to support a heavy monolithic slab roof which mirrors a thick plinth beneath it. They sandwich a recessed two-storey glazed facade around the main part of the building, creating a belvedere in the hilly landscape. Thinner horizontal wood at different heights creates window frames that vary with a gently jazzy rhythm. The clubhouse's long rectangular horizontal form stretches no less than 123 metres, and it floats on a landscape that is so up and down that the ground actually drops away from under the building at one end. The form of the 7,500 m^2 building has something of the long, low Prairie style of Frank Lloyd Wright, but with a simpler geometry. Inside, there are walls and floors of the same travertine marble as in the roof and plinth, its smoothness a contrast to the rugged rock outside. There is a conversation between this building and its location. The expanses of glazing bring the full panorama of the golf course, forests and mountains into the building itself. And out there, we also find three small satellite tea houses with different forms, nestling in the hillsides. One of them is particularly sculptural — an organic cocoon pavilion with circular entrances at each end. Wright said of his Prairie houses that they are 'married to the ground'. That certainly applies to the horizontal clubhouse, but here the marriage creates a striking juxtaposition.

Mecanoo's architectural prowess shines through in their design of the **Taekwang Country Club Café** (2015), a 36-hole golf course situated just outside Seoul in Gyeonggi-do. Tucked within the hilly terrain, the new two-floor café serves as a distinctive landmark on the course, seamlessly integrating with the picturesque Korean landscape and local flora. The café's design invites golfers to catch glimpses of it from various vantage points across the course. While still maintaining an element of concealment, it adds a touch of intrigue. Adorned with an intricate pattern of interlocking circles, the striking oversized black steel roof creates a spacious and encompassing canopy. And that's not all… With floor-to-ceiling windows, the Country Club Café's transparent facade offers beautiful panoramic views of the golf course and the city, just like a picture-perfect postcard of the golfing world.

Giving Justice its Place

Eurojust, the home of the EU's judicial agency for cross-border crime completed in 2017, is another composition of straight lines and right angles. Security is paramount, and the landscape helps provide it. Situated in the Dutch city of The Hague, Eurojust sits beside undulating sand dunes, which have been colonized by vegetation and stretch inland towards the downtown high-rise skyline. Eurojust has two volumes, one a mid-rise square tower that makes a monumental presence from the road. Adjoining it is a long box, with the same rhythms of full-height, subtly tilted windows, which are framed in the same crisp, white solid envelope.

What makes Eurojust specific to its location is the way Mecanoo and landscapers DS landschapsarchitecten have extended the sand-dune terrain. It lies behind embankments threaded by walls of corten steel that line the otherwise dull major road on one side and bend to become the building's access gate, which is actually buried in a new dune around the corner. Inside this fortification, hardy biodiverse plantings erupt all around the building. Two glass curtain-walled basement levels face a wall over which water trickles, nurturing plants growing in its layers of natural stone. At Eurojust, nature not only helps build a protective security buffer around the building, it also brings sustainability and beauty deep inside the building.

In completely urban environments, local inspiration can lurk in the buildings that already characterize the city. Another great justice building, also completed in 2017, is the **Palace of Justice** in Córdoba, Spain. Designed with local practice Ayesa, it seems to be sculpted from a long bright white monolithic block. Its sheer size transforms its neighbourhood of repetitive high-density apartment blocks. Luckily, the city has another urbanism to draw inspiration from — the UNESCO World Heritage site of the historic centre, full of vernacular buildings. They date from the centuries up to 1236, when Islamic Córdoba was one of the world's most important cities of learning. Features of the Islamic architecture that brought relief from the local hot, dry climate have inspired features in the new building. Its glass-fibre reinforced concrete cladding is perforated with geometric screens that filter bright sunshine into gentle interior light. The vast block has vertical cuts that create cool, shady patios, some beneath overhangs, which reach into the volume to the central circulation spine. They are like twenty-first century updates of Córdoba's ancient courtyards, and are surfaced with gold-coloured perforated ceramic panels. The entrance is in a shady void beside a new plaza apron. It cuts deeply into one corner of the block, beneath a cantilever that carries the auditorium, and opens out from the building at the same angle of the auditorium seating above it.

Tower and Plinth

So far, we have looked at entirely new buildings, but the question of fitting in with the location applies to the transformation of existing buildings too. The **De Nederlandsche Bank** (DNB) project is an excellent example. In 1961, architect Marius Duintjer unveiled his design for the Dutch national bank's new headquarters building beside the Singel canal in central Amsterdam. The overall shape seemed to follow the 1950s American modernist office block formula of 'tower and plinth', in which a rectilinear slab tower rises from a low, wide building. The DNB's tower rose from the ground over a car park within the lower three-storey rectangular building. The bank moved in in 1968 and subsequently, a cylindrical tower was added as well as a third floor on top of the plinth building. DNB was an Amsterdam landmark, but people didn't like it. It felt disconnected from the neighbourhood and the historical city. Holding the Netherland's gold reserves, it was a functional requirement that this building would be impregnable and self-sufficient, a fortress in the city.

Mecanoo's transformation opens up the building, to make it a Place for both People and Nature. The whole plinth building has been reglazed for maximum transparency, showing off the airy interior, and a large new entrance facing the park has been cut through the concrete structure of the vault, which had once stored gold reserves. A bridge cuts across a new, naturally lit underground exhibition space for art and historic coins and banknotes. Atria up to three storeys high extend down to the basement level. An accessible sculpture garden grows where the car park had been, bordered by a restaurant, café, and learning centre, and overlooked by a double-height meeting centre that retains distinctive original columns (which are 'high-tech', years before it became an architectural style). The original slab tower remains as offices. Photovoltaics are placed on all its roofs. Another garden on the other side of the tower is on the first floor. These gardens do more than offer visitors tranquillity and proximity to nature, they also boost biodiversity, and include insect hotels and bird boxes. Along with a top-floor terrace garden on one side of the plinth and an extended public quay adjacent to the canal on the other side, the DNB is now animated with greenery.

The building itself is super-charged with sustainable features, from a geothermal heat pump and a heat recovery system to openable windows that breathe air in the cupboard-like gaps between inner and outer glass. All this helps reduce DNB's energy demand and CO_2 emissions by four-fifths. But just as significant, the building architecturally embraces the concept of 'circularity', which aims to create zero waste, and everything is recycled or re-usable. The principle applies from the use of circular certified materials in construction to dismantling the entire round tower and shipping it off for use elsewhere.

Does the new DNB fit in with Amsterdam's traditional urban fabric, which the original building disrupted in many ways, such as height and separation from the street? No, but the transformed building strongly fits in with a new idea of urban fabric, which applies to cities everywhere. That idea is to open it up to the public, integrate nature ever deeper into the city, and dissolve barriers to the movement, interaction, and pleasures of people in its built environment.

Connecting to City and Park

Mecanoo are crafting the transformation of another twentieth-century landmark building in the Netherlands' other world city, Rotterdam. The **Museum Boijmans Van Beuningen** has one of the Netherlands' greatest art collections. 'The Boijmans', as it is known, was originally a 1935 building designed by architect Ad van der Steur. Inspired by the Stadhuset (1923) in Stockholm, he designed a similar iconic tower rising over austere brick facades. The museum was expanded in 1972 with another great brick wing, designed by Alexander Bodon. After two more extensions, this great museum became a challenge for visitors to navigate, and even finding the entrance was not obvious. Its solid walls disconnected it from the city centre, just minutes away to its east, or even the adjacent Museumpark, a green oasis with water gardens, lawns and trees. The museum had turned its back on the park, but that was already changing. The MVRDV-designed Depot (2022), the latest Boijmans building, which displays art held in storage, reflects the park in the mirrored surface of its distinctive vase-like shape. But it is a new, separate building, while Mecanoo, on the other hand, takes the pre-existing museum as its starting point.

Francine Houben summarizes the design approach as 'opening up the museum, connecting it to the city and park, and strengthening the museum as part of the Museumpark'. The architecture of Van der Steur and Bodon is respected and more extensively revealed, while a new volume will create a new, open exhibition space. A new entrance that is clear, obvious and inviting will draw people into and through the museum. The loading bay, which frankly was an intrusion in the heart of Boijmans, will be relocated. The park is the key to fitting in. A passage through the heart of the museum will lead from the city and street directly into it. A new piece of park, and a belvedere designed to see and be seen from the park, will banish the museum-park disconnection of the past. At the same time, there is now access to an underground loading dock. The reborn Boijmans will belong to the People, and they will animate both park and museum. As Houben says, it is in how it will 'imagine, amaze, inspire within a historical inner-city context' that the Poetry of the project lies.

Creating Wonder

The very different Mecanoo-designed **Natural History Museum** is coming to Abu Dhabi, which like its sister emirate Dubai has rapidly urbanized. In 2017, it stepped onto the international cultural stage with the Louvre Abu Dhabi designed by Jean Nouvel, housed under a huge scintillating, perforated dome. Not far along the waterfront, Mecanoo's new volume is under construction and it will be vast. Its 35,000 m² area puts it in the same size league as the world's greatest natural history museums in London and New York, making it the second largest of the five museums which the Saadiyat Cultural District will eventually host. They will include Frank Gehry's Guggenheim Abu Dhabi, which echoes the shapes of his iconic original Guggenheim in Bilbao, and the Zayed National Museum designed by Foster+Partners, whose five curving ventilation towers are shaped like the wings of a falcon, a symbol of the UAE. How does Mecanoo's new grand new museum fit into an emerging quarter with such expressive architectural wonders?

The answer lies in both its Purpose and Place. The museum's mission, to explain and create wonder about the natural world, also inspires a form suggesting vertical rock outcrops, abstracted in white and like clusters of pentagonal columns. The idea resonates with the exposed ancient dolomites and volcanic rocks of Abu Dhabi's islands. These islands are also home to 436 native plant species, and mangroves, so greenery also inspires the design. Imagine the Hanging Gardens of Babylon, which was one of the Seven Wonders of the World compiled by the Ancient Greeks, re-evoked in the twenty-first century! In reality, we don't know what the original structures looked like, where they were, or even if they actually existed. But a consistent thread runs through the idea of how they should have looked — there were tiers of garden terraces. The new museum will feature exactly that, with vegetation spilling down across the facades from its roof terraces, which step down all the way to shady waterside gardens. Amongst its futuristic, often high-tech neighbours, Mecanoo's landmark building honours the poetry of an ancient architectural legend — but it also visibly messages that Nature is part of the future we must build.

Each of these projects contains an intuitive leap — the recognition that there is something out there in the particular location to inspire the design. That approach is what makes a project fit in, and helps to keep the contemporary world a world of distinct, local Places.

Museum Kaap Skil

Texel, the Netherlands

Discipline:

Architecture

Typology:

Museum/Exhibition

Size: 1,200 m²
Design: 2007-2009
Realization: 2010-2011
Client: Maritiem & Juttersmuseum

Design team: Mecanoo

Programme: Museum building of 1,200 m², exhibition galleries, café and offices.

Link

FITTING IN

The vertical wooden slats are made of sawn hardwood sheet-piling from the North Holland Canal

The four playfully linked zig-zag roofs echo the steep pitched roofs of the surrounding village.

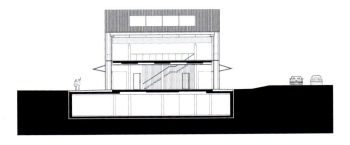

The size of the basement is defined by an 18 by 4 metre model about the history of the island.

RECLAIMED WOOD

2007-2011　　　　　　　　　　Texel, the Netherlands　　　　　　　　　15

The upper museum gallery is full of light, filtered by the dark wooden slats, creating a beautiful play of light and shadow.

The museum's rich collection of washed-up objects surfaced by divers are on display in movable glass and steel showcases.

FITTING IN

The museum shop and restaurant connect to the open-air museum.

A large model showcases the anchorage of ships of the Dutch East India Company before sailing from Texel to Asia in the seventeenth and eighteenth century.

In the open-air museum, you can experience life on Texel as it was in the past and visit fishermen's cottages, a smithy and a mill.

2007-2011   Texel, the Netherlands

Whistling Rock Golf Clubhouse

Chuncheon, Republic of Korea

Discipline:

Architecture

Typology:

Leisure

Size: 11,400 m²
Design: 2007-2009
Realization: 2010-2012
Client: Dong Lim Development Co.

Link

Design team: Mecanoo (lead architect),
Gansam Architects & Partners (local architect)
and Pinnacle Landscape Company (landscape architect).

Programme: 11,400 m² golf clubhouse on a 27-hole golf course including a start house, three tea houses, restaurants, pro shop, wine cellar, banquet rooms, bathing areas, multiple lobbies, and a parking garage.

We took the beautiful mountain landscape as the design inspiration for the golf clubhouse

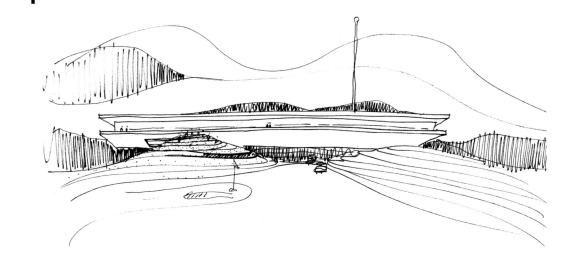

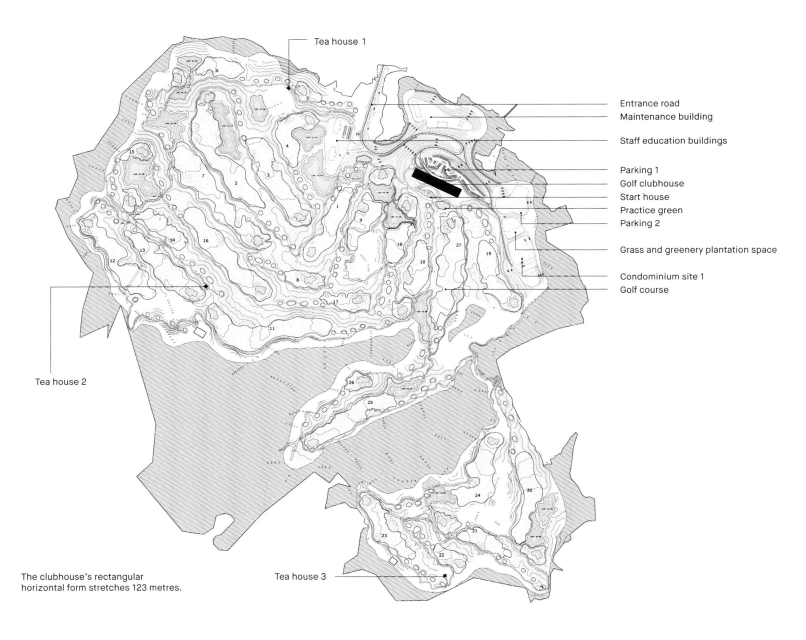

Tea house 1

Entrance road
Maintenance building

Staff education buildings

Parking 1
Golf clubhouse
Start house
Practice green
Parking 2

Grass and greenery plantation space

Condominium site 1
Golf course

Tea house 2

Tea house 3

The clubhouse's rectangular horizontal form stretches 123 metres.

Whistling Rock Golf Clubhouse

The transparent facade is set in between two horizontal natural stone slabs.

The golf clubhouse has been designed as a room with a view

FITTING IN

The clubhouse is rather like a museum, where members and visitors are invited to celebrate culture and nature.

The restaurant has a bamboo patio.

Three tea houses, designed as sculptural objects, serve as visual icons within the landscape.

2007–2012   Chuncheon, Republic of Korea

Taekwang Country Club Café

Gyeonggi-do,
Republic of Korea

Discipline:

Architecture

Typology:

Leisure

Link

Size: 300 m²
Design: 2014
Realization: 2015
Client: Taekwang Leisure Development

Design team: Mecanoo

Programme: 300 m² pavilion on a 36-hole golf course including café, kitchen, and service areas.

FITTING IN

The two-floor café is nestled in a steep hill, acting as a visual point of reference on the golf course.

The expressive black steel roof of interlocking circles produces a generous all-sided canopy for the Country Club Café

The Country Club Café's transparent facade offers a beautiful panorama of the golf course and the city.

Eurojust

The Hague, the Netherlands

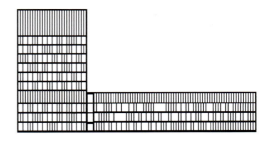

Discipline:

Architecture, Interior

Typology:

Office, Government/Civic

Size: 18,500 m²
Design: 2011-2014
Realization: 2014-2017
Client: Rijksgebouwendienst (Central Government Real Estate Agency) and Ministry of Security and Justice.

Design team: Mecanoo (lead architect) and DS landschapsarchitecten (landscape design).

Programme: 18,500 m² high security office building for the agency of the European Union dealing with judicial co-operation in criminal matters among agencies of the EU member states, including office and conference facilities, restaurant, underground parking for 272 cars, and integrated landscape design, BREEAM-NL Very Good.

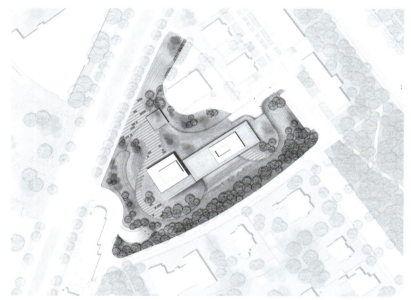

Eurojust is linked to The Hague's International Zone by an undulating dune landscape with grassy vegetation and wild flowers

Eurojust, the home of the EU's judicial agency for cross-border crime, is a composition of two volumes: a mid-rise tower and a low-rise plinth.

FITTING IN

The facades have a rhythm of full-height, subtly tilted windows, which are framed in a crisp, white solid envelope.

Visitors are welcomed in a spacious, double height lobby with views out onto the dune garden.

2011-2017　　　　The Hague, the Netherlands　　　　31

↗ A wide staircase, overlooking the dune landscape, descends to the two-floor conference centre.

↑ Representatives of the EU-member states meet weekly in the College Meeting Room with its characteristic double oval layout.

↓ The Conference Centre on -1 and -2 has breakout spaces with private meeting rooms as well as informal seating areas.

FITTING IN

↑ The two glass curtain-walled basement levels face a wall which water trickles over, nurturing plants growing in layers of natural stone.

Nature not only helps build a protective security buffer, it also brings daylight and green deep inside the building

Palace of Justice

Córdoba, Spain

Discipline:

Architecture

Typology:

Office, Government/Civic

Size: 48,000 m²
Design: 2006
Realization: 2014-2017
Client: Junta de Andalucía

Design Team: Mecanoo (lead architect) and Ayesa (engineering).

Programme: 48,000 m² courthouse including 26 courtrooms, wedding room, Forensic Institute, offices, café, archive, jail cells and parking garage.

Link

Vertical cuts create cool, shady patios in the vast block

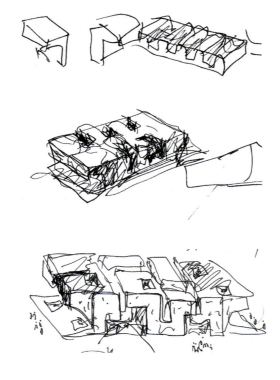
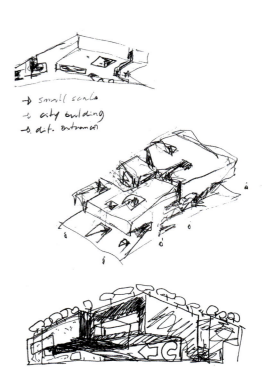

The massing strategy follows the spontaneous growth of medieval Córdoba with its informal, green patios.

Inspired by geometric patterns, the glass-fibre reinforced concrete cladding is perforated, filtering the bright sunshine into gentle interior light.

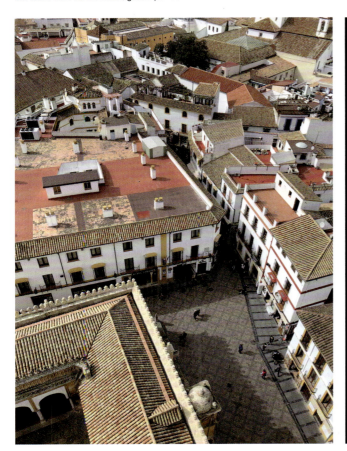

The building volume was condensed to allow space for a generous entrance square.

→ The patios have distinctive facades, reminiscent of Córdoba's typical filigree-worked jewels.

SHELTERED PATIOS

The entrances cut deeply into the corners of the building

FITTING IN

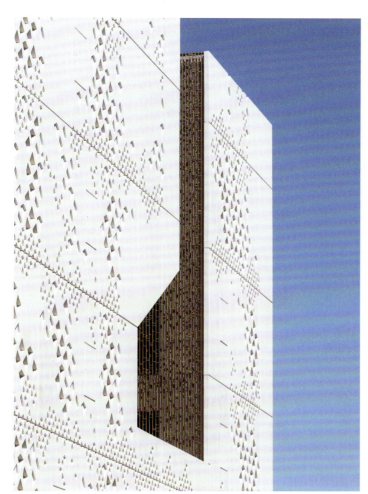

2006–2017 — Córdoba, Spain

FILTERING SUNSHINE

The Palace of Justice has 26 courtrooms of different sizes and shapes.

A central axis cuts through the building and connects to the various courtrooms.

FITTING IN

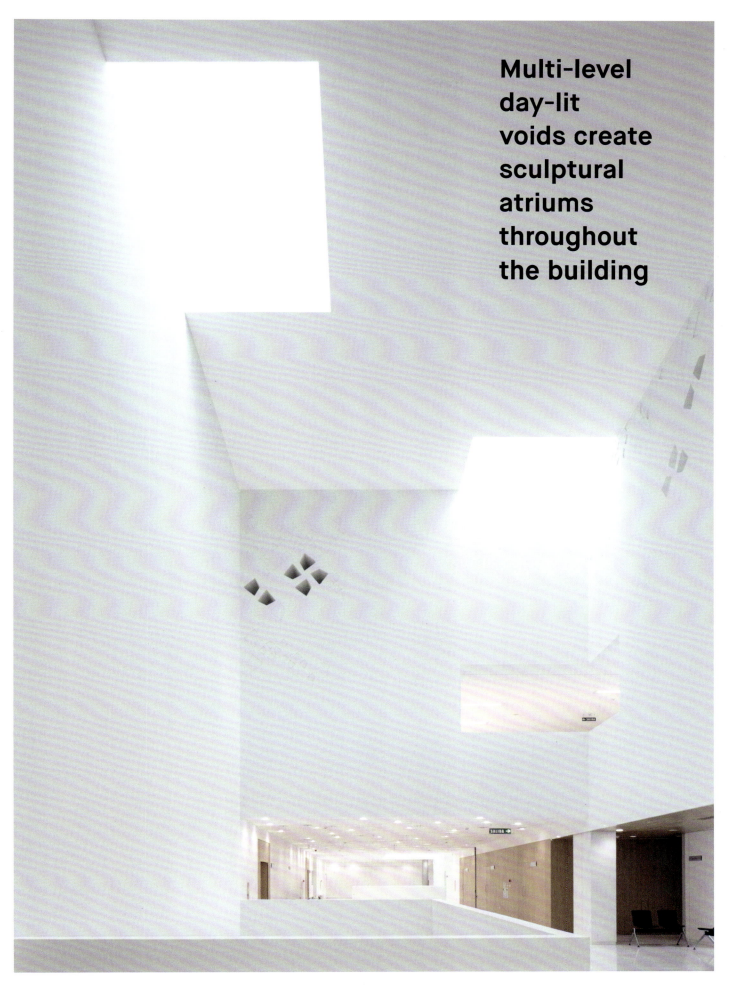

Multi-level day-lit voids create sculptural atriums throughout the building

2006-2017 — Córdoba, Spain

De Nederlandsche Bank

Amsterdam, the Netherlands

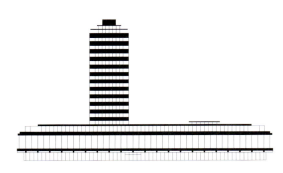

Discipline:

Architecture, Interior, Landscape, Restoration

Typology:

Transformation, Office, Government/Civic

Size: 67,000 m²
Design: 2018-2020
Realization: 2020-2025
Client: De Nederlandsche Bank

Design team: Mecanoo

Programme: 67,000 m² renovation and transformation of the 1968 building of the central bank of the Netherlands in the historic city centre of Amsterdam, including new entrance area, information, exhibition and education spaces, lobby, auditorium, reception areas, staff restaurant, staff fitness room, work space environment, new atrium of 400 m² with stairs, three zones of security from public to high security zones, and landscape design park, patios and roof gardens, BREEAM Outstanding and WELL Platinum.

2
TRANSFORMATION OF A MODERNIST BUILDING

6 November 1961: Architect Marius Duintjer, Mayor Gijs van Hall and DNB President Marius Holtrop around the model of the new Nederlandsche Bank headquarters.

1968

A cylindrical tower was added in 1991.

FITTING IN

In Mecanoo's vision, Frederiksplein transforms from a square into a neighbourhood park.

Circularity plays an important role in the Nederlandsche Bank project. The cylindrical tower has been dismantled and will be reused.

Distinctive columns form a characteristic element in the old and renovated building.

On the Singel Canal, people can sit on a wooden jetty and watch boats sail by

Employees have their office in the low-rise as well as in the tower that is being renovated to become highly sustainable.

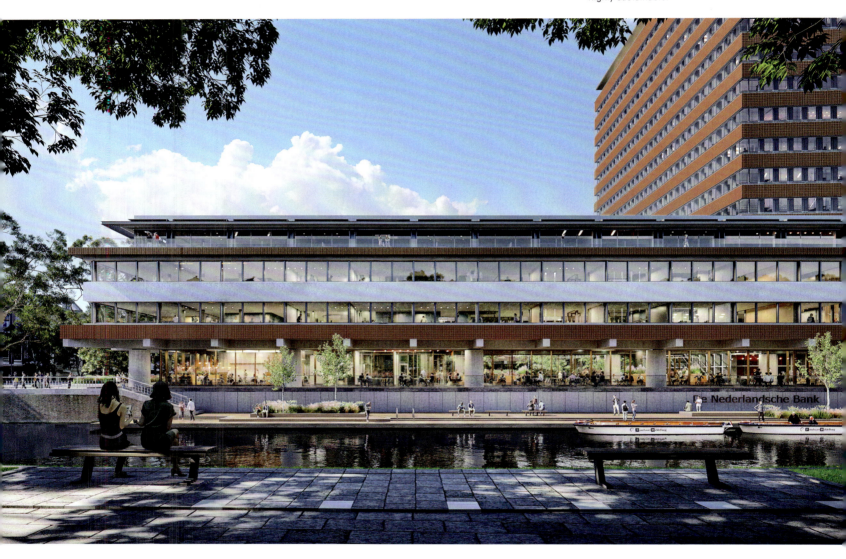

The car park for employees on the ground floor makes way for a spacious staff restaurant with a view to the Singel canal.

FITTING IN

The former Cash Centre transforms into a Meeting Centre with the historic columns and spiralling staircase as iconic features.

A spectacular atrium connects the floors of the low-rise building from level -2 to +2. The stepped seating invites people to informally meet.

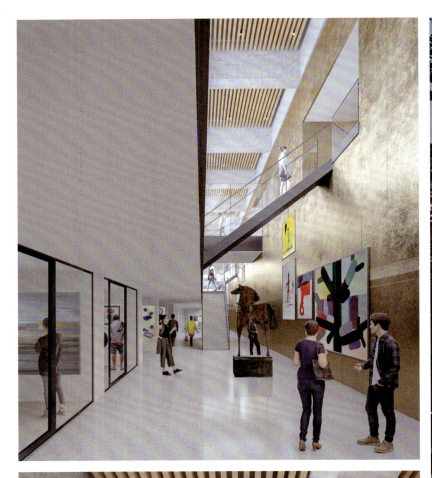

↖ Voids create a free-standing theatrical space for exhibitions, seminars, lectures and debates that extends from level -2 to the ground floor.

↑ The large patio has been freed up by removing the cylindrical tower and is now a public green oasis in the buzzing city where part of the bank's art collection can be seen.

FITTING IN

CITY GARDEN

Mecanoo's transformation opens up the building, to make it a place for both people and nature

2018-2025 — Amsterdam, the Netherlands

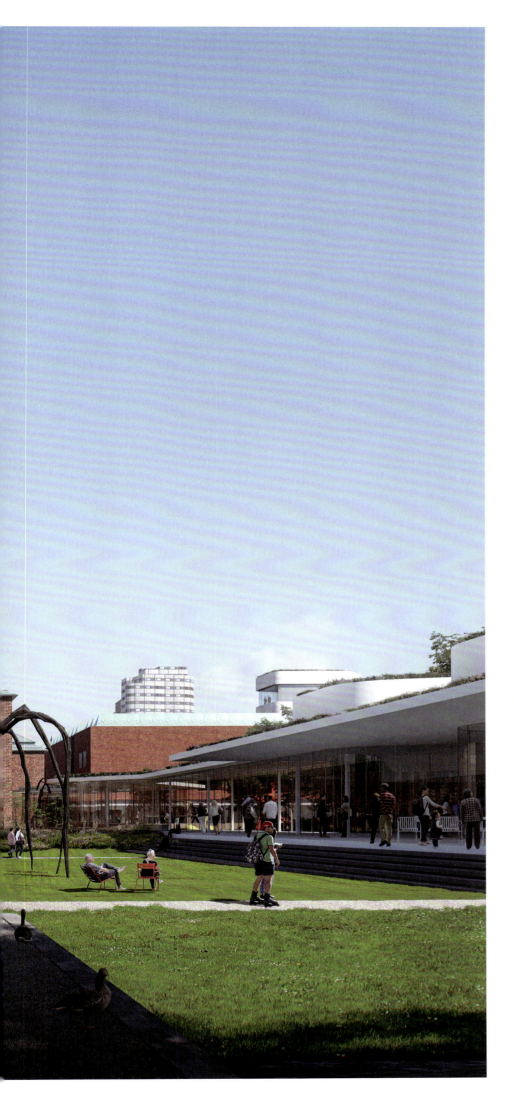

Museum Boijmans Van Beuningen

Rotterdam, the Netherlands

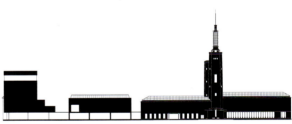

Discipline:

Architecture, Interior, Landscape, Restoration

Typology:

Transformation, Museum/Exhibition

Size: 25,000 m²
Design: 2019-2024
Realization: 2024-2029, expected
Client: Municipality of Rotterdam

Design team: Mecanoo (lead architect) and BBM architecten (restoration architect).

Programme: Winning competition design for the restoration and transformation of an approx. 25,000 m² partly listed museum building and associated outdoor space, including a new entrance area with museum shop, exhibition spaces, flow of people and goods, educational spaces, café, event space, logistics centre, depots, offices, workshops, facility spaces, and landscape design.

53

VAN DER STEUR

↑ In 1935 the Museum with Museumpark opens its doors. The building was designed by city architect Adriaan van der Steur (1893-1953).

← ↓ In 1972, a new wing is added, designed by architect Alexander Bodon (1906-1993) for temporary modern art exhibitions, including three flexible, white halls with diffuse skylight.

& BODON

In 2019 Mecanoo wins the competition for the renovation and restoration of the Museum Boijmans Van Beuningen. Its collection of 151,000 objects is among the top 50 in the world. The competition design will be further developed.

Competition design: the new entrance is clear, obvious and inviting, and draws people into and through the museum.

Opening up the museum to the city and the public

2019-2029   Rotterdam, the Netherlands

Competition design: the patio in the Van der Steur wing, formerly a logistics yard, transforms into an outdoor exhibition and event space.

Competition design: the new Park Pavilion in the park will have a partly double-height exhibition space.

A meandering route leads to a new pavilion in the Museumpark

Competition design: the café is integrated in the new entrance zone and overlooks the museum garden.

Competition design: the Van der Steur (right) and Bodon (left) wings are being restored to their original strength. With the addition of the Mecanoo wing, the museum better connects to the city and park, including good logistics for both visitors and back of house.

CONNECTING TO CITY & PARK

Natural History Museum Abu Dhabi

Abu Dhabi, United Arab Emirates

Discipline:

Architecture, Landscape, Interior

Typology:

Museum/Exhibition

Size: 35,000 m²
Design: 2020-2022
Realization: 2022-2025
Client: Department of Culture and Tourism, Abu Dhabi (DCT Abu Dhabi) in partnership with Miral.

Concept design team: Mecanoo (architecture, interior and landscape design), Aurecon (architect of record), Arcadis (engineering), Theateradvies (theatre consultant), Trinity Design (landscape consultant), Plan A (design management).

Programme: 35,000 m² iconic museum on a 82,000 m² site, including plaza, gardens and waterfront, galleries, display areas, café, education centre, laboratories, logistics and operations, public spaces, research and administrative facilities, V.I.P. areas, multipurpose and event space and parking (206 spaces).

2

GEOMETRY

Every element of the design uses geometry as an overriding theme, with pentagonal shapes resembling cellular structures

The museum will showcase the world-famous 'Stan', a 11.7-metre-long Tyrannosaurus rex, the Murchison Meteorite specimen, and other spectacular collections.

Natural History Museum, Abu Dhabi

FITTING IN

Vegetation spills down across the facades, from the roof terraces to the shaded waterside garden

2020–2025 · Abu Dhabi, United Arab Emirates

2

In the museum, visitors will travel on a 13.8-billion-year journey through time and space, which will include a thought-provoking perspective into a sustainable future for planet Earth.

Natural History Museum, Abu Dhabi

The Natural History Museum has Abu Dhabi's Louvre, Guggenheim and Abrahamic Family House as its neighbours

3

Home
Sweet
Home

Shelter is a basic human need, like food, water, sleep, and companionship. To come home and feel secure in your own private space is one thing, but to come back to a beautiful home is something else, bringing pleasure in addition to filling needs. The Dutch were the first to frame this feeling, literally, in the paintings of domestic interiors from the Netherlands' Golden Age. They intimately reveal the contentment, protection, comfort, order and stillness of being at home. It was in Delft that Pieter de Hooch captured these elements in the 1650s, and inspired another masterful painter, Johannes Vermeer, also of Delft.

Of course, Delft is the home of Mecanoo. Their very first project, completed in 1985 at Kruisplein, was a flexible housing complex in nearby Rotterdam. It started from the optimistic proposition that, as Francine Houben says, 'social housing should be beautiful, and pleasant to live in'. That sense of optimism still drives Mecanoo's residential designs, whether they are new housing for local communities or students, secluded villas or hip, cosmopolitan lifestyle developments in the big city. What does an urban neighbourhood have in common with a rural retreat? Something rather big — they are both places for humans!

Eclectic Neighbourhood

In Manchester, England, a boom in high-rise living is transforming the skyline and abandoned Victorian industrial buildings are being converted to meet the demand for loft-style living. At **Kampus**, Mecanoo not only combines both these contemporary lifestyle trends, but creates an eclectic neighbourhood that's just about the coolest downtown place to meet, drink, eat and hang out. Surprisingly, although it distils the energy and heritage of Manchester, Kampus also has some very Dutch elements.

Completed in 2021, the 44,000 m² development is on a city-block site near Piccadilly, Manchester's main station, and directly across a canal from the Gay Village quarter. There are six buildings, the oldest two mid-nineteenth-century warehouses that have been converted to apartments by Shed KM architects and retain original cast-iron columns and brick inside them. The cobbled passage between them has been re-opened as a street, with a single original iron fire escape suspended above it, like so many in New York or Chicago, but older. The site's biggest heritage building was the 12-storey Manchester Metropolitan University square concrete office tower, built in 1964. Dull and sad when it was vacated, its facades have been jazzed up with steel sandwiched between brighter, renewed horizontal concrete banding, with just a few cantilevering balconies teasingly disrupting the regularity of the block's shape. Three new steel-clad storeys are added. On either side, two new 15-storey blocks supercharge the site's density, giving it a dense, downtown feel and delivering 352 of the 533 apartments across Kampus. Manchester is a city dominated by brick, and it clads the new blocks. Again, there is an occasional teasing disruption in the facades, this time with protruding concrete rectangles which angle inwards to frame windows as if zooming in on them. Most surprising are the penthouses, which occupy forms with pitched roofs like Dutch-style houses — but elevated to Manchester's skyline.

That's not the only Dutch echo at Kampus. Between the canal and the secluded public garden, lush and enclosed by the residential blocks, there is the sixth building, a plain bungalow curiously raised off the ground. Now painted black and repurposed as a bar, it is at the heart of the hip social buzz that animates Kampus. Sitting at its waterside tables below, there is something about it like being next to a canal in the heart of Amsterdam...

Referencing the Industrial Past

In the Netherlands, with the second highest national population density in the EU, land is in short supply. So brownfield sites such as disused gasworks are especially good opportunities to build homes for the Dutch, and they come with memories of the industrial past that can be woven into new neighbourhoods. In the **Villa Industria** (2018) project in the town of Hilversum, Mecanoo has masterplanned a new neighbourhood on the site of a former gasworks. The development of 357 homes and spaces for small-businesses includes three towers of eight, ten and 12 storeys with 120 apartments, which rise within open cylindrical lattices of slender steelwork that are the same shape as the gasometers that once loomed there. The buildings, which include affordable housing, are characterized by red brick, some marked by bold V brick reliefs. Red brick extends to a new sports hall, which stands on a steel support with a strong presence at street level. It sits on top of a renovated swimming pool. The contaminated soil was removed to create an underground parking garage. Villa Industria is a walkable neighbourhood where children are safe from traffic, and its materials and forms referencing the industrial past in contemporary architecture make it a wonderful place to call home.

Affordable Key Worker Housing

Both Kampus and Villa Industria create high-density urban housing by building mid-rise — and elsewhere we will meet Mecanoo high-rise residential projects, such as Rotterdam's Montevideo (see p. 350) Icoon at Frankfurt Grand Central (see p. 358), and Amsterdam's Brink Tower (see p. 370). But building high is unacceptable in many historic settings, such as Cambridge, England, which is also one of the world's top academic hubs. That brings pressures and the University of Cambridge struggles to fit into its small host town. In 2018, in a brand-new district called Eddington, Mecanoo's **Key Worker Housing** was completed, so named because the complex offers 232 affordable housing units for the university's researchers and key workers. Up to five storeys high, the seven yellow brick buildings are inspired by the layout of the Cambridge colleges with their courtyards, but with windows that vary in size, frame and off-grid positions. They hide an integrated acoustic and ventilation system to provide protection from the noise of the nearby highway. The five-sided site they occupy gives an angled configuration to the blocks and the courtyards they enclose. These courtyards are landscaped as communal gardens, with paths, stone surfacing, lawns, and peripheral plantings. The central spine block bridges a two-storey opening between them. At Cambridge, Mecanoo builds on its long history of Dutch housing projects, addresses the urgent issue of affordability and shortage in English housing, and with features like photovoltaic roofs, shows the way for dense sustainable housing on a human scale.

Healthy Campus

Another high-density university project, the **Lawson Center for Sustainability** in Toronto, Canada, is a collaboration with local practice RDHA. It is situated adjacent to the neogothic-styled heart of Trinity College at the University of Toronto. Approaching the design, Francine Houben raised a question closely related to sustainability: 'How to make a healthy campus?' As we shall see, the solution involves nature … and food. The new 14,500 m² four-storey building with a 'T'-shape plan is positioned to frame the north end of the campus as a continuation of the forecourt and courtyard typologies, while implementing Houben's vision for a future central pedestrian spine as part of the campus masterplan. The new design aims for the Canada Green Building Council Zero Carbon and LEED Platinum certifications. The scale and social connectivity of Mecanoo's design offer a very different vision from the high-rise development of the site which the college had previously envisioned. The Lawson Center houses dormitories for 343 students in the east and west volumes. To break up the long north facade, the building volume shifts with student lounges at each end framing different views along Devonshire Place and Philosopher's Walk, a neighbouring urban park. From the main entrance at Devonshire Place, the first* floor seminar rooms connect to the academic wing housing a café, a community kitchen, meeting rooms, offices, a lecture hall and event space with views towards Toronto's distant, iconic CN tower and the immediate surrounding campus. The academic wing extends south to frame new landscaped courtyards, giving new life to a previously under-utilized, fenced-off sports pitch now replaced with drought tolerant grass and plantings.

The first-floor* 'plinth' is clad in limestone, while above it are locally sourced calcium silicate bricks with a tonal variety to complement the limestone. Champagne-coloured aluminium cladding accents the entrances, window surrounds and event pavilion. The residence windows shift their positions along the facade, with aluminium-clad operable panels that subliminally enliven the facades, which are simultaneously contemporary yet sympathetic to their historic neighbours. The facade and roof create a high-performance envelope, which balances daylight and energy efficiency. The envelope combines with numerous features including structural mass timber, ground source heat pumps, photovoltaic panels, rain harvesting, native droughttolerant planting and food production to help achieve the Lawson Center's exceptional sustainability. Plants highlight Houben's vision of a healthy campus. The smaller courtyard is like an urban pocket park, a peaceful, shady enclave under a great tree, while biodiversity flourishes in the larger, café courtyard planted with local species. Wellbeing is always boosted by proximity to Nature, which surrounds the entire building and the new paths that boost walkability in the campus. Meanwhile, the roof taps into another gift that nature gave us — sustenance from the soil. We use 38 per cent of all Earth's land used to feed us, so we urgently need to embrace urban farming, because it relieves pressure on rural land and reduces the carbon cost of food transport. The Lawson Center's rooftop farm shows students and the community the way forward, and also supports the café and the students' own communal kitchen, where they will learn how to take the food from farm to table. Farming and cooking become social activities, weaved into student life on a happy campus that is home.

Glass and Water

Mecanoo's mastery of creating the sense of home applies at all scales. In the English village of Lechdale, upstream from London on the Thames, Mecanoo has designed the **Glass Villa on the Lake**, completed in 2018. The house is surrounded on three sides by woodland beside the lake that it appears to float on, although its basement is grounded underwater. It is accessed by a footbridge, so no trees had to be felled to create a site. The house is a two-storey box, resting on a basement level, faced not just with glass but also with dark, burnt wood produced by a traditional Japanese treatment. Inside, dark wooden flooring and dark metal stairs contrast with white walls, and there is a three-dimensional play of space as stairs and light from skylights descend into the interior. Rooms have a minimalist, modernist feel, and indeed the villa revives the modernist idea of living in a glass box that was pioneered in the 1940s at Mies van der Rohe's Farnsworth House in Illinois and Phillip Johnson's Glass House in Connecticut. Clearly, they all share the transparency that immerses domestic life in the surrounding nature, but the villa also has something in common with a third modernist icon — the more organic and materially-varied Eames House (1949) in Los Angeles by Charles and Ray Eames, who Francine Houben visited there. The villa has solar panels around its rooftop patios, a heat pump and heat recovery systems, and triple glazing. It is an update on a modernist ideal, but designed for the contemporary energy-conscious world.

Rural Home

A very different rural home is the **Villa Vught** (2019) in the Netherlands, where three wooden volumes are clad in dark bronze anodized aluminium. The villa's composition follows that of a traditional farmstead, called a 'hoeve', which groups buildings around a courtyard. Particularly striking is the volume with the family bedrooms — a steep pyramid shape cut flat above the third storey to make a roof terrace. This dark form, like all of Villa Vught, echoes the vernacular of the Dutch countryside — in this case, tapering windmills now stripped of their sails. The two lower buildings are shaped like barns. One, with the living room, connects to the tall building via a passage that is buried under sloping grass, and the other one is detached and includes a cooking school and guest bedroom. Its large sliding doors can be opened to the courtyard. Wood has been used for both the structure and interior finish. It creates a warm atmosphere and is sustainable as well. Villa Vught's overall effect is striking and slightly mysterious, but simultaneously familiar in its context, tied together by a circular path in the landscape.

Mecanoo's philosophy built on People and Place is especially relevant for projects whose Purpose is housing. Like de Hooch, Vermeer and other Golden Age painters, Mecanoo also understand the gentle poetry of domesticity, as well as that in the spectrum of rhythms from the city to the countryside that animate the world outside the window. That Poetry makes home a sweet Place to live.

*US/Canadian floor numbering.

Kampus

Manchester, United Kingdom

Discipline:

Architecture, Urbanism, Landscape

Typology:

Transformation, Residential

Size: 44,000 m²
Design: 2016
Realization: 2017-2021
Client/Property Developer: Capital & Centric and Henry Boot Developments.

Design team: Mecanoo (urban plan including landscape design, lead architect new buildings and transformation tower), Shed KM (architect listed canal warehouses), Exterior Architecture (delivery landscape architect), Chapman Taylor (delivery architect new buildings and transformation tower).

Programme: Urban plan for a garden neighbourhood in the city centre, next to Manchester Piccadilly Station, for 533 apartments and leisure/retail spaces across five buildings of which two grade II listed warehouses, transformation of an existing office tower (1964) and two new buildings, totalling 44,000 m², and landscape design for gardens and public realm; architectural design for the two new apartment buildings including 352 apartments and the building transformation with 123 apartments, BREEAM Very Good.

↑ Once the home of Manchester Metropolitan University, Kampus is an eclectic mix of architecture that repurposes two Victorian warehouses, a brutalist 1960s tower and a disused security cabin later left on stilts, referred to as 'the bungalow'. ↓

Bringing a forgotten part of the city back to life

HOME SWEET HOME

↑ New waterside access from the street brings people into Kampus.

↑ Two new 15-storey blocks with protruding window frames supercharge the site's density.

↑ Three steel-clad storeys were added to the 12-storey office building, which was converted into apartments. The Bungalow became a bar in the heart of Kampus.

↑ The Victorian warehouses have been converted into loft-style apartments by Shed KM.

← Little David Street is transformed into a gateway into the Kampus bars, cafés and restaurants. →

2016–2021 · Manchester, United Kingdom

HOME SWEET HOME

In the heart of Kampus is a secret garden, the perfect backdrop for social events.

The existing building has been jazzed up with steel, concrete bandings and balconies jutting out dramatically.

Concrete window frames playfully emerge from the brick facades.

Inviting pocket parks connect the urban fabric to the secret garden in the centre of Kampus.

← Kampus is one of the coolest downtown places to meet, drink, eat and hang out.

2016–2021   Manchester, United Kingdom

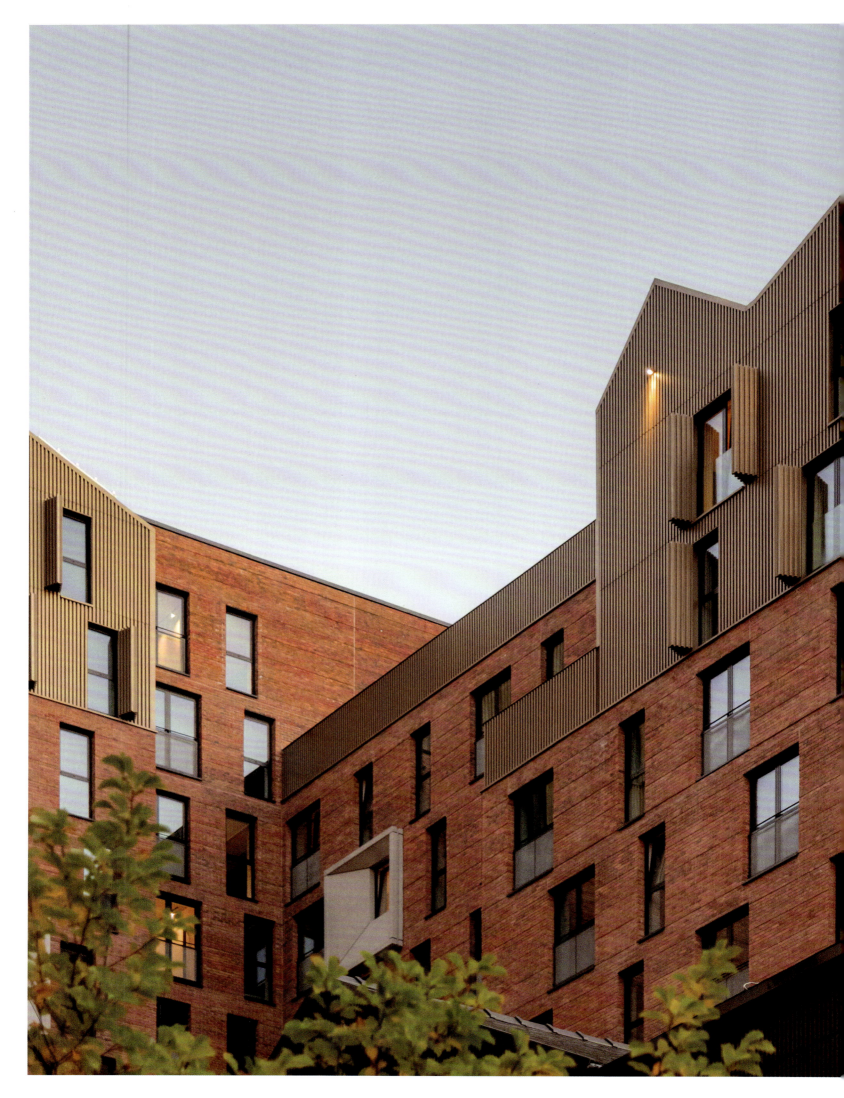

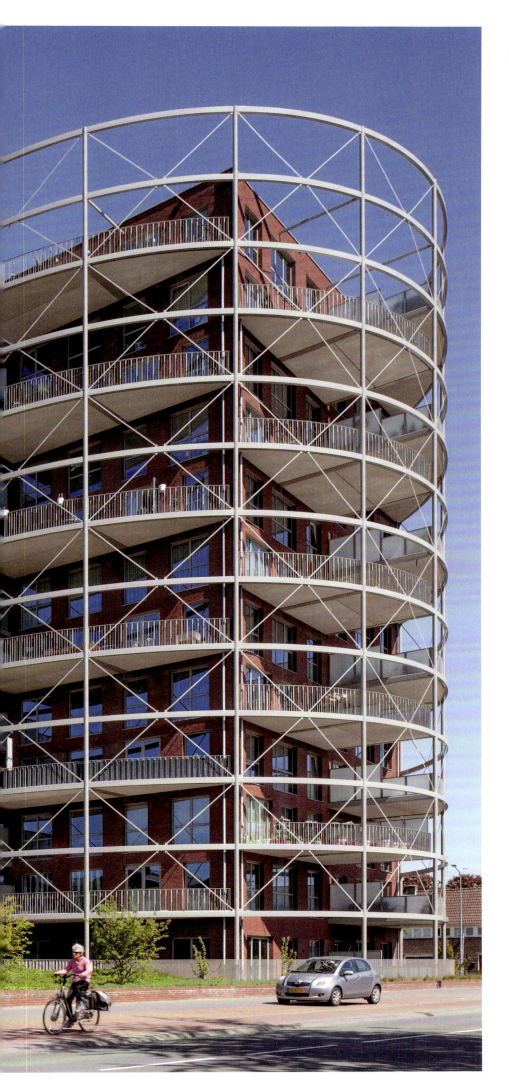

Villa Industria

Hilversum, the Netherlands

Discipline:

Architecture, Urbanism, Landscape

Typology:

Residential, Masterplan

Size: 74,000 m²
Status: completed
Design: 2004-2015
Realization: 2007-2013
Client: Heijmans; De Alliantie.

Design team: Mecanoo

Programme: Urban plan and design of 357 dwellings, 400 m² small-scale businesses, and 4,000 m² sports facilities, totalling 74,000 m².

FROM GASWORKS

The gasworks site was in use until 1962. In the years after, mainly businesses occupied the buildings. In 2004 Mecanoo created a masterplan for a new neighbourhood with 357 homes and small businesses.

HOME SWEET HOME

TO NEIGHBOURHOOD

2004-2018   Hilversum, the Netherlands

HOME SWEET HOME

← An eye-catching ensemble of three cylindrical residential buildings refers to the old gasometers that once stood on the site.

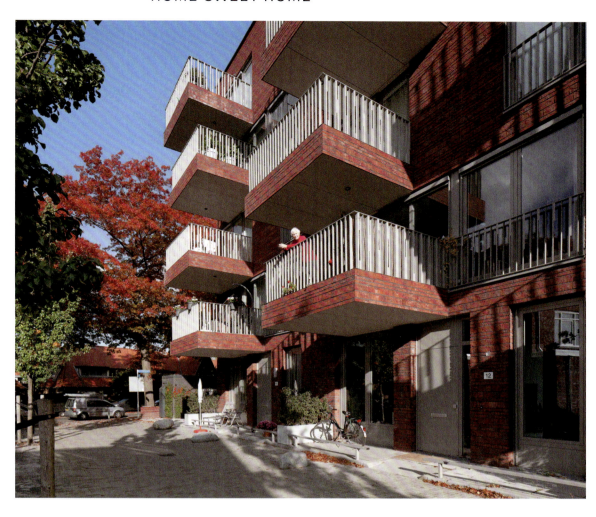

Cool materials - steel and glass - are combined with warm materials such as red or red-brown bricks with subtle relief.

The design language and detailing are inspired by the site's industrial heritage

Robust steel columns support a new sports hall and fitness centre built on top of the swimming pool. The artwork on the windows has been designed by artist Berend Strik.

2004-2018   Hilversum, the Netherlands

Key Worker Housing, University of Cambridge

Cambridge, United Kingdom

Discipline:

Architecture, Landscape

Typology:

Residential, University/Campus

Size: 19,500 m²
Design: 2012-2014
Realization: 2014-2018
Client: North West Cambridge Development, University of Cambridge.

Design team: Mecanoo

Programme: 232 sustainable dwellings for researchers and key university employees, totalling 19,500 m², 3,100 m² parking and 5,100 m² public realm design, Code For Sustainable Homes Level 5.

COMMUNITY

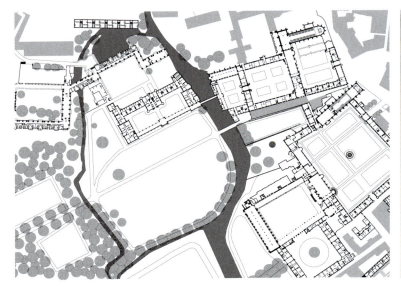

We took the Cambridge colleges and courtyards as an inspiration

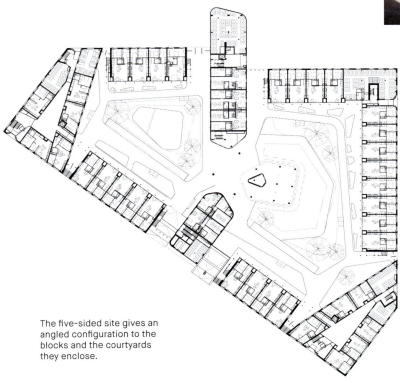

The five-sided site gives an angled configuration to the blocks and the courtyards they enclose.

Affordable housing for international researchers and key employees at the university

Key Worker Housing, University of Cambridge

HOME SWEET HOME

2012-2018 · Cambridge, United Kingdom

Windows vary in size, frame and off-grid positions and at the same time hide an integrated acoustic ventilation system to mitigate the noise of the nearby highway.

HOME SWEET HOME

Two internal green courtyards are sheltered by galleries forming covered outside community spaces.

The courtyards are landscaped as communal gardens, with paths, stone surfacing, lawns and planting.

Lawson Center for Sustainability, Trinity College

Toronto, Canada

Discipline:

Architecture, Interior, Landscape

Typology:

Residential, University/Campus

Size: 14,450 m²
Design: 2019-2022
Realization: 2022-2025
Client: Trinity College in the University of Toronto

Design team: Mecanoo (design architect and landscape architect), RDHA (architect of record), NAK (delivery landscape architect).

Programme: 14,450 m² student residence and academic building, a mass timber facility including full-service cafeteria, academic offices, meeting rooms, lecture hall, seminar rooms, community kitchen, event pavilion, 343 bed dormitory, student lounges, study spaces, and rooftop farm, LEED Platinum and CaGBC Zero Carbon.

89

SUSTAINABLE

The main entrance of the new building leads to the academic building and residences of the students and is connected to a modernist building (left) of the 1960s and an auditorium of the 1970s.

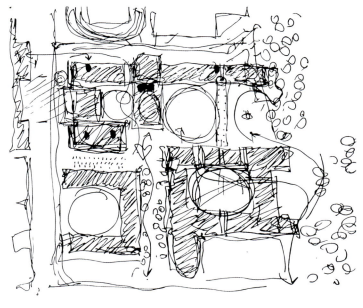

The new addition of the Lawson Center is a walkable building, tailored to the urban scale of the campus

Lawson Center for Sustainability, Trinity College

HOME SWEET HOME

Teaching and learning with a focus on healthy living and sustainability

Vegetables harvested in the urban farming fields on the roof are part of the educational food programme that also includes a community kitchen.

The use of mass timber in the building's structure helps to target LEED Platinum and CaGBC Zero Carbon.

COMMUNITY

2019-2025 Toronto, Canada

Glass Villa on the Lake

Lechlade, United Kingdom

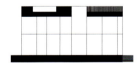

Discipline:

Architecture, Interior

Typology:

Residential, Private Houses

Link

Size: 600 m²
Design: 2015-2016
Realization: 2016-2018
Client: private

Design team: Mecanoo (concept design) and Arquitectura y Ordenación Urbana S.L. (executive architect).

Programme: Three-storey house of 600 m² with one level below water with screening room, games/bar area, wellness/spa area, 80 m² roof terrace and 176 m² ground floor terrace.

3

The villa enjoys panoramic views through full-height glazing.

Glass Villa on the Lake

HOME SWEET HOME

Dark wooden flooring and dark metal stairs contrast with white walls. Light from skylights descends into the interior.

GLASS

The villa and surrounding nature merge into one continuous space

The guiding design principle was to create a house that combines transparency with sustainability, forging a strong relationship between the villa and the landscape.

Glass Villa on the Lake

HOME SWEET HOME

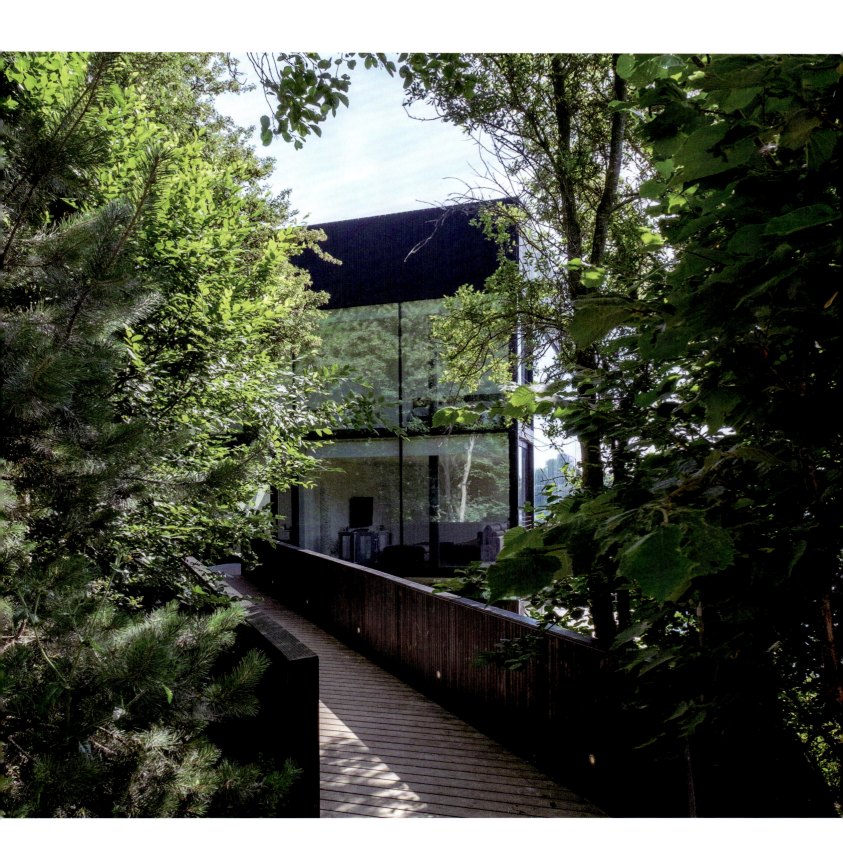

& LIGHT

2015-2018 — Lechlade, United Kingdom

Villa Vught

Vught, the Netherlands

Discipline:

Architecture, Interior

Typology:

Residential, Private Houses

Size: 683 m²
Design: 2016-2018
Realization: 2018-2019
Client: private

Design team: Mecanoo (design architect) and Anne Laansma (landscape architect).

Programme: 683 m² mass timber, highly sustainable private villa complex with a separate professional cooking studio and a guest suite with extensive gardens.

HOME SWEET HOME

The composition follows the layout of a traditional farmstead, with buildings around a courtyard

The steep pyramid building with family bedrooms is cut flat above the third storey to make a roof terrace. The lower buildings contain the living room and a cooking school.

2016-2019 Vught, the Netherlands 101

The three buildings have a cross-laminated timber structure and European silver fir interior surfaces which create a warm atmosphere and are sustainable as well.

HOME SWEET HOME

2016-2019 — Vught, the Netherlands

The three wooden volumes are clad in dark bronze anodised aluminium.

Throughout the building, views from each floor carefully frame the surrounding landscape

2016-2019 Vught, the Netherlands 105

4

The Big
Picture

If we stand outside and look around, we form a picture of where we are. We see the built environment around us, and we can say what sort of place we are in — suburban or central, residential or commercial, office or industrial, or mixtures of any of these. Beyond the city, we see countryside, which comes with its own varieties — agricultural, parkland, natural landscape, wilderness, and so on. Walking around, we build a bigger picture, connecting places up to make a mental map of an area. But the big picture of an area, without gaps or blind spots, is the view from above. To have the bird's-eye view, you need a map. One that describes land use is a powerful planning tool, and if we plan change, we can create a new, future map. This big picture is at the heart of a masterplan, which is the design of a framework for what is to be built.

The Power of Masterplans

Powerful masterplans have a vision of how everything fits together to make life better for People, in which the different Purposes of buildings are zoned to work efficiently, and where new Place is created. There is a long history of masterplans, including rebuilding great cities after disasters such as the Great Fire of London of 1666 or the Great Lisbon Earthquake of 1755. Obviously, disasters are not the only opportunities to build a better city. Visions of the Ideal City have a long history, and can echo down through the centuries. Italian architect-artist Fra Carnevale's vision, represented in a painting from around 1480 that is actually called *Ideal City*, shows classical and neo-classical buildings and monuments formally set in public space, and such formal arrangements persisted in cities around the world until the twentieth century. In the 1920s Le Corbusier, architect of the some of the most extraordinary and beautiful buildings of the modernist era, developed a utopian masterplan called Ville Radieuse with vast standardized blocks aligned along a grid. It would have drastically changed the centre of Paris and thankfully it was never realized. His big picture epitomized top-down planning indifferent to human scale and social connectivity, and it drove the strategies of planners and architects worldwide for decades afterwards. The result was often soulless new cityscapes carved up by highways with menacing social housing that destroyed the sense of community of those rehoused there. British architect Cedric Price was an early voice rejecting these imposed plans, proposing a strategy called *Non Plan* in 1969.

Nowadays, masterplans and visions are still with us, but we have mostly learnt the lessons of planning's past arrogances. Rather than plan idealistic utopian dreams, Mecanoo's human-centred approach, making places to belong to and enjoy, is far more realistic. Social aspects, mobility, economy, facilities, landscaping and ecology are considered as a coherent whole. The masterplan may still be top-down, but in this holistic approach, human scale pervades the make-up of the whole site, and individual human experience is the baseline on which entire projects are measured. A masterplan can even be an act of social justice, especially applied to neglected, devalued or overlooked areas. Such areas include those cut off or divided by barriers such as railway lines, roads, rivers — and in the Netherlands, dykes. To make them better, you need to get the big picture.

South Side of Town

The great metropolis of Rotterdam has a north-south divide, and Francine Houben has developed not a masterplan, but something wider and more holistic — **A New Perspective for Rotterdam South.** The bustling centre of the city lies to the north, and the Erasmus Bridge (1996), a unique landmark suspension bridge designed by UN Studio, crosses the wide Maas river via the historic, reborn Wilhelmina Pier, where Mecanoo's Montevideo (see p. 350) is one of the projects that have revitalized the waterside on the south side. But the new urban vivacity there and in the adjacent Katendrecht peninsular is yet to spread deep into Rotterdam South. As Francine Houben has said, it 'has a negative image, but I think that's wrong'. This is a vast territory that stretches out behind the barrier of a dyke embankment, which blocks even a view of the water and runs right up to the active docks in the west. It is home to 200,000 people and while there is deprivation, neglect and poor educational prospects, there is also beauty, for example in its canals and schools. It has fascinated Francine Houben for years, and driven her to personally undertake research and fieldwork, talking to a spectrum from the Port Authority and education institutes to people on the street, barge skippers and artists. There have been plenty of localized plans, but Houben asked, 'where's the big picture? It needs an integral vision'. A New Perspective for Rotterdam South is precisely that. It envisions a new Purpose as a region for education and the knowledge economy, a transformation of Place into a green city, and a healthier and hopeful future for its People.

The Perspective proposes interventions that build into a big new picture. Two campuses come together with student housing across the water from Katendrecht on the southern side of Maashaven, and connected to it by a new pontoon bridge. In the east, Charloisse Poort and Waalhaven (Waal Harbour) are transformed with a mix of manufacturing, housing, and education. The dyke that separates them from the Waalhaven docks becomes part of a beautiful ten-kilometre-long Dyke Park, where nature and citizens come together. It runs along the waterfront to connect South Rotterdam all the way west to Feyenoord Stadion (Stadium) and beyond. There are rail shunting-yards at the Stadion — they became a new park. The vision tackles the transport poverty of Rotterdam South. The main railway passes the Stadion, and a new InterCity station is proposed there. An existing metro line would include two stations – an upgraded existing station in the middle of two overlooked neighbourhoods, and a new Park-and-Ride stop at Charloisse Poort that will help reduce the number of cars coming into the city. Superbus routes would connect across the river in the east and west. A circular route for cycles and people, which incorporates the Erasmus Bridge and Maas Tunnel, would not only link to Rotterdam's great museum zone (including the Boijmans – see p. 52), but extend the idea of Central Rotterdam as a Place that spans the river.

Those north of the river, gradually seeing a green, attractive and hopeful city emerge across the water, may well become jealous. No need — they will find Rotterdam South completely accessible with its new, convenient routes, uniting the whole metropolis!

Sustainable Green City

Not far from Rotterdam is Dordrecht, an 800-year-old port city on the Oude Maas river. Here, rail and road have disconnected territory. In this case, the railway is like a barrier effectively dividing the city, and its southern half seems to be wholly elsewhere from the picturesque historical centre. Mecanoo sees the **Dordrecht Railway Zone** as a line of opportunity to connect and bind the whole city, and it has a vision of how we can live and thrive in a future-proof, sustainable green city.

The railway enters the city from the north on one of two adjacent bridges across the river, the other a box girder bridge, carrying a road called the Brugweg. Of course, vehicles need to cross the river, but there is a nearby motorway tunnel, so Mecanoo will transform Brugweg into a sort of High Line (the famous linear park that threads through Manhattan neighbourhoods on an old elevated railway line). The Brugweg green corridor will be for pedestrians and cyclists, and sweep into a new, socially mixed and car-free neighbourhood. It will be peppered with interestingly shaped and varied mid-rise blocks that connect the elevated level of the bridge to ground level, built not with steel and concrete, but locally sourced wood. Residents of the new 6000 homes will live 'with their feet in the water', enjoying a waterside plaza, promenade and moorings beside them. A landmark office tower will rise by the water. The Brugweg diverges from the railway, and the shunting-yards between them will become an urban park blending into the neighbourhood.

The railway continues east to the central station, with the charms of the historic centre, easily accessible to the north. But just to the south, cut off by the tracks, is the beautiful but almost ignored Weizigtpark. Mecanoo proposes a landscaped platform floating above the station's platforms that forms a wide, green bridge to the park as well as to the city centre, so that the station zone will become a bridge across the divide. Weizigtpark also becomes a gateway to Dordrecht's assets to the south — a tree-lined canal leads to the Health and Learning Park, a parkland campus that is also a hub of innovation. A green route by the railway leads further south to the Amstelwijck neighbourhood, where new development opportunities for homes and business lie on the frontier of nature in the Dutch delta lands, and beyond that the Brabant countryside.

Alight Here for Nature

The Brabant countryside is old, but in Flevoland, east of Amsterdam, almost none of the land existed before the 1950s. It has been reclaimed from the sea and now supports agriculture and is a powerhouse of wind energy. Here, Mecanoo have a masterplan for the **Nieuw Land National Park**, situated between two thriving new towns, Almere and Lelystad. The national park is the world's largest national park on new land, and contains four nature reserves, which are now binding together into a unified ecosystem.

Imagine a railway station that serves no homes, work places or shopping, but instead floats a few metres above a tranquil natural landscape where woodlands meet wetlands rich in birdlife, and marsh and grasslands where wild horses and deer roam. This unusual train stop is called Nature Land. The station doesn't exist yet, but it will bring people to the very heart of the park.

Houben's approach to the masterplan was to 'deal with it like a big public building'. That means addressing access and facilities. As Houben explains, the plan is 'very much driven by nature, by sustainability, by mobility'. The four nature reserves largely consist of inaccessible nature areas. Instead of making these accessible, Mecanoo created nature zones around the reserves where people are welcome to visit. There are gateways and visitor centres. New paths include a dyke that becomes a high-line for walkers towards the water, where ferries connect to new islands that host more human-made nature. The Mecanoo plan not only brings the park together, but connects it to the Netherland's greatest concentration of urban population. Its children may never have seen nature like this before, and it may change their lives forever.

Co-existence

All these projects have been in the Netherlands, but of course Mecanoo projects find the big picture further afield too, such as planning the newest high-rise business district in Shenzhen (see p. 380). A common thread in all visions and plans is how Nature is woven into the design, and in the elegance and intelligence of the weave, we find Poetry. These masterplans address not just the benefits of proximity to nature, but ultimately they respond to the biggest picture of all — the invasion of nature's land by human activity. We need to live in balance with nature, or face extinction. The vision of co-existence with nature must thrive in every masterplan.

A New Perspective for Rotterdam South

Rotterdam, the Netherlands

Discipline:

Architecture, Urbanism, Landscape

Typology:

Masterplan/Mobility, University/Campus

Design: 2016-2021, ongoing
Initiative: Francine Houben; Manifesto Group Rotterdam South.
Client: Municipality of Rotterdam; Bernard van Leer Foundation.

Design team: Mecanoo

Programme: An integral vision for better connections between Rotterdam South, the port area and Central Rotterdam with, amongst other interventions, an education strip, a cultural campus, new forms of living, working and mobility interconnected by an adaptive 10-kilometre dyke park.

111

4
ROTTERDAM SOUTH

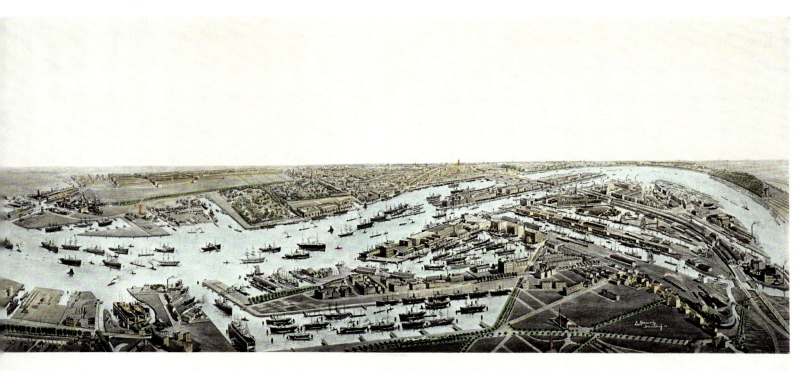

1895

Construction of new large ports

To accomodate larger vessels, Rotterdam transformed agricultural land into new and larger harbours.

Work, living and leisure were intertwined with the harbours

112   A New Perspective for Rotterdam South

THE BIG PICTURE

1953

Flood disaster

The 1953 flood disaster necessitated the implementation of higher river dykes within the city. ↓

The Strevelsweg road near the Lange Hilleweg road during the flood disaster.

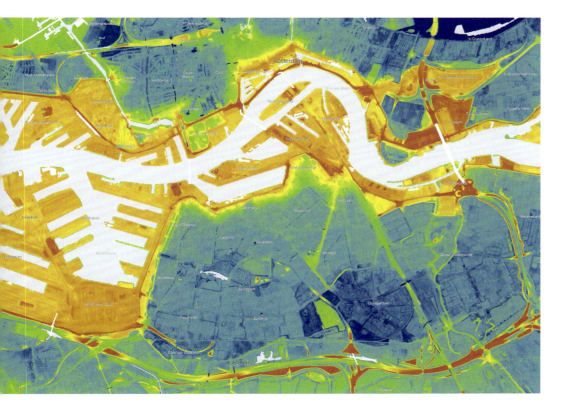

1960s

Building dykes up and better water management

The river dykes constructed in the 1960s in Rotterdam South create barriers between neighbourhoods and the port, as well as between the Maas River and the city. But what if these dykes were to transform into connectors and catalysts, fostering vibrant and appealing spaces to inhabit?

PORT & CITY CONNECTED

The Manifesto Group Rotterdam South wants to enhance the quality of life for the next generation. The group consists of Francine Houben; Gijs van den Boomen, KuiperCompagnons; Jesse Flink, Hart van Zuid; Hamit Karakus, Feijenoord XL; Maurice Unck, RET; Miriam Hoekstra, Woonstad; Ron Kooren, Albeda and VNO-NCW Rotterdam-Rijnmond; Marco Pastors, NPRZ; Wietske Vrijland, Maasstad hospital; Dominic Schrijer, citizen; Ron Bormans, Hogeschool Rotterdam; Bob de Baedts, BOOR; Peter van der Gugten, Heijmans; and Job Dura, Dura Vermeer.

Beautiful city behind the dykes

Youngsters do not hold a positive view of working in the harbour, but the Port of Rotterdam is transforming into an innovative, healthy, safe, and sustainable harbour, powered by renewable energy.

The dykes act as barriers between the neighbourhoods with high unemployment and the harbour with many job opportunities.

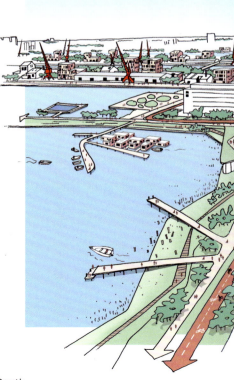

THE BIG PICTURE

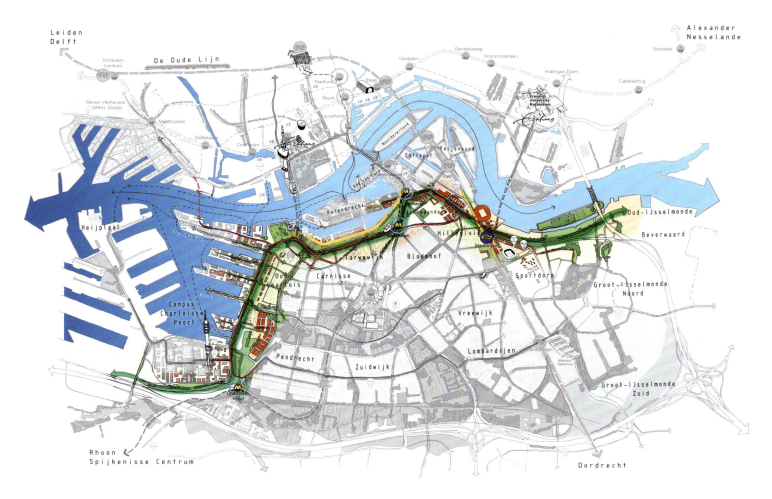

A ten-kilometre long dyke park that meanders from the harbour to the stadium.

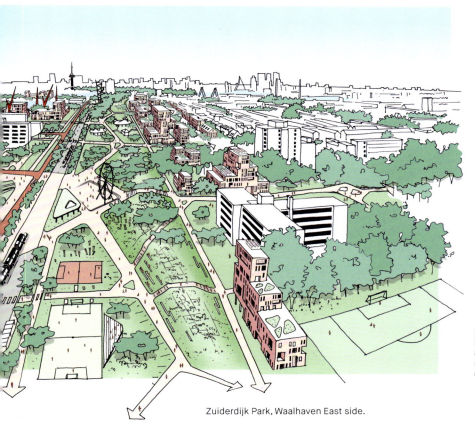

Zuiderdijk Park, Waalhaven East side.

Rotterdam South: a better place to live, learn, and work; a place to grow and pursue your dreams

Imagine the dykes transformed into a long linear park for people and nature, and connecting the residents of the South with job opportunities in the harbour.

115

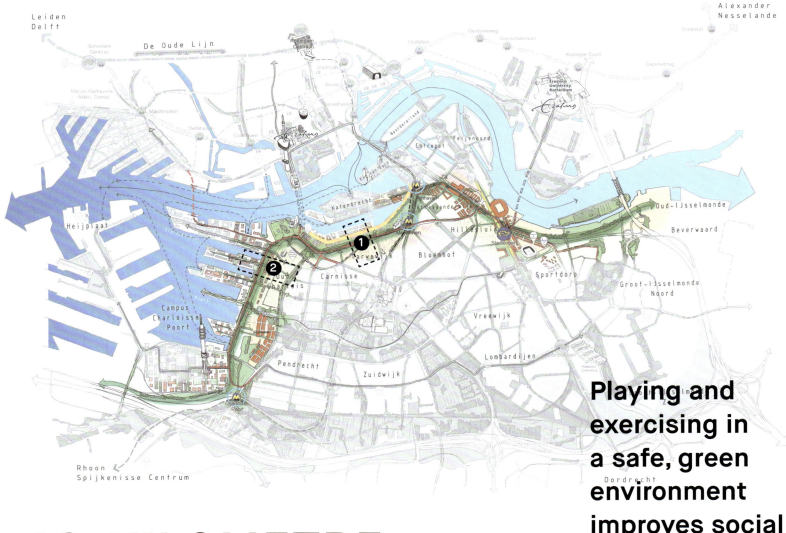

10-KILOMETRE DYKE PARK

Playing and exercising in a safe, green environment improves social cohesion, health and happiness

Creating a balcony along the Maas river for the inhabitants of the Tarwewijk neighbourhood.

Two visions were crafted in partnership with the Bernard van Leer Foundation. Their Urban95 programme prioritizes the well-being of young children, emphasizing access to nature, clean air, public spaces, and mobility in urban environments.

THE BIG PICTURE

Waalhaven East Side.

Imagine allotments with herbal gardens, flower beds and playgrounds.

Tarwewijk/Balcony on the Maas. Just as Waalhaven East Side, this study takes the perspective of 95 cm, the height of a three year old.

The linear dyke park provides a safe playground for children as well as gardens and paths for jogging.

10 ASPIRATIONS OF MANIFESTO ROTTERDAM SOUTH

1. Giving the residents of Rotterdam South perspective: school, work and housing.
2. Connecting South with an innovative, healthy and innovative harbour.
3. Connecting to the waterfront: a 10-km dyke park, easily accessible for neighbourhoods and harbour.
4. Three focus areas on both sides of the Maas river.
5. A 5-km walking and cycling route crossing Maas Tunnel and Erasmus Bridge.
6. A renewed train track with a central station for Rotterdam South: marshalling yard becomes Stadium Park.
7. New metro station Charloisse Poort and existing metro station Slinge as attractive centres for the Pendrecht and Zuidwijk neighbourhoods.
8. Transformation of Waalhaven (Waal harbour) and introduction of Charloisse Poort Campus.
9. A high-quality public transport network in the short and long term with superbus, trams and metro.
10. Transformation of Maashaven (Maas harbour) and adding an informal bridge connecting the Katendrecht and Tarwewijk neighbourhoods.

THE BIG PICTURE

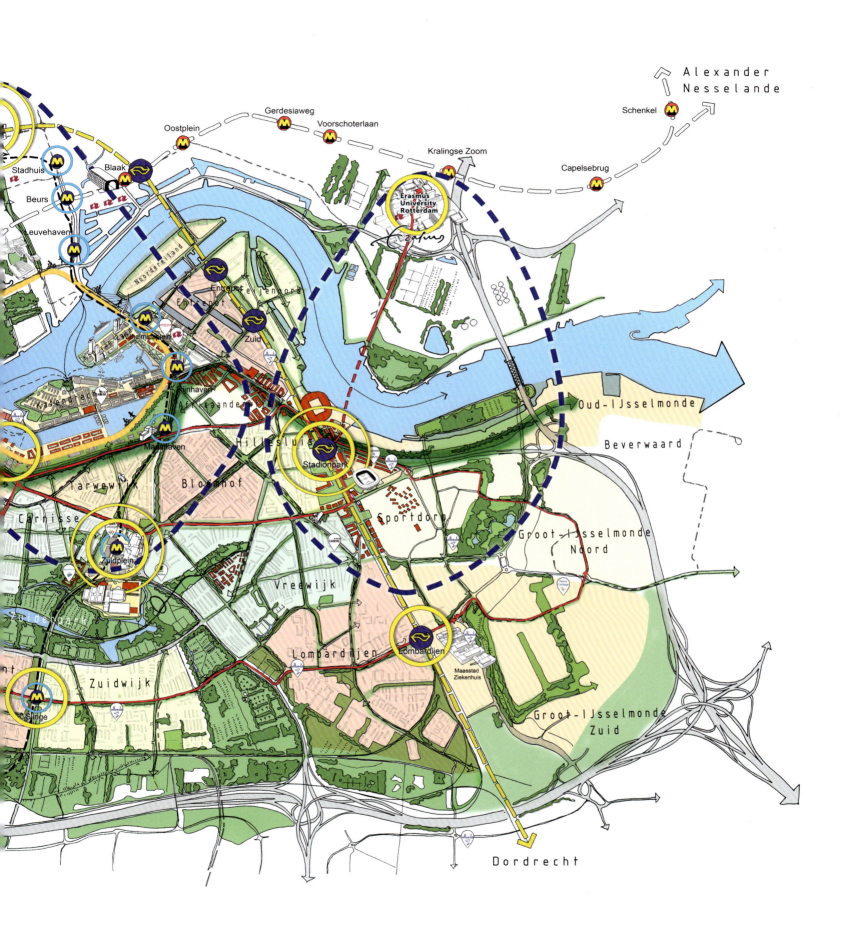

Dordrecht Railway Zone

Dordrecht, the Netherlands

Discipline:

Architecture, Urbanism, Landscape

Typology:

Residential, Masterplan/Mobility

Design: 2020-2021
Client: Municipality of Dordrecht

Design team: Mecanoo

Programme: Urban masterplan for the railway zone in Dordrecht including five development areas: Maasterras, Spuiboulevard, Central Station area, Learning Park and Health Park with 6000 homes, commercial functions, community amenities, parks and stations.

4

← ↑ Dordrecht is an 800-year old port city on the Oude Maas river. The masterplan for 6000 new homes transforms an infrastructural barrier into a sustainable, green and car-free neighbourhood.

→ Dordrecht Central Station is set to become the Netherlands' greenest station, featuring a raised green bridge connecting Weizigt Park to the city centre.

THE BIG PICTURE

2020–2021   Dordrecht, the Netherlands

The Railway Zone masterplan transforms former industrial areas into resilient city districts with spectacular green areas prepared for climate change.

The Brugweg road will be a green corridor for pedestrians and cyclists. It sweeps into a new, socially mixed and car-free green neighbourhood with mid-rise blocks built with locally sourced wood.

THE BIG PICTURE

SPATIAL CHALLENGES

2020-2021 — Dordrecht, the Netherlands

THE BIG PICTURE

The Dordrecht Masterplan connects with another Mecanoo masterplan for the town of Zwijndrecht on the river's north side, where a green garden village character is promoted.

The masterplan connects several major development areas and 7.5 kilometres of opportunities along the railway track

2020-2021   Dordrecht, the Netherlands

Nieuw Land National Park

Flevoland, the Netherlands

Discipline:

Landscape

Typology:

Leisure, Masterplan/Mobility

Size: 29,000 ha
Design: 2018-2019
Client: Province of Flevoland, Municipality of Almere, Municipality of Lelystad, Staatsbosbeheer and Natuurmonumenten, Stichting Flevo-landschap, Rijkswaterstaat, Waterschap Zuiderzeeland.

Design team: Mecanoo

Programme: Masterplan vision for a 29,000-ha national park bringing together four core nature reserves: the Oostvaardersplassen, the Lepelaarplassen, Marker Wadden and Trintelzand.

4
NATURE CONNECTS

Render of the view from Oostvaarders dyke towards Markermeer lake with its new shallows and islands.

Nieuw Land is the largest man-made natural park in the world and located in the former Zuiderzee (Southern Sea)

Nieuw Land is a bird paradise of international significance.

The National Park brings children in close contact with the wonderful world of nature.

THE BIG PICTURE

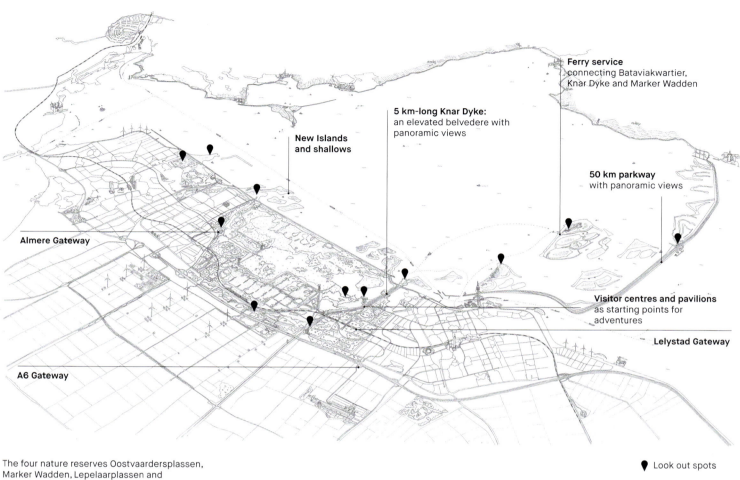

The four nature reserves Oostvaardersplassen, Marker Wadden, Lepelaarplassen and Trintelzand will gradually grow into the continuous National Park Nieuw Land.

● Look out spots

The nature reserves will be expanded across the Knar Dyke to include publicly accessible nature areas om that side of the dyke, allowing visitors to enjoy the reserve while hiking, canoeing or camping without disturbing the flora and fauna in the nature reserves. (Render)

2018-2019 — Flevoland, the Netherlands

5

Wisdom
and
Wizardry

Ask people to imagine a library, and many think of something like that in Hogwarts in the Harry Potter books — a gothic caricature of historic libraries shrouded in gloom and a respectful, almost sacred silence, a repository of endless arcane books written by people long dead. It's certainly poetic, but not much good for today's needs. Libraries have been changing ever since the Babylonians stored documents on clay tablets in rooms five millennia ago, and in this century the changes have accelerated. Nowadays, libraries are more than just warehouses for words. They are coming alive as venues of culture, and education not just for scholars but for all. They are hubs for community services and events. Their core function — to give access to printed publications — is transforming to the exchange of knowledge in many ways: digital, classes, lectures or meeting other people. The buildings which libraries occupy should be anchors and catalysts for urban renewal, not just of the built environment, but of the life and interaction of people, inside and out. Francine Houben even says that 'libraries are the most important public buildings' of all. They are, she declares, 'the cathedrals of our time'.

Breakthrough Library

Mecanoo's breakthrough project, the first to catch the attention of the architectural world beyond the Netherlands, was actually a library. Mecanoo's 15,000 m² **Library Delft University of Technology**, at Francine Houben's Alma Mater, changed the idea of what a library could be. The main library room itself is a vast open hall stretching under a sloping ceiling that is penetrated by light falling around a giant cone. It's like a spacecraft that has arrived and put down legs. You can enter into the reading spaces of this conical building-in-building, accessed by gangways from a stunning 60-metre-wide, four-level wall of books.

Outside, the 42-metre-high cone breaks through an inclined lawn sweeping across the roof down towards Delft University of Technology's previous stand-out building, the 1968 brutalist Aula Auditorium designed by Jo van den Broek and Jaap Bakema. This grass roof is peppered with people when the sun shines, and it also insulates the building, thus saving energy, and absorbs CO_2, pollution, and rainwater. In 1998, the Library Delft University of Technology was a radical break from all the post-war modernism of the Delft campus, and a giant leap towards today's drive for sustainability. It is also a dramatic poem writ large, in the languages of space, form, and landscape.

Beyond the Library

What you won't find in the Delft University of Technology Library is a book of poetry, but in **LocHal Library** (2018), you are sure to. This library in the Dutch town of Tilburg incorporates the Midden-Brabant public library. Two cultural institutions and a co-working office space provider share the structure, once a locomotive repair shed but now restored and reconfigured by CIVIC, Braaksma & Roos and Inside Outside. The volume is large — 90m x 60m and 15 metres high. Mecanoo's contribution to the project is the interiors, breathing life into the refreshed structure. It is a re-interpretation of the identity of Tilburg and its textile industry, Locomotive Hall and popular Efteling fantasy amusement park. LocHal brings public space inside, with a warm entrance café at ground level. Tables made from old railway chassis can be moved along retained heritage rail tracks within and outside the building, and they can join to make a stage for performance. Beyond them is a wide set of stairs and terraces to sit on, and the higher you stop, the more there is to see. In an internal passage that runs deep into the old shed, Mecanoo created a long 'book street', where old iron structural columns became reading stations. The children's library is like a colourful playground, inspired by the Efteling, with bookcases shaped like pencils, brushes and pens, and even one that can be walked through. The floor to ceiling curtains designed by Petra Blaisse and produced by the local Textile Museum create flexible rooms. Learn-and-try rooms called 'labs' pop up. For example, the Foodlab explains and even offers food, while in the Digilab you can try things like virtual reality or 3D printing. Even the gamers have a facility, called GameLab. Is there a lab with books? Of course! It's called the WordLab, and its walls are packed with books and book-spines are even mounted on ceiling panels. This spatial immersion in books is perfect for enjoying literature and creative writing, which people can share in groups around the central table and the benches below the bookshelves.

LocHal goes far beyond the idea of a library as just somewhere to access books. A shed for the dynamic machines of the past becomes a dynamic box of contemporary interaction and ideas for the future. It offers visual drama, and crucially, it reaches out to the community with attractive, relevant offerings. It has become the new icon of Tilburg and its citizens are proud of it, as if it is their home. Mecanoo had the same approach in their first library beyond the Netherlands.

Golden Crown

When the **Library of Birmingham** in England opened in 2013, it was an instant hit with locals, and a new icon for the city. In 2008, when Houben walked and observed the city and its citizens, she was inspired to make a People's Palace, something for all of Birmingham. It faces Centenary Square, adjacent to the brutalist 4,000 m² REP Theatre (1971) by Graham Winteringham, which Mecanoo reconfigured and connected with the new 31,000 m² library. The new landmark rises in three stacked boxes, each behind an intricate, elegant filigree screen of aluminium circular rings (5,357 in total), and it is crowned by a golden cylinder reaching 60 metres up, which rehouses the nineteenth-century Shakespeare Memorial Room. The library itself is entered under the 11-metre cantilever of the largest box, and long escalators rise into a cathedral-scaled internal space. Its composition came to Houben in a dream — a series of staggered circular voids, connected by escalators and moving walkways, which diminish in diameter towards light that falls from the sky above. Continuous bookshelves behind balconies line the 24-metre-wide Book Rotunda, from which the floors spread out.

The rooftop Discovery Terrace on level 3 is an L-shaped public garden of benches and islands of vegetation containing 3500 plants. Level 7 has another terrace, the Secret Garden, with many different herbs that with their scents touch your senses. These terraces are not just fantastic viewing platforms, but urban oases of biodiversity that attract birds and pollinating insects. The level 10 roof over the Shakespeare Memorial Room is designed for a wild meadow to grow.

There is much more to this project, such as a joyful bank of big yellow steps for children, and an 18-metre-wide circular performance space sunk into the plaza outside. Birmingham's library is a dynamic spatial adventure, but it delivers practical services. It is inclusive, reaching out to all, recognizing for example that some come to search for jobs, or may even need a refuge to do homework away from a troubled home. On the big scale, the Library is place-making at its best, powerful enough to transform the city itself.

Inverted Ziggurat

In Taiwan, the **Tainan Public Library**, delivered in collaboration with local practice MAYU, opened in January 2021. Here, the rectangular-plan building's highest level is supported by pillars, and it is wrapped with a screen of vertical aluminium louvres, acting as brise-soleil to filter light, and poetically carved to create a pattern evoking Taiwanese window frames. The libraries' imposing crown shelters three glazed floors, each stepped back as they descend. The whole form is like an inverted ziggurat and is inspired by the subtropical climate of the city, protecting visitors from the sun and rain. Step through the entrance, and there is the drama of looking up into the library floors, as in Birmingham. Set in landscaped gardens, the 37,000 m² project includes a conference hall, auditorium and café. Again, inclusivity for all is built in, with areas especially dedicated for teenagers and elderly. The children's library looks out on a children's playground, visually connecting play and reading. Four sunken plazas offer spaces for outdoor events and exhibitions. Tainan Public Library will be a catalyst for a rapidly building neighbourhood, and a new hub for the city of Tainan.

Bringing Light to Legacies

In Europe and Taiwan, Mecanoo re-invented the library as a place for 'more than words'. But transforming a historic library to meet twenty-first-century needs is a different matter. It requires a certain wizardry to respect the legacy of the architecture, yet at the same time create a vehicle for future wisdom. In the United States, Mecanoo has transformed three of the nation's greatest central libraries, and each of them has history.

Washington DC hosts the only library designed by the master of minimalist modernist architecture Ludwig Mies van der Rohe. In Germany, he was the last director of Bauhaus, the deeply influential pre-war design school, but in the US, after the war, Mies perfected a distinctive black, rectilinear glass-and-steel architecture, celebrated in iconic skyscrapers in New York and Chicago. His last commissioned design was the Washington Central Library, and he died three years before it opened in 1972. The library was named the **Martin Luther King Jr. Memorial Library** (MLKML) after the towering African-American civil rights leader, tragically assassinated in 1968. Gradually, MLKML deteriorated physically and became functionally outdated. Frankly, the old MLKML was like a dark overcrowded book warehouse sitting on top of an outdated corporate lobby, all disguised as an office block. When Francine Houben first visited it, she found that it 'was not a good building technically and not a good library... all the books got daylight and all the people didn't get any at all'. She realized that the building simply needed a human touch, a 'female touch'.

Houben knew that the transformation of MLKML had 'to highlight the library's social gathering purpose and its strong presence as a social landmark in the city'. It also had to balance the very different legacies of Mies van der Rohe and Dr King. Mecanoo's 2020 transformation of MLKML, delivered in collaboration with OTJ Architects, brings a new, humanistic environment. Designed and programmed for the future, it has exciting new facilities from roof to basement and major new interventions between them.

The 39,600 m² project respects the powerful simplicity of the original building. Mecanoo has not been afraid to introduce organic surfaces and softer lines to Mies van der Rohe's hard, rectilinear design. The MLKML's rectangular form has three storeys of dark-glazed facades that float above a first* (ground) floor recessed behind a colonnade of black steel columns. The main entrance leads into the Great Hall, a typically modernist Miesian lobby. Below a magnificent restored mural by Don Miller celebrating Dr King's life, Mecanoo have recessed the wall, lined it with vertical wooden slats, and inserted bench steps, drawing people to sit, chat, read, and watch. The intervention brings warmth, better acoustics, and a social dimension. As with all the library's new features, it is clear what is Mies and what is Mecanoo. Removing a brick wall enables the view to a new café and for it to extend outside, into the city.

Mecanoo has revolutionized the MLKML's vertical circulation with two beautiful new sculptural wood-lined staircases, carrying wide terrazzo-surfaced stairs. They have a fluid feel as they curve gracefully from the lower ground floor towards skylights above a new fifth* floor — and they invite people to get exercise instead of taking elevators!

The lower ground floor has been opened to library users for the first time. It hosts a wide range of facilities offering resources and skills training. The new Fabrication Lab is a suite of workshops with hands-on equipment, and as Houben comments, 'this is a space where you can make noise and a mess!' In contrast, the Studio Lab's rooms are quiet, conducive to activities such as music, dance and yoga.

Upstairs, book stacks had previously spread right up to the windows. Now, there is clear space and natural light flows into the building. A 220-metre-long wooden counter, a 'reading ribbon', threads around the reading rooms, on every floor overlooking the street. A colourful children's library, divided into three age zones, includes a slide beside a staircase. Fun is something new Mecanoo have built into the library.

On the third* floor, the most impressive feature is the Grand Reading Room. A doubleheight void cut through the steel frame now visually connects the fourth-floor* main reading room above it. A dynamic installation by artist Xenobia Bailey spans the ceiling.

The fourth* floor hosts a new double-height 283-seat auditorium. It has wood-lined walls that curve around the corners, and banked seating rising into an entirely new fifth* floor. Up there, a glazed trapezoid pavilion, sheltered by a roof cantilevering out around it, hosts an auditorium lobby, conference rooms and an events space. The pavilion is invisible from the street, because it is set back from the edges and surrounded by a new sky-garden, which brings biodiversity into the heart of Washington. This hidden yet public oasis offers everyone tranquillity, proximity to nature and an open sky. 'The rooftop was a bleak desert', comments Houben. 'Now, it has become a park for the city.'

With its new facilities and spaces reaching out to the whole community, MLKML embodies the spirit of advancement, inclusivity, and hope that Dr King brought to the nation. King's oratory had a poetic power. Now, at last, so does the library named after him.

Mothership of Research

The New York Public Library (NYPL) system includes two historic buildings. One is a global icon, and NYPL's mothership of research. The other is its long-estranged sister library, the mothership of NYPL's circulating (lending) libraries. They stand diagonally opposite each other across the junction of Fifth Avenue and 40th Street in Manhattan. Mecanoo's first step was to produce a masterplan which viewed the buildings not in isolation, but as a Midtown Campus. Its aim was to increase space for books and people, expand life-long learning, enhance user experience, and create a synergy between NYPL's research and circulating flagships, and Bryant Park. Mecanoo's New York collaborator was architects Beyer Blinder Belle. Let us look at each building in turn.

The New York Public Library opened in 1911 with a glorious design by Carrère & Hastings in the grand neo-classical 'Beaux-Arts' style. It is now called the **Stephen A. Schwarzman Building** (SASB). A major strategic overhaul was needed. With over 1.7 million visits a year, visitors surge through a three-dimensional maze which has a long history of complicating changes. Spaces had filled with clutter, natural light was blocked, and even a courtyard was lost. Mecanoo's concept started with 'listening to the logic of this Beaux Arts building', says Houben. Re-opening spaces to the people would reveal the full internal architectural glory, and tackle the crucial issues of its circulation, both vertically between the different building's functions at lower and higher levels, and horizontally in the lower floors. Mecanoo's solutions not only solve these challenges, but deliver new facilities and infrastructure too.

Grand stairs facing Fifth Avenue lead to the main entrance on the library's main floor, which is a 'bel-étage', an above-ground high-ceilinged floor of grand rooms. A new Mecanoo desk greets visitors in the magnificent marble Astor Hall lobby. This entrance and another on 42nd Street are not enough for channelling visitors. Mecanoo's plan creates a new 40th street entrance for staff, researchers and school and student groups, and it will lead to a new Center for Research and Learning. Unlocking the first* floor spaces for public use takes pressure off the bel-étage, as well as deepening educational engagement. The bel-étage floor also includes a new café, a spacious new shop, a visitor centre, and a new gallery. Just behind the Astor Hall, the great columned Gottesman Hall has become a museum showcasing NYPL's own treasures. The elegant glass-domed Bartos Forum will be upgraded for functions.

The upper levels are a place of quiet research. New elevators to it shortcut today's complex access routes. Mecanoo's design has transformed the balcony floor (between the top floor and the bel-étage floor) with a suite of nine rooms called the Center for Research into the Humanities. It includes the Lenox and Astor Room for seminars. With long classical tables, double-level walls of books, restored marble, and mindful choices in colours and lighting, the rooms are now perfect for study and sharing wisdom. The third* floor includes the original, world-famous Rose Main Reading Room, 90 metres long and 16 metres high.

There has always been a majestic, baroque Poetry in the Beaux-Arts style of the SASB, and Mecanoo brings an upbeat shift. New spaces seamlessly clarify and counterpoint the rhythms and grandeur of the original architectural language.

Across Fifth Avenue

The buildings that are visible across Fifth Avenue from the SASB once included a six-storey department store built in 1914, designed by James T. Bartley. NYPL started moving books into it in the 1970s, and acquired the whole building in 1982. It became NYPL's largest and busiest circulating branch, known as the Mid-Manhattan Library. In 2020, after Mecanoo's complete transformation, it was reborn. This 16,722 m² powerhouse of wisdom is now called the **Stavros Niarchos Foundation Library**.

The sheer volume of millions of items makes access, organization and storage a challenge. Now the library has more space, more books, more seats, as well as accommodating a business library and new zones for youngsters. It also adds a conference centre, a café, and a sensational public open space. To fit all this in, Mecanoo dramatically restructured the space behind the facades, stratified the programs vertically, and built one of Manhattan's most extraordinary roofs ever.

Entering the library from Fifth Avenue, a colonnade of columns formed by the old structural steelwork has become an internal street beneath a floating linear canopy of timber beams, leading to welcome desks. To one side are elevators and stairs, and a new mezzanine terrace. On the other side, light from 40th Street now enters and reaches down through a void to a new Children's Library in the newly-opened lower ground floor. A separate Teen Center is accessed by its own dedicated staircase, and its study and media rooms are decorated with a mural by Melinda Beck. An internal window in the lower ground floor allows children to see the book-sorting machine in action.

On the second* floor, we find the heart of the library in the staggering Long Room. Francine Houben's idea was inspired by the Long Room Library at Trinity College in Dublin, Ireland. As at MLKML, a void has been made by cutting into the old horizontal steel beams. Now, a dramatic, airy 9-metre-wide linear atrium rises 26 metres, under a ceiling with vibrant artwork by Hayal Pozanti. This atrium separates three floors of flexible, day-lit reading areas on its Fifth Avenue side. On the other side, five levels of book stacks give open access for library users.

The Long Room's southern wall is deep red, and has new windows to bring light from a pocket park to the south. Gently sloping ramps connect the different floor heights of the book stack levels and reading areas. Bespoke oak-surfaced reading tables up to 20 metres in length were assembled in situ, many supported by the building's original steel frame. Readers' chairs were designed in collaboration with Thos. Moser, exclusively for NYPL. Above the Long Room, the fifth* and sixth* floors host the Business Center and Adult Learning. The design of the SNFL reflects that of the SASB: long tables with special chairs, artistic ceiling, and the Long Room as a reinterpretation of the stacks of SASB. But the stacks of SNFL are accessible and the book shelving is not structural and therefore flexible and future-proof. A new seventh* floor now stands on the building's original roof level. It has pitched wood slat ceilings and includes a flexible space for conference and events, and a public café. Best of all, the floor opens onto the only free-access rooftop public terrace in Manhattan. The L-shaped terrace, including a roof garden, runs above the 40th Street and Fifth Avenue facades. The views across Fifth Avenue to the Stephen A. Schwarzman Building and surrounding skyscrapers are simply staggering.

A Wizard Hat

The Stavros Niarchos Foundation Library's most visible sensation is a new sculptural crown. Covering the conference centre and mechanical equipment, a new roof now slopes up to a sharp apex 56 metres above street level. Its angled pitches and copper-coloured aluminium surface are inspired by Manhattan's copper-clad Beaux Art mansard roofs, and its shape nods to the tapering spires of New York's art deco skyscrapers and the faceted facades of contemporary towers. On a site visit, Francine Houben declared this spectacular roof to be 'a Wizard Hat for all New Yorkers!'

Mecanoo has brought ideas to America that range from re-imagined roofs and multi-storey walls of books, to designing in opportunity for all sectors of society, and making learning a pleasure. Houben once said that the hearts of America's most powerful cities 'are super-charged with energy, diversity and hope'. Now, at least in New York and Washington, they have the libraries precisely designed to channel those fantastic assets.

Mecanoo's wizardry in re-inventing the library in the real world is very different from the wizardry found in the world of Harry Potter. The Purpose of the contemporary library is now more than storing and sharing words of wisdom, it is to equip People with skills and access to everything from the knowledge economy to community support. Mecanoo's libraries from Delft to Manhattan are also spaces of activity and the shared life of their community. Each Library is a Place that transforms its location with its Poetry of form and light. Mecanoo's wizardry lies in architecture that creates a sense of belonging in the storehouse of wisdom, which, like magic, becomes a gateway to anyone and everyone's future.

*US floor numbering.

Library Delft University of Technology

Delft, the Netherlands

Discipline:

Architecture, Landscape, Interior

Typology:

Library, University/Campus

Link

Size: 15,000 m²
Design: Library 1993-1995, learning and working environment upgrades 2008-ongoing.
Realization: Library 1996-1997, learning and working environment upgrades 2010-ongoing.
Client: ING Real Estate; Delft University of Technology.

Design team: Mecanoo

Programme: University library of 15,000 m² with reading rooms and study spaces, trésor for historical books, archive, offices, university publisher, book binder and bookshop; ongoing interior upgrades learning environment, café, and new media centre.

GRASS AND GLASS

A library that doesn't want to be a building, but a landscape

The library is a building of glass and grass. A 42-metre-high cone breaks through an inclined lawn sweeping accross the roof down toward the 1968 brutalist Aula designed by Van den Broek and Bakema.

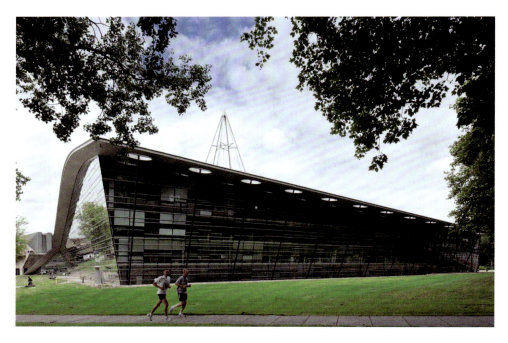

Library Delft University of Technology

WISDOM AND WIZARDRY

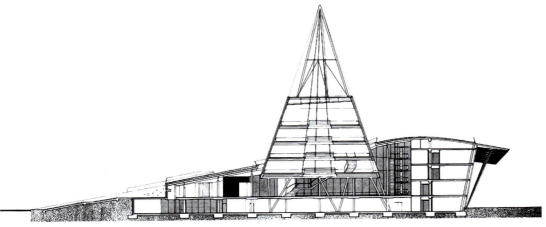

The eco-engineered library has an insulating grass roof, a climate wall, cold and heat storage, and a sunken book depot where books are kept just like good wine.

1993-2010   Delft, the Netherlands

5

A huge cone pierces the sloping ceiling, allowing daylight to filter into the library

WISDOM AND WIZARDRY

→ You can enter into the reading spaces of this conical building-in-building, accessed by gangways from a stunning 60-metre-wide, four level wall of books.

LocHal Library

Tilburg, the Netherlands

Discipline:

Interior

Typology:

Transformation, Library, Office, Government/Civic Link

Size: 7,000 m²
Design: 2016-2018, ongoing
Realization: 2018, ongoing
Client: Bibliotheek Midden-Brabant and Kunstloc Brabant.

Design team: Mecanoo (interior design), CIVIC (architecture), Braaksma & Roos (restoration), Inside Outside and TextielMuseum (interior concept and textiles).

Programme: 7,000 m² interior design for the Midden-Brabant public library and two cultural institutions, Kunstloc Brabant and Brabant C, in a former locomotive hall of the Dutch National Railways including 1,300 m² of offices.

CITY LIVING ROOM

LocHal (1932) was built as a locomotive repair shed and reconfigured into a library. Mecanoo designed the interiors, breathing life into the refreshed structure.

Tables made from old railway chassis can be moved along retained rail tracks within and outside the building, and they can join up to make a stage for performance.

Libraries are more than just warehouses of words; they are venues of culture, education, community services and events

A modular system of re-used books can be adjusted for book presentations, celebrations or a literary café with the stairs as tribune seating.

The industrial columns are fitted with wooden tables where visitors can read, meet and study.

LocHal Library

WISDOM AND WIZARDRY

In the WordLab books wrap the entire space, turning it into an immersive world of literature and language.

Inspired by the fairy-tale environments of the nearby Efteling theme park, the furniture of the Children's Library encourages children to read, imagine and dream.

The KennisMakerij or dialogue room hosts film screenings and presentations. Seated on curved benches, the public can be engaged in discussions.

The oval shaped GameLab is for teens, where you can learn everything about gaming.

2016-2018 Tilburg, the Netherlands

WISDOM AND WIZARDRY

← Together with the Textile Museum, Inside Outside created ceiling-heigh textiles that help to shape the immense hall.

A former oil pit has made way for a two-storey orange object with desks, a lecture area including stepped seating and a quiet mezzanine where you can work, with an overview of the space.

A shed for dynamic machines of the past becomes a dynamic box of contemporary interaction and ideas for the future

Tilburg, the Netherlands

Library of Birmingham

Birmingham, United Kingdom

Discipline:

Architecture, Urbanism, Landscape, Interior

Typology:

Library, Theatre/Concert Hall

Size: 35,000 m²
Design: 2008-2009
Realization: 2010-2013
Client: Birmingham City Council

Design team: Mecanoo

Programme: Central library of 31,000 m² with adult and children's library, study spaces, music library, multimedia, city archives, integration of the historical Shakespeare Memorial Room, offices, exhibition gallery, resources for health and wellbeing, cafés and lounge space, three roof terraces, 300-seat auditorium (shared with the REP Theatre); 4,000 m² renovation and extension of the REP Theatre including new back of house, rehearsal spaces and stage building workshops; urban plan for Centenary Square, BREEAM Excellent.

A PEOPLE'S PALACE

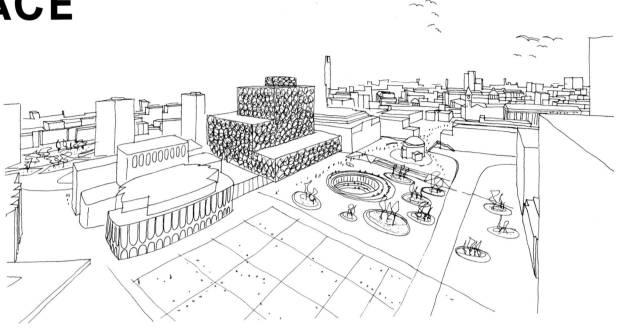

The new Library fits the rythm of the city. The library, REP Theatre (left) and Baskerville House (right) face Centenary Square like three palazzos.

1970: The brutalist library is under construction and the new building for the REP Theatre by architect Gramham Winteringham is about to open in 1971.

Library of Birmingham

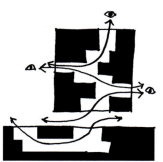

The city has a rich industrial history. Scattered around the city, the steel skeletons of gasometres catch the eye.

Based on a dream vison of a sequence of rotundas, the building creates a journey of discovery

Inviting, welcoming and inspiring for all ages and backgrounds

The library embraces you with a circular frieze creating an interior panorama of circles and shadows.

On the joyful bank of big yellow steps children can read a book, play or hang out.

The Book Rotunda in the heart of the library is an iconic space that is detailed like a circular book case with five levels.

Visitors travel through the Book Rotunda. A cylindrical lift leads up towards the Secret Garden and the Shakespeare Memorial Room.

The Shakespeare Memorial Room, that was part of the 1882 Victorian library, is integrated into the new library to showcase the library's unique Shakespeare collection.

Special 50-pence piece to celebrate the Birmingham 2022 Commonwealth Games. Designed by Natasha Preece of the Royal Mint, the coin features the library's facade design. The Library of Birmingham also features on a stamp.

The Discovery Terrace on level 3 is a public garden of benches and islands of vegetation containing 3,500 plants

ADDING PUBLIC SPACE

The outdoor circular amphitheatre is connected to the Music Library on the lower ground floor. It brings daylight into the building and can be used as a performance space.

Tainan Public Library

Tainan, Taiwan

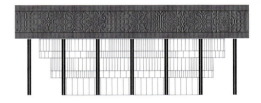

Discipline:

Architecture, Landscape, Interior

Typology:

Library, Government/Civic

Size: 37,000 m²
Design: 2016-2017
Realization: 2018-2020
Client: Cultural Affairs Bureau, Tainan City Government.

Design team: Mecanoo (lead architect) and MAYU Architects (architect of record).

Programme: 37,000 m² library with areas for the children's, teenagers and general collections, exhibition spaces for the modern art and heritage collection, 24/7 study room (130 seats), multimedia library, café, theatre (324 seats), conference hall (123 seats), offices, multipurpose rooms, maker space, bookshop, archive, parking garage, four patios, roof gardens and a square.

The design of the library is inspired by the rich history of Taiwan's oldest city

↑ Slender columns support the cantilevers in rhythmically placed quartets, giving a feeling of weaving your way through a modern bamboo forest.

The concept is inspired by the canopies of the historical temples and the creative window patterns that can be found in the city. ↓

The building's highest level is wrapped in a screen of vertical aluminium louvres, acting as brise-soleil to filter light. It is poetically carved to create a pattern evoking Taiwanese window frames.

A DELICATE SECOND SKIN

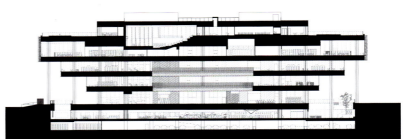

2016-2020   Tainan, Taiwan

On entering, visitors are welcomed with the artwork of London-based artist Paul Cocksedge, freezing the instant in which white paper is blown into the air.

Stepping into the library, a surprisingly transparent and warm interior unfolds

WISDOM AND WIZARDRY

A red sculptural staircase evokes a red lantern and adds an exciting element to the geometric building. It intersects all levels and is visible everywhere through the subtle wooden-slatted flight of stairs.

The library features a 324-seat auditorium for lectures and performances. ↓

Various reading areas are recognizable by different atmospheres. ↓

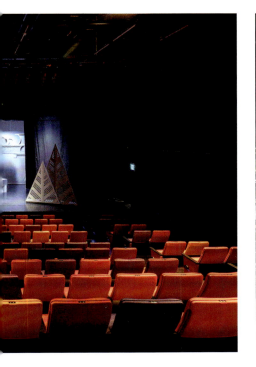

The lower-ground-floor houses lively functions such as the Children's Library with reading areas, playing areas, a kitchen for cooking lessons and a café.

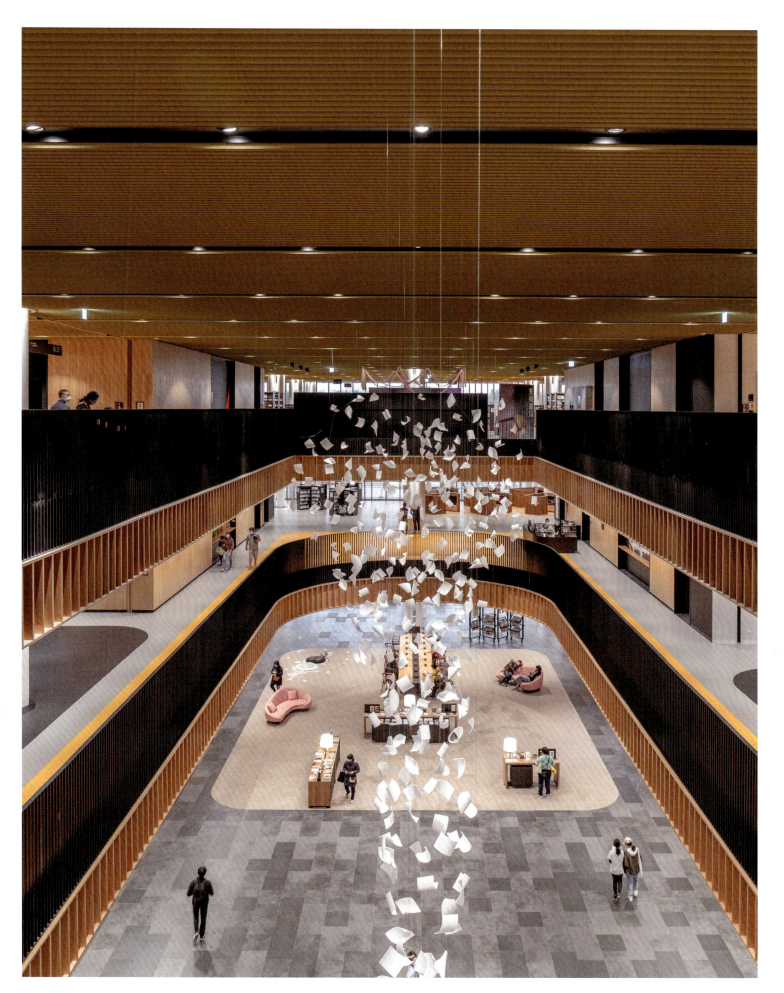

5

Beneath the cantilevers, there are four sunken patios designed for outdoor activities and to introduce natural daylight to the lower-ground-floor. The forest of columns extends down to this level.

WISDOM AND WIZARDRY

The inverted ziggurat shape of the library stands as a landmark within the new neighbourhood

2016–2020 — Tainan, Taiwan

Martin Luther King Jr. Memorial Library

Washington DC,
United States of America

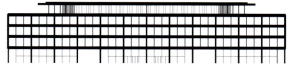

Discipline:

Architecture, Interior, Landscape, Restoration

Typology:

Transformation, Library

Size: 39,600 m²
Design: 2014-2016
Realization: 2017-2020
Client: District of Columbia Public Library, Washington DC.

Design team: Mecanoo (lead architect) and OTJ Architects (executive architect).

Programme: 39,600 m² central library renovation (1972, Mies van der Rohe) including children's library, teen's space, digital commons, main reading room, DC Welcome Center, Conference Center, Special Collections archives, exhibition and performance spaces, fabrication lab, creative lab, auditorium (291 seats), event spaces, café, and roof garden, LEED Silver certified.

5
TWO STRONG IDENTITIES

Washington DC hosts the only library by the master of minimalist modernist architecture, Mies van der Rohe. It opened in 1972. The library was named after Martin Luther King Jr., the African-American civil rights leader, tragically assasinated in 1968. Bringing these two strong identities together was the challenge for this library.

The transformation should highlight the library's social gathering purpose

Martin Luther King Jr. Memorial Library

WISDOM AND WIZARDRY

The 1972 library was a modernist masterpiece, however all the books got daylight and all the people didn't get any at all.

What if we transform the dark, unsafe staircases into pleasant and warm circulation spaces…

What if we create a rooftop as a public destination…

What if we open the building up to the city…

What if we bring daylight to the workfloor…

2014-2020 Washington DC, United States of America

A library for people and not just books

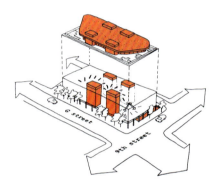

↑ The concept: transformation of the four cores, opening up the corner of 9th Street and adding a pavillion and garden on the roof.

By taking away a part of the brick walls and replacing them by glass, the main entrance on G Street has become transparent and welcoming.

Martin Luther King Jr. Memorial Library

WISDOM AND WIZARDRY

Below a mural from 1986 by Don Miller, which celebrates Dr King's life, the wall was recessed and lined with vertical wooden slats while stepped seating was added.

The granite floors of the Great Hall have been restored and the walls are partly transparant to better connect inside and outside.

The glazed perimeter is now for people instead of just books.

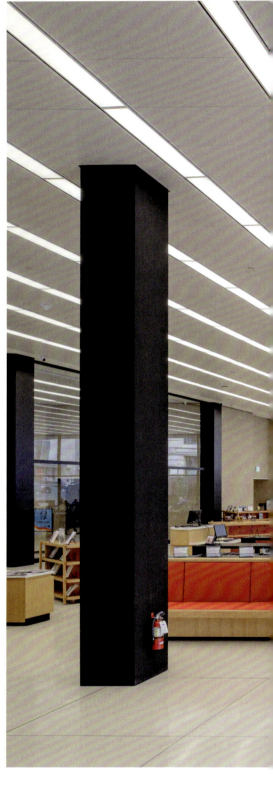

Book stacks had previously spread right up to the windows. Now, there is clear space and natural light that flows through the building.

Martin Luther King Jr. Memorial Library

WISDOM AND WIZARDRY

The transformation brings a new, humanistic environment at all levels

2014-2020 — Washington DC, United States of America

5

A new café extends to an outside area on the library's north-east corner. Brick walls have been cut back so that it is open to the sidewalk, connecting the library with the city.

The new café with outdoor terrace opens up the library to the city

SOCIAL LANDMARK

Martin Luther King Jr. Memorial Library

WISDOM AND WIZARDRY

The Grand Reading Room features an installation by Xenobia Bailey, an artist known for her strong traditional African and contemporary urban aesthetics.

The Children's Library is colourful with playful elements.

Instead of taking the stairs, children can take the slide!

The fourth* floor features a new 291-seats auditorium with warm wood-lined walls curving around the corners, and banked seating which rises into the new fifth* floor. (*US floor numbering)

2014-2020　　Washington DC, United States of America

A brick wall has made way for a transparent facade with a view into the new, inviting public interior with sculptural staircases.

Two sculptural wood-lined staircases curve gracefully from the lower ground floor towards the skylights above a new fifth* floor. (*US floor numbering)

Martin Luther King Jr. Memorial Library

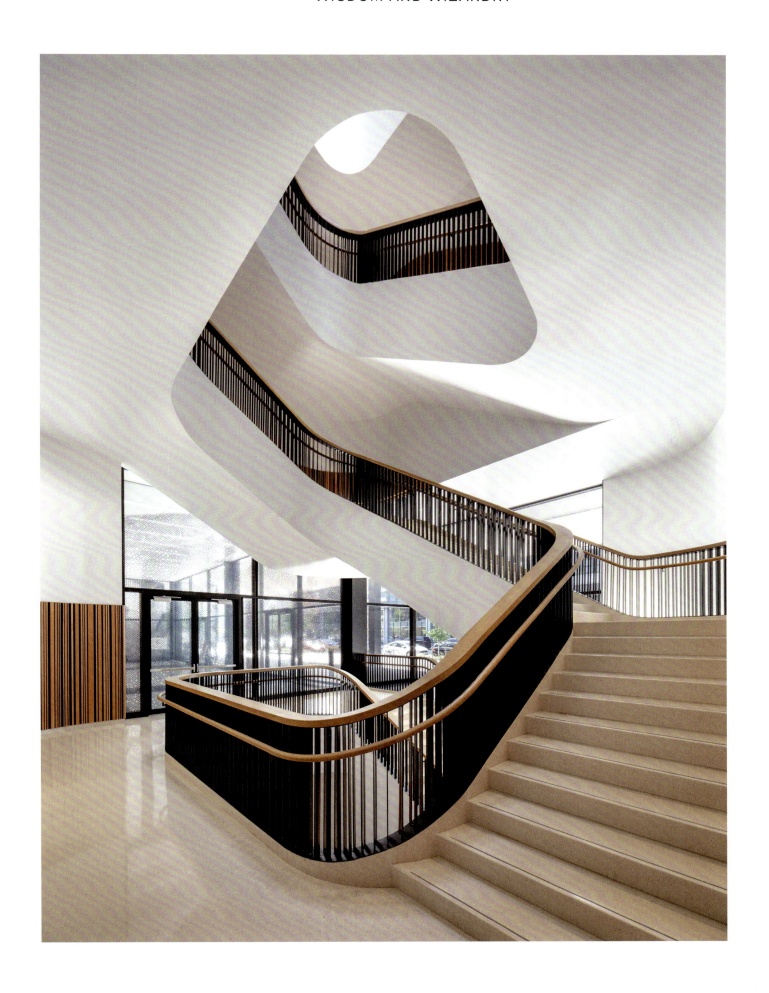

5

Surrounding the new pavilion is a roof garden with paths criss-crossing between angular planters which bring biodiversity into the heart of Washington.

190   Martin Luther King Jr. Memorial Library

TRAPEZOID CANOPY

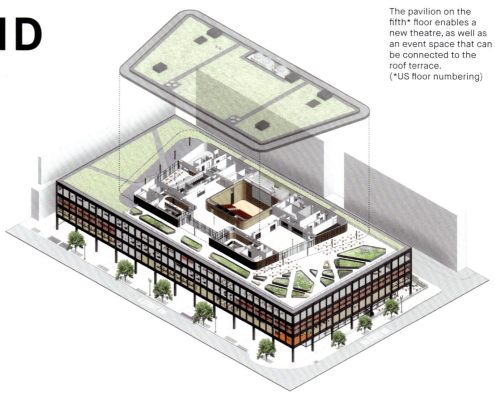

The pavilion on the fifth* floor enables a new theatre, as well as an event space that can be connected to the roof terrace.
(*US floor numbering)

2014–2020 — Washington DC, United States of America

The New York Public Library

Stephen A. Schwarzman Building

New York,
United States of America

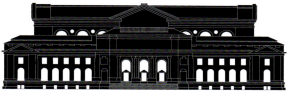

Discipline:

Architecture, Interior, Restoration

Typology:

Transformation, Library

Size: 23,226 m²
Design: 2015-2018, ongoing
Realization: 2017-2023, ongoing
Client: The New York Public Library

Link

Design team: Mecanoo and Beyer Blinder Belle Architects & Planners.

Programme: Central research library, part of the Midtown Campus masterplan, including app. 23,000 m² interior restoration and transformation, a new entrance on 40th Street, new stairs and elevators, Visitor Center, welcoming desks, Library Shop and Café, The Polonsky Exhibition of The New York Public Library's Treasure in Gottesman Hall, photo gallery, Center for Research in the Humanities, Center for Education, reading and study rooms, staff spaces, back of house logistic improvements, public and staff restrooms.

5
RESEARCH LIBRARY

The New York Public Library's flagship, the Stephen A. Schwarzman Building, is celebrated for its exceptional historical collections and dedication to free and equal access to its resources. (Photo 1915)

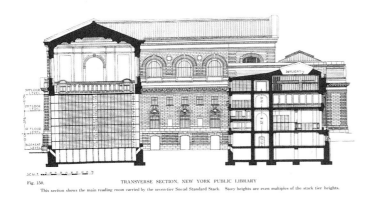

The Rose Main Reading Room, located under the pitched roof, is supported by seven-tier stacks.

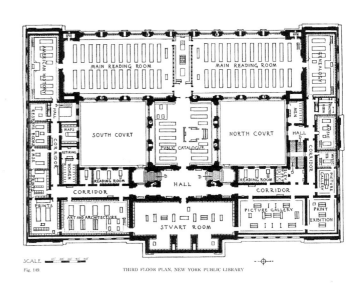

The original layout is a symmetrical three-storey building with a grand entry hall, two courts and stacks.

Stephen A. Schwarzman Building

WISDOM AND WIZARDRY

1905: The workshop of architects Carrère & Hastings. Their design was lauded for its practicality, monumentality, functionality, and beauty.

2015: Architects Francine Houben, of Mecanoo, and Elizabeth Leber, of Beyer Blinder Belle, are responsible for the largest renovation in the history of the New York Public Library.

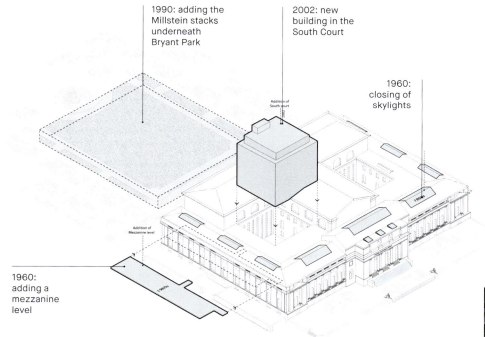

The design process started with 'listening' to the logic of this Beaux-Arts building

↑ Many transformations have been made over the years, according to its Zeitgeist.

2016: The Maps Division Collection storage space has large windows and is not a logical place to store daylight-sensitive documents.

MIDTOWN CAMPUS PLAN

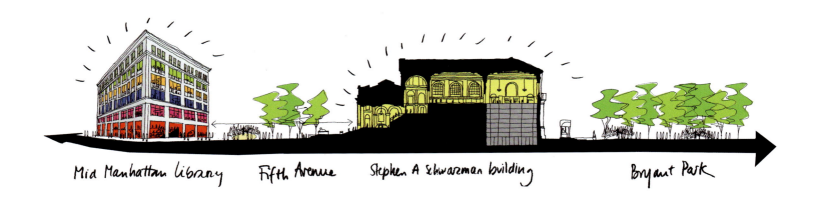

Mid Manhattan Library — Fifth Avenue — Stephen A Schwarzman building — Bryant Park

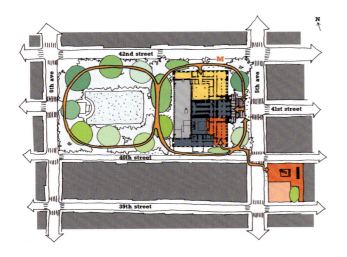

The Midtown Campus Masterplan connects the Stephen A. Schwarzman Building (research library), the Stavros Niarchos Foundation Library (circulating and business library) as well as Bryant Park by reshuffling the programme, adding a new entrance and creating a public rooftop destination (the Wizard Hat) for all New Yorkers.

WISDOM AND WIZARDRY

The Beaux Arts principles of symmetry, balance and clear lines are being reinforced

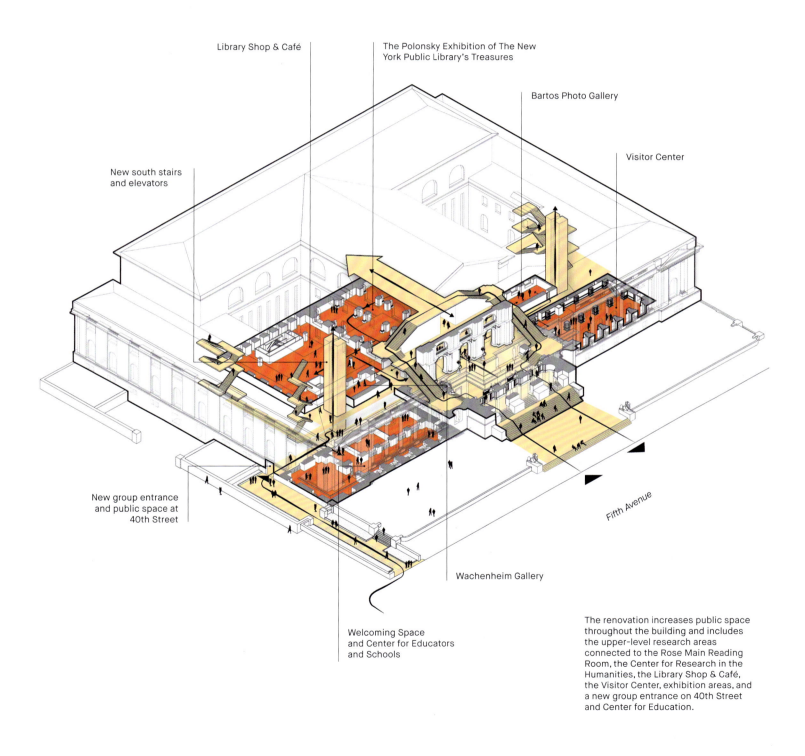

The renovation increases public space throughout the building and includes the upper-level research areas connected to the Rose Main Reading Room, the Center for Research in the Humanities, the Library Shop & Café, the Visitor Center, exhibition areas, and a new group entrance on 40th Street and Center for Education.

2015-2023 — New York, United States of America

The Rose Main Reading Room on the third* floor is an unforgettable space where researchers can quietly work in the centre of the Big Apple. Bottom left: McGraw Rotunda on the third* floor with paintings on the ceilings and walls. Bottom right: Astor Hall on the first* floor. (*US floor numbering)

→ The new timeless, brass reception desk fits the Beaux Arts design language of Astor Hall. The desk is flexible, allowing Astor Hall to be transformed into an event space.

ICONIC HALLS

Stephen A. Schwarzman Building

The treasures in the Polonsky Exhibition tell the stories of people, places, and moments spanning 4,000 years - from the emergence of the written word through to the present day. Visitors will encounter manuscripts, artworks, letters, still and moving images, recordings, and more that bring voices of the past to life.

WISDOM AND WIZARDRY

The renovated Gottesman Hall showcases the permanent 'The Polonsky Exhibition of The New York Public Library's Treasures'

A new Library Shop & Café is situated on the first* floor in the South Court, next to the exhibition galleries.
(*US floor numbering)

Circularity and identity: disused tables and cabinets were given a second life as displays in the Library Shop.

LIBRARY SHOP & CAFÉ

WISDOM AND WIZARDRY

5

The new Center for Research in the Humanities inspire, support, and connect a growing community of scholars worldwide

WISDOM AND WIZARDRY

The Lenox and Astor Room are designed for small seminars and hands-on interaction with collection materials. They've been renovated with computer and AV facilities and upgraded finishes inspired by the original Beaux Arts building's design.

The stripped space during construction in 2019.

The Maps Division Collection storage space has been transformed into a Visitor Center, inviting visitors, including those visually impaired, to touch and feel the building and the collection.

New stairs and elevators lead to the Celeste Auditorium on -2. The original brick walls of the former water reservoir are on display.

The New York Public Library was built on the location of the Croton Reservoir that held over 75 million litres of water (photo around 1898). ↓

WISDOM AND WIZARDRY

The new south stairs connect all floors from street level with the new 40th Street entrance to the third* floor, enhancing access and flow of visitors and employees. (*US floor numbering)

← Francine Houben and Tony Marx, President of The New York Public Library, at the construction site of the new south stairs in 2021, a highly complex intervention.

A new group entrance on 40th Street

Stephen A. Schwarzman Building

WISDOM AND WIZARDRY

The new 40th Street entrance for staff, researchers and student groups, also provides access to the new Center for Educators and Schools.

A new public space at 40th Street has been designed to safely accommodate groups entering the building.

To connect the new 40th Street entrance and south stairs, a wall opening was created. ↓

The iconic Stephen A. Schwarzman Building is one of the most loved buildings of New York

WISDOM AND WIZARDRY

Bryant Park, on the other side of the research library, is a popular place for people to meet and hang out.

The research library and the circulating library stand diagonally opposite each other across the junction of Fifth Avenue and 40th Street in Manhattan.

2015-2023　　　　New York, United States of America

The New York Public Library

Stavros Niarchos Foundation Library

New York,
United States of America

Discipline:

Architecture, Interior, Restoration

Typology:

Transformation, Library

Link

Size: 16,722 m²
Design: 2015-2018
Realization: 2017-2021
Client: The New York Public Library

Design team: Mecanoo (lead architect) and
Beyer Blinder Belle Architects & Planners
(architect of record, historic preservation and wayfinding).

Programme: 16,722 m² renovation and transformation of the central circulating library (former Mid-Manhattan Library) including circulating library, 400,000 books, Children's Center, Teen Center, Business Center, Adult Learning Center, general reading and study spaces, multipurpose space for events and lectures, café and rooftop terrace and garden, LEED Gold certified.

5
CIRCULATING LIBRARY

The 1914 building along Fifth Avenue was once the Arnold, Constable & Company department store. In 1982 it became the largest and busiest circulating branch of The New York Public Library.

The main challenges were how to create more study areas, cleverly organize book shelving, create more light and add a Children's Center and Teen Center.

The building had a bright presence on Fifth Avenue in the 1920s.

Re-imagining the Mid-Manhattan Library to a space of activity where learning is a pleasure

WISDOM AND WIZARDRY

The transformed library received a new name, Stavros Niarchos Foundation Library, and has more space, books, seats and daylight. It accommodates new zones for youngsters (-1), a Long Room with book stacks, a Business Center, (fifth and sixth floor*), and new functions on the roof. (*US floor numbering)

A void, cut into the old horizontal steel beams, creates a Long Room of 9-metre-wide and 26-metre-high were a large part of the book collection can be found.

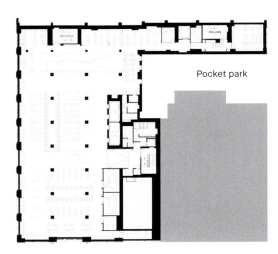

Second floor*   Pocket park

Fifth Avenue

Entering the library from Fifth Avenue, the colonnade of columns has become an internal street beneath a floating canopy of timber beams, leading to welcoming desks.

The columns are transformed from obstacles into a colonnade defining an inviting internal street, as well as carriers of tables and benches, and wayfinding posts

Light reaches down through a void to a new Children's Center and Teen Center on the lower ground floor

Stavros Niarchos Foundation Library

WISDOM AND WIZARDRY

The study and media rooms of the Teen Center are decorated with a mural by Melinda Beck.

An internal window allows children to see the book-sorting machine in action.

The Children's Center and Teen Center have a dedicated stairs to the lower ground which is designed with lots of playful and colourful detailing.

The Long Room, a dramatic 9m-wide linear atrium, rises 26m under a ceiling with vibrant artwork by Hayal Pozanti

Just as for the Stephen A. Schwarzman Building, special chairs were designed for the circulating library. The chairs were designed in collaboration with Thos. Moser.

Bespoke oak-surfaced reading tables up to 20 metres in length were assembled in situ, many supported by the building's original steel frame.

Five levels of book stacks give open access for library users.

The library has an abundance of study areas: beside the voids, along the windows and at the many large reading tables.

The Long Room truly brings the idea of a library into the old structure, which was originally designed as a department store

5
PUBLIC TERRACE

The sculptural crown of the library is inspired by Manhattan's copper-clad Beaux Arts mansard roofs. It covers mechanical equipment but also a 268-occupant conference and events centre.

The library is crowned with one of Manhattan's most extraordinary roofs

WIZARD HAT

The Stavros Niarchos Foundation Library is a powerhouse of wisdom, and its street presence brings drama and magic to Manhattan, visibly expressed with its Wizard Hat.

2015-2021 New York, United States of America

6

Come Together

Togetherness is a human need. The Covid-19 pandemic reminded us that we need human contact in the real world. The company of others delivers mental health, enables social bonds to prosper across the scale from personal friendships to whole communities, and is still the best way to share experiences and ideas. The real world offers a far richer 'bandwidth' for this to happen than channelling everything digitally onto a screen. Digital encounters are constrained by format and protocol whereas real-world encounters are more open and the unexpected is far more likely to happen. The environment itself is integrated into real-world encounters, which can be multi-sensory experiences. Being there with others in spaces such as a street, café, lounge, gallery, classroom or laboratory is physically impossible with digital technology.

Good design for Places where People come together can not only enhance personal experience, it can transform work, learning and neighbourhoods. We start by looking at an example that brings a neighbourhood together, in the eastern reaches of China's booming mega-city of Shenzhen.

A Chain of Buildings

China is a stage for extraordinary architectural geometry on a grand scale. The **Longgang Cultural Centre** completed in 2019, takes a truly fantastic form — a 400-metre-long chain of four angular buildings clad in red aluminium, like an enormous red train crossing the landscape. Each building is 50 metres wide and 25 metres high with fluidly curved edges, and each has inclined trapezoid sides. Each is essentially a hollow concrete container, like the cores that carry lifts and services in standard buildings. Mecanoo calls the Longgang structures 'supercores'. The volumes almost kiss across the narrow gaps between them at roof level, and as the gaps between them open up towards the ground, they create passages through the long site and create sheltered public space. These gaps are like gateways in a vast red wall and connect a park on the north-east side with, on the other side, a dense urban neighbourhood, including a traditional 'hakka' walled village, high-rise housing, and a new commercial centre to the west. The flow of people drives civic life around the cultural centre.

Each of the five-storey volumes brings people together for different purposes. At one end is a 13,500 m^2 arts museum, which includes urban planning displays, and next to it is an 8,000 m^2 youth centre. In the middle is the 10,000 m^2 science centre, full of exhibits designed to thrill and physically engage young visitors, while stairways and bridges create spatial drama as they cross a vast atrium. The largest volume is a 35,000 m^2 book mall, which also hosts lectures and shows. A triangular arch cuts through it, making a covered plaza where book trading can spill into the open. Every building makes the inside of the concrete 'core' shell part of its experience, creating awe-inspiring spaces defined by tilting walls and curving corners. A sunken shopping street runs beneath the buildings, connecting them and bringing street life. The futuristic form, colour and scale of the whole structure is a visible expression of the sheer dynamism of Shenzhen as it races towards tomorrow, and the cultural centre's public offerings extends to the whole city, with easy access thanks to an adjacent metro station. At the same time, it is also a place where the locals come together — to linger between city and park, to shop, to share life.

A Place for People

A city hall should also be a Place that brings a city's people together, but too often it operates from buildings that don't exactly offer a welcome to the citizens it serves. As we have seen with libraries (in Wisdom and Wizardry), Mecanoo's designs make an art of drawing People into public buildings, bringing them and the services they provide into city life. An excellent example of this approach is at the **City Hall and Municipal Offices** in Heerlen, a town in the southern Dutch province of Limburg, completed in 2023. Modernist architect Frits Peutz left a remarkable pioneering legacy there, including the all-glass Glaspaleis (1935), once a department store, and nearby City Hall (1942), a handsome limestone building. Mecanoo's project restores the latter, adds a major new building for its municipal offices beside it, and transforms the town centre space around them.

White-painted brick is a characteristic of facades in Heerlen's province of Limburg, and forms the cladding of a four-storey solid volume, penetrated by big square windows that echo those of Peutz's City Hall. The new volume floats above the ground on a glazed plinth. Entering at street level from the northern side, you can see right through to the public town hall. Descending wide stairs, which echo the City Hall's striking stair banks, bring people into a double-height main lobby, which is like an urban living room where they can linger as well as access city services. There is flow as well, because this underground level is an axis connecting northwards into the City Hall. Above it, voids penetrate into the higher municipal office floors, bringing natural light into the whole building, and an interior green wall climbs into it. Wood and natural stone bring warmth to all floors and resonate with Peutz's use of materials. The internal spaces have an informality that promotes interaction and connection, but there is also privacy in the booths where citizens can interface city services, such as we have seen in Washington's Martin Luther King Jr. Memorial Library (see p. 178). Outside, the rectangular volumes of both buildings complement each across and around the restored and landscaped car-free new public space. Seating, biodiverse planting, stone walls and connecting cross-routes give it a fascinating urban sense of Place, an outdoor stage for city life.

Street of Brands

We now turn to a project that innovates how a workplace can bring People together. The social element of office life makes workers happier, and spatial proximity boosts communication and collaboration. In Rotterdam, we find both in Mecanoo's design of the **Unilever Benelux Headquarters,** completed in 2020. It occupies the top six floors of a contemporary 10-storey office slab, located on a roundabout near the city's central station. There is also an entrance zone on the ground floor. This 8,400 m² project is a purely internal campus, although it enjoys great outward city views. The design approach was to emulate a smaller version of humanity's most pervasive coming-together environment, the city, but all contained within Unilever's walls.

The exposed concrete structural frame of the building defines the spaces, all under industrial ceilings with exposed services, but the overall neutrality is varied by different materials and colours. Black steel stairs to all Unilever's floors rise through voids cut through the floors. Wooden panelling and furnishings bring warm textures. As well as signage, design agency Silo (who Mecanoo also collaborated with at Eurojust, see p. 28 and Delfland Water Authority, see p. 340) have created a wide range of reliefs, drawings and graphics that celebrate both Unilever and the idea of a city. Green tiling and plants also crop up, for example at the bar designed to enjoy tea situated where one enters the campus on the sixth floor. It opens onto a double-height space, the 'Town Hall' auditorium, where a tier of wooden step seating rises at one end. We find curtains that can enclose the space for events, this time in Mecanoo's distinctive blue colour.

The curtains in the single-storey theatre space that is also on the sixth floor are orange-red, as is its bank of informal, tiered seating and furniture.

Brand hubs provide the opportunity to test products, and they are designed like shop service counters. The hub for soaps and washing products even has washing machines, and you can't help wondering if the foods hub doesn't run short on Unilever products like Ben & Jerry's! Because the building takes the form of a slab, each of the long floors is connected by a central corridor, but up on the eighth floor, it becomes an 'internal street', lined with displays of products in cabinets, like shopfronts. Connecting brand hubs for food and refreshments, and with break-out spaces and work areas, the flow of employees and the places to stop make it the high street of this mini-city floating above the big city.

A Big, Warm House

Architecture in the educational sector has a special responsibility for the future, because those who are now students will shape it. And the better their learning environment, the stronger and happier their learning experience will be. At **Amsterdam University College** (2012) in the city's Science Park, we find a refreshing new variation of an academic building. From outside, there is the poetic evocation of something unexpected yet instantly familiar — a big, warm house in the plain modernist campus surroundings. The square-plan, 5,800 m² volume is clad in corten steel and rises four storeys to a complex gabled green roof, which is laid with sedum, even though no part is horizontal. Inside, the building is about openness, reflecting the interdisciplinary spirit of the faculty's liberal arts and sciences programme. Its heart is two airy double-height voids that connect and carry staircases up towards wood-clad ceilings, through which light falls from skylight windows. The voids are overlooked from walkways and internal windows, some of double height, of rooms with views into the lively heart. More light comes through double-height windows at the generously large common room, the library and study area at the first floor and the ground floor café, all areas where people come together. The complex but calming spaces makes you feel connected to the whole faculty. You can study in the attic, as if this was a home away from home. Any place within the extraordinary geometry visually connects you to the whole place, and the people throughout it.

New Engineering Hub

Mecanoo's biggest academic project yet, for which they were lead designers, is the 81,000 m² **Manchester Engineering Campus Development** (MECD), completed in 2023. This new home of Manchester University's four engineering schools and two research institutes covers a site parallel to Oxford Road, the city's academic corridor. MECD's central building, the MEC Hall, is Manchester's longest building since industrial times, but it's not the only new building with wow factor.

A car-free passage runs beside the MEC Hall, separating it from other buildings, which include the new brick-clad Upper Brook Street Building, where double-height windows reveal heavy engineering laboratories. To the north, the Oddfellows Hall has been extended and refurbished behind a 1916 facade by architects Penoyre & Prasad, under supervision of Mecanoo. On the other side of MEC Hall is the new brick-clad, green-roofed York Street Building. This hosts the breathtaking High Voltage Lab, where generator structures rise towards the 20-metre-high ceiling and discharge up to two million volts. It feels like a 1950s sci-fi movie set that should be manned by boffins in white coats, but the lightning-like discharge flashes are real and anyone can see them, again through double-height street windows.

A major part of how MECD connects with the public is to reveal its laboratories, and there's much more of that in the vast MEC Hall. This 59,000 m² eight-storey rectangular box stretches 238 metres from a new southern landscaped garden plaza towards the city centre in the north. It is clad in black steel and dark glass, not unlike Mies van der Rohe's modernist American style such as the Martin Luther King Jr. Memorial Library (see p. 178), but on the upper levels, it steps back in its steel frame. The MEC Hall is much more than a state-of-the-art technical box for laboratories, clean rooms, lecture rooms and offices — it is also like a massive social machine. Let's step inside and see.

From the northern lobby, an extraordinary internal public street runs the entire length of the building. On one side, full-height glass reveals workshops, and on the other is a continuous strip of study and collaboration space with work tables. Above, acoustic baffling panels hang like books from the ceiling, and black staircases climb three storey voids through the visible concrete structural frame. The street is so long, it feels like walking into an infinite matrix simulation — but this place is busy with real people. The MEC Hall can host 9,000 students, staff and visitors. Past a huge Makerspace, where anyone can come to construct their idea, the street opens on one side into the triple-height Event Space, with tiered seating steps and a stage lighting rig above. A sewer crosses underneath, so this part of MEC Hall is free of heavy concrete. Elsewhere underground, vibration-sensitive labs are buried. The southern entrance opens to a new square that can host outdoor events, and like another new garden on Upper Brook Street, it hosts biodiversity. Also at the MEC Hall's southern end is one of MECD's two blended lecture theatres, where tables rather than rows of seats are on gently rising tiers. That's handy for students taking their coffee in.

Two levels of balcony run above the internal street, and they too have a street feeling. On the higher one, people gather around a café beside a covered bridge to the Upper Brook Street Building, and the larger blended theatre inside it. Two other large double-height theatres, with 450 and 600 seats, are near the Event Space. The third floor interfaces to the higher, non-public levels, accessed by four 'cores' that are skylit atriums with tiered seating, which creates more social space.

The MEC Hall hosts three cafés, and their names tell how it brings People together. To 'Change' how different disciplines are traditionally walled off from each other, they need to 'Connect'. The transparency of the laboratories breaks down visual barriers, but connections are also made between the people that use the building. The long internal street is a social as well as spatial connector. Connection opens the way to 'Collaborate', and cross-disciplinary collaboration is a fundamental driver of innovation. Manchester became the world's first industrial city through innovation, and now, as Francine Houben comments, the MECD will 'become a centre for twenty-first-century innovation'. The social aspect is crucial too, and MECD's social space reaches out to the city. As Houben says, the MECD 'physically extends the city centre into its academic axis, combining epic scale with connectivity, heritage and new public space for everyone'.

There are common threads that run through the very different Mecanoo projects we have looked at, such as voids that create visual connection across buildings so that shared space becomes three-dimensional, and features with a social dimension such as the tiered seating, internal streets and free spaces. All of them create opportunities to encounter others and work, study or simply hang out together. Of course that sounds good, but it is also carries a poetic hope for humanity's future. To survive, we, the People, need to come together. The best places to do so are not on a screen or in a metaverse, but in a real Place designed — as Mecanoo always has — for humans.

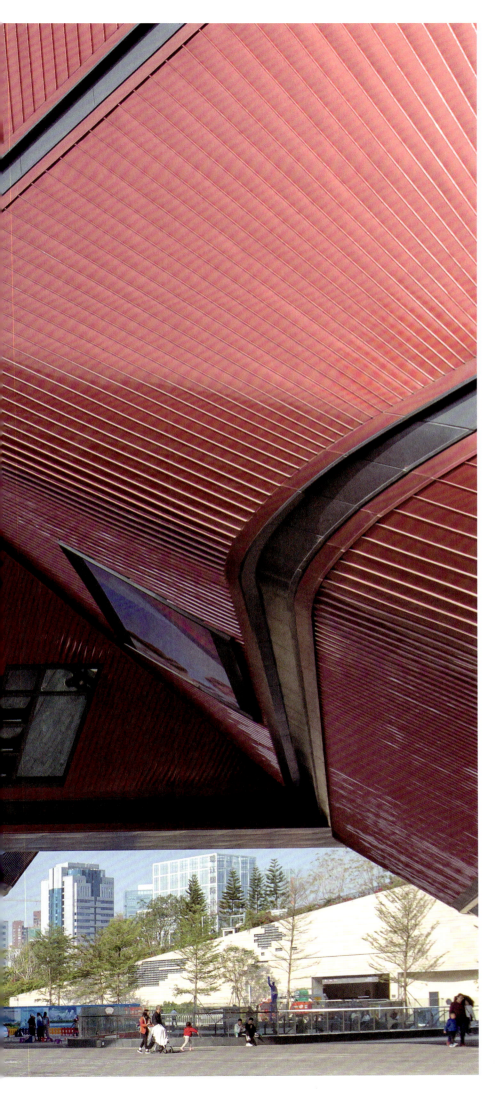

Longgang Cultural Centre

Shenzhen, China

Discipline:

Architecture, Urbanism

Typology:

Museum/Exhibition

Link

Size: 95,000 m²
Design: 2012-2016
Realization: 2015-2019
Client: Longgang Government, Vanke and SPDG.

Design team: Mecanoo (lead architect) and CCDI (local architect).

Programme: Cultural complex of 95,000 m² with 13,500 m² public art museum, 10,000 m² science museum, 8,000 m² youth centre, 7,000 m² retail and a 35,000 m² book mall with cafés and restaurants, 21,500 m² of underground parking and a 3.8-ha public square.

6
ARCHITECTURAL GEOMETRY

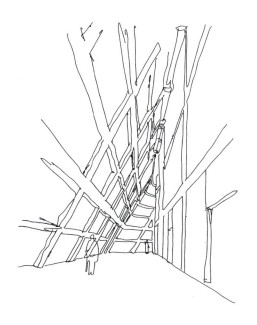

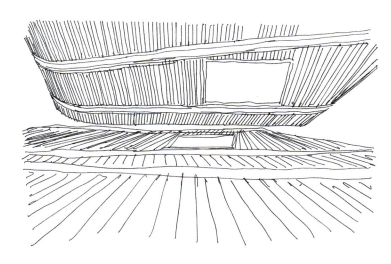

The Longgang Cultural Centre is a 400m-long chain of four angular buildings clad in red aluminium. ↓

Each of the buildings is 50 metres wide and 25 metres high. The concrete construction is part of the building's experience.

Longgang Cultural Centre

COME TOGETHER

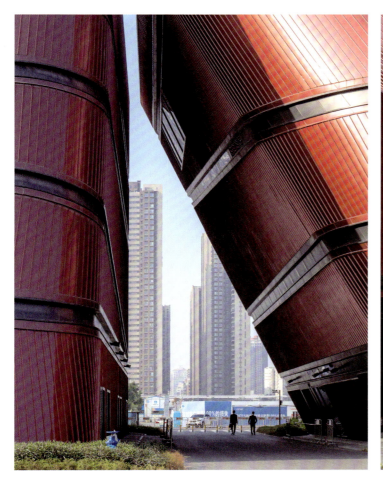

The tilting facades frame dynamic views, shelter public squares and naturally guide pedestrian flows.

The arches create covered squares for outdoor activities

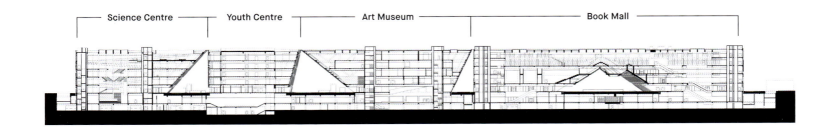

2012–2019   Shenzhen, China   237

The gigantic Book Mall includes cafés and restaurants.

The Youth Centre provides a place for meeting and activities such as music and sports.

Science Centre

The Science Centre focuses on popular science for children and young adults.

→ The Public Art Museum combines art exhibitions on the upper floors and an urban planning centre on the ground floor and lower ground floor.

Longgang Cultural Centre

6

The gaps are gateways that connect the park to the neighbourhood on the other side, including a traditional 'hakka' or walled village with low-rise housing.

Longgang Cultural Centre

COME TOGETHER

A rich and varied cultural programme housed in an iconic urban connector

2012-2019 — Shenzhen, China

Heerlen City Hall and Municipal Offices

Heerlen, the Netherlands

 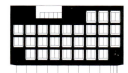

Discipline

Architecture, Interior, Landscape, Restoration

Typology

Transformation, Office, Government/Civic

Size: 16,000 m²
Design: 2017-2018
Realization: 2019-2023
Client: Municipality of Heerlen

Design team: Aannemersbedrijf Jongen B.V. (contractor), Mecanoo (architect, interior and landscape), ABT (structural and M&E engineer, acoustic, building physics and fire safety consultant) and Dijkoraad (landmark consultant).

Programme: Renovation of the existing landmark City Hall of 6,900 m² and new municipal offices of 9,100 m² with public lobby, call centre, offices, meeting centre, entrepreneurs house, co-working space and council chamber including landscape design, totalling 16,000 m².

FRITS PEUTZ

Frits Peutz (1896-1974) has left a remarkable modernist pioneering legacy including the Heerlen City Hall.

The iconic 1942 City Hall has the shape of an elongated shoe box with playful elements in its limestone facade. Typical for architect Peutz are the asymmetrical placement of doors and windows, and a balcony jutting out above the main entrance.

The 1942 City Hall is designed as a Roman villa

Situation in 2018: the large building with municipal offices on the right side of Peutz's City Hall was demolished to make way for a compact building connected to Peutz's monument.

Heerlen City Hall and Municipal Offices

COME TOGETHER

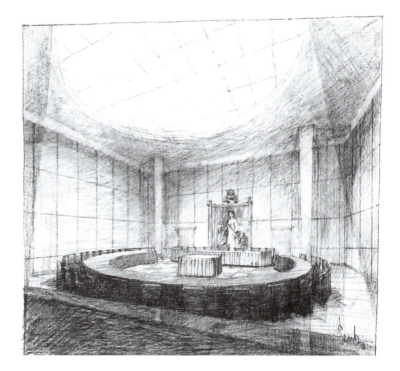

Handsketch by Frits Peutz of the Council Chamber, app.1938. →

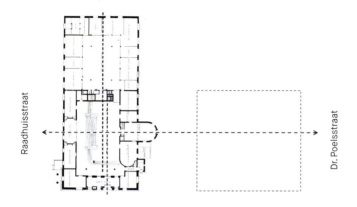

Mecanoo introduces a new axis perpendicular to the symmetrical axis of the existing City Hall.

Renovating and extending a pioneering legacy

Peutz wanted to bring the public, politics and art together. Therefore, he designed a wide staircase leading to the Council Chamber and gave the hall the atmosphere of an art exhibition space.

2017-2023 — Heerlen, the Netherlands

6

Francine's Heerlen childhood in the thriving mining town was filled with optimism, but when her family relocated to Groningen when natural gas was discovered there, the mining industry faced a downturn. Francine aimed to revive Heerlen's childhood optimism and its scenic beauty.

Bringing back optimism and the beauty of the landscape to Heerlen

246   Heerlen City Hall and Municipal Offices

COME TOGETHER

↑ The new Municipal Offices form a balanced composition with the existing City Hall, and with its varying heights it connects to the rolling landscape of South Limburg.

A central axis connects the City Hall on the right with the new Municipal Offices on the left. The main entrance links to the level of the inner city. ↓

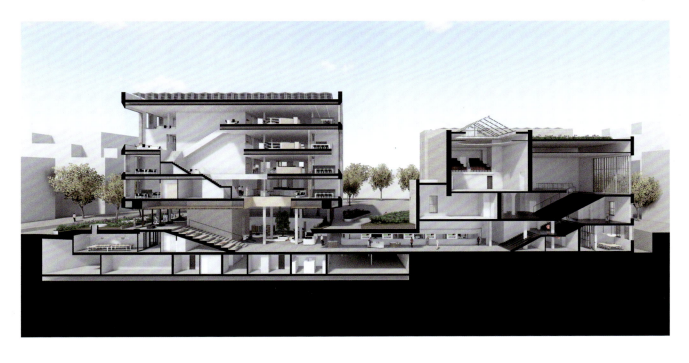

2017-2023 · Heerlen, the Netherlands

The white limewashed brickwork in the interior of Peutz's City Hall now graces the facades of the new Municipal Offices, while the City Hall's natural stone facades are echoed in the cores of the Municipal Offices.

Peutz's City Hall, featuring distinctive rounded columns and white limewashed brickwork, has been carefully renovated.

Mecanoo mirrors Peutz: its special brickwork, natural stone and the composition of windows

COME TOGETHER

The main hall showcases the modern art collection of Heerlen.

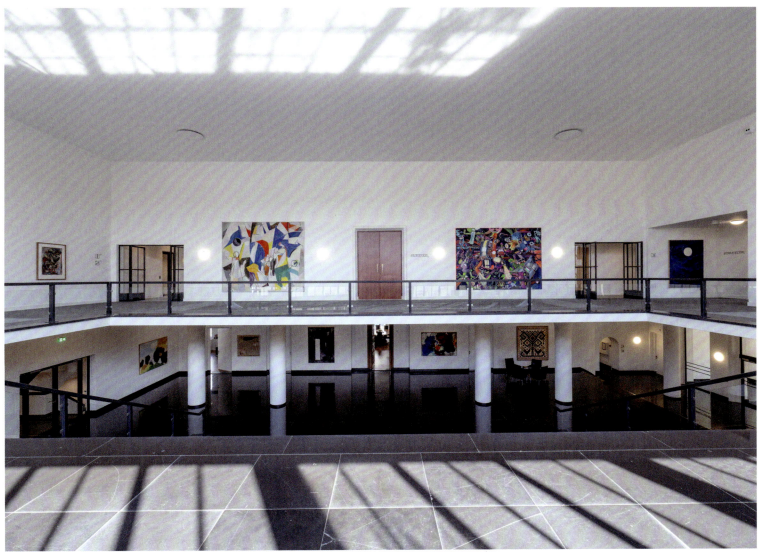

Oak detailing characterizes the Mayor's room as well as the Council Chamber.

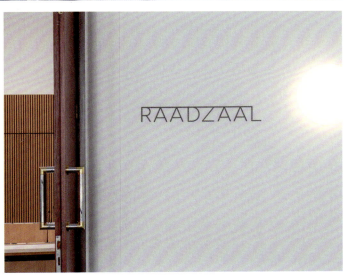

The timeless signage has been designed by Ritzen-Design-Consult.

2017-2023   Heerlen, the Netherlands

COUNCIL CHAMBER

The new layout of the Council Chamber offers increased space for speakers, audience, and press. Oak-clad walls enhance acoustics, while a bespoke chandelier highlights the original oval skylight.

COME TOGETHER

The former public hall is transformed into a public Conference Centre with its own entrance at the lower level of the Geleenstraat. Glass facades, once moved and now restored, align once again between columns.

With its public hall on the lower level, the Municipal Offices make clever use of the topography

The double-height public hall serves as a welcoming living room for the citizens of Heerlen. Its transparent plinth allows passers-by to catch glimpses of the interior.

COME TOGETHER

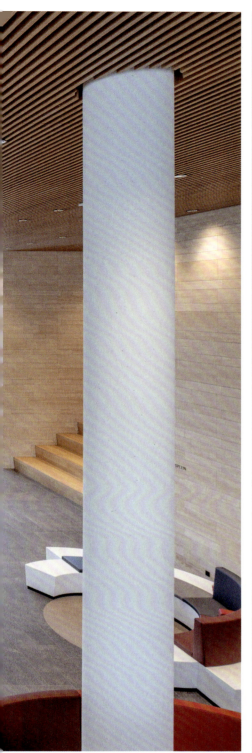

On either side of the central axis are wide staircases: the oak staircase leads to the offices, while the black stone staircase leads to Peutz's City Hall.

2017-2023 — Heerlen, the Netherlands

COME TOGETHER

A void with a green wall links the office area and public hall, fostering visual connections among employees, the public hall, the city and the rolling landscape.

The office floors have a middle zone for informal meetings. →

The dynamic office layout promotes informal meetings and exchange

2017-2023   Heerlen, the Netherlands

Unilever Benelux Headquarters

Rotterdam, the Netherlands

Discipline:

Interior

Typology:

Transformation, Office

Size: 8,400 m²
Design: 2019
Realization: 2019-2020
Client: Unilever Nederland

Design team: Mecanoo

Programme: Interior design for the new Unilever Benelux headquarters on the fourth to ninth floors of a mid-century modern building, including an entrance on the ground floor, a variety of activity-based workplaces, staff restaurant and bars, auditorium, brand hubs, kitchens for development of Unilever brands and displays for Unilever products, totalling 8,400 m².

Unilever occupies the top six floors of a 10-storey office slab (1960, architect C.A. Abspoel) including entrance zone on the ground floor.

The building is located along the Hofplein, an area that was bombed during World War II. Now it is one of the busiest roundabouts in the city centre of Rotterdam.

Breakthroughs create voids connecting the various departments and employees.

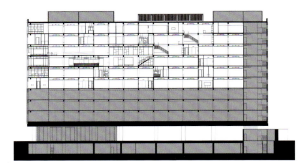

COME TOGETHER

Upon entering the sixth floor, visitors are welcomed in a bar from which all floors are accessible via internal stairs.

Brand hubs of Unilever products each have their own identity. In the brand hub of Beauty & Personal Care, products can be presented and tested.

The theatre on the sixth floor is for presentations, and informal working and meeting.

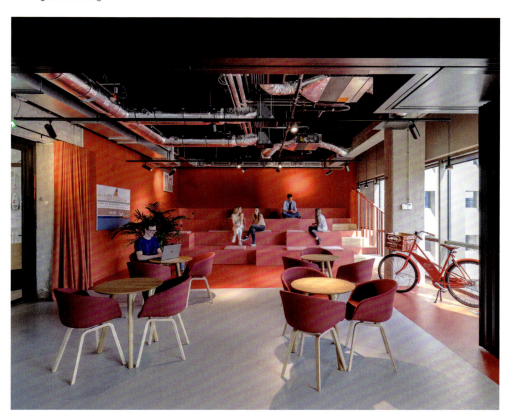

Transforming a 1960s office building into a community-together environment

2019-2020 Rotterdam, the Netherlands 261

Breakthroughs were made in the floors creating voids with stairs that connect the various departments and employees.

The interior is designed as a city with streets and shops: Unilever City.

Unilever Benelux Headquarters

COME TOGETHER

The auditorium is multifunctional and can be used for events, lectures, meetings, working, or to have lunch.

Amsterdam University College

Amsterdam, the Netherlands

Discipline:

Architecture, Interior

Typology:

Educational, University/Campus

Link

Size: 5,800 m²
Design: 2008-2010
Realization: 2010-2012
Client: University of Amsterdam;
VU University Amsterdam.

Design team: Mecanoo

Programme: 5,800 m² liberal arts and sciences college, a compact, sustainable building with class rooms, library, restaurant, living room, project rooms, conference rooms and workstations.

265

Diagonally placed gabled roofs

Amsterdam University College

You can study in the attic, as if this was a home away from home

ROBUST AND HOMELY

The building's heart has two airy double-height voids which connect and carry staircases up towards wood-clad ceilings with skylight windows.

Quieter study areas and the library are located on the first floor, directly under the gabled roof.

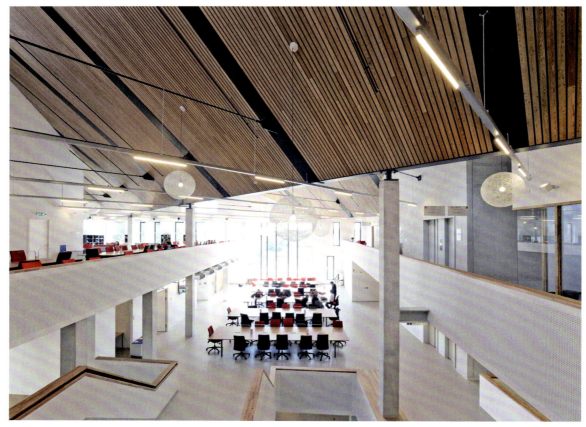

The double-height common hall has tall, expansive windows that offer beautiful views of the surroundings.

An inspiring home for a community of international students and their professors

The compact mass of the building allows for an optimal ratio between wall and floor surface.

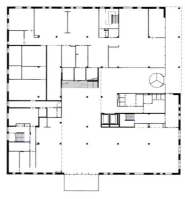
Ground floor

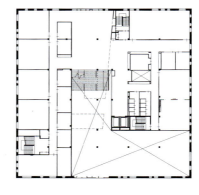
First floor

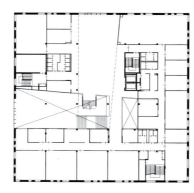
Second floor

Third floor

The heart of the building is a lively meeting place: homely and flooded with daylight.

Amsterdam University College

COME TOGETHER

The voids are overlooked from walkways and from the internal windows of rooms with views into the central space. The wood-clad ceilings and walls create a warm atmosphere throughout the building.

Manchester Engineering Campus Development

Manchester, United Kingdom

Discipline:

Architecture, Landscape

Typology:

Office/Research, University/Campus

Size: 81,000 m²
Design: 2014-2016
Realization: 2017-2024
Client: University of Manchester

Design team: Mecanoo (lead architect), Penoyre & Prasad (refurbishment and extension of Odd Fellows Hall), BDP (detailed design).

Programme: Technical University of 81,000 m² integrating four engineering faculties (Chemical, Material, Electrical and Mechanical engineering) and two research institutes merged into six buildings, including 76,000 m² of new construction and 4,300 m² renovation. The six buildings include a state-of-the-art new learning environment MEC Hall of 59,000 m², four lecture halls (600, 450, 250 and 150 seats), a wide range of laboratories (1,161 m² laser labs, 8,784 m² dry labs, 2,412 m² chemical labs, 630 m² biochemical labs, 1,141 m² laboratory for electron microscopy and cleanrooms), meeting and conference rooms, workshops, offices, student facilities, café, restaurant, and storage areas, BREEAM Excellent.

FOUR FACULTIES & TWO RESEARCH INSTITUTES

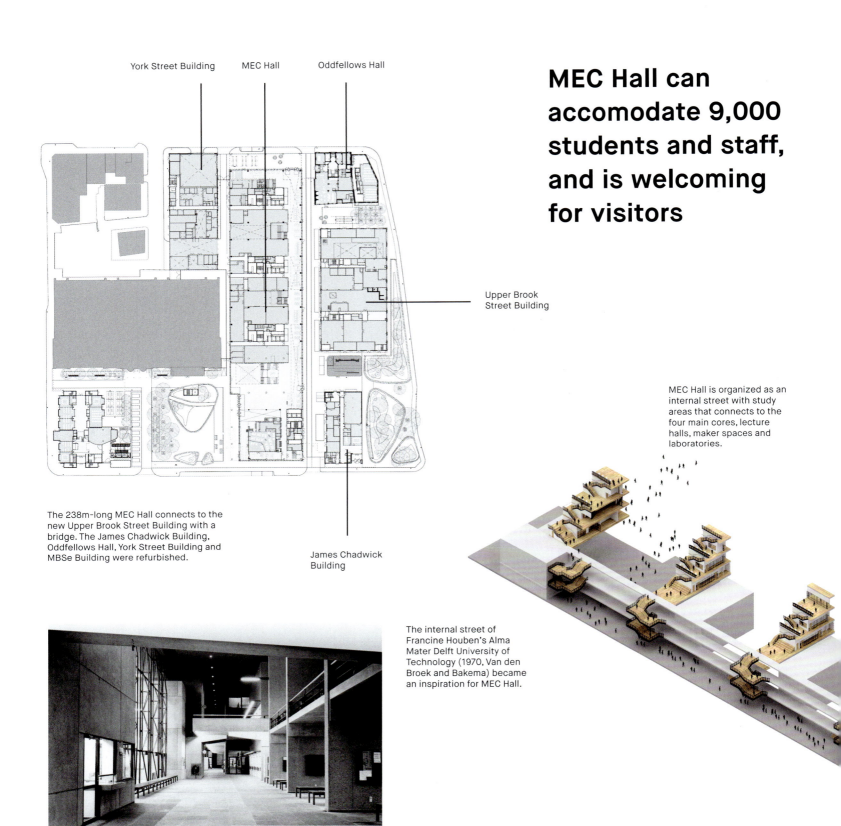

MEC Hall can accomodate 9,000 students and staff, and is welcoming for visitors

York Street Building

MEC Hall

Oddfellows Hall

Upper Brook Street Building

The 238m-long MEC Hall connects to the new Upper Brook Street Building with a bridge. The James Chadwick Building, Oddfellows Hall, York Street Building and MBSe Building were refurbished.

James Chadwick Building

MEC Hall is organized as an internal street with study areas that connects to the four main cores, lecture halls, maker spaces and laboratories.

The internal street of Francine Houben's Alma Mater Delft University of Technology (1970, Van den Broek and Bakema) became an inspiration for MEC Hall.

Manchester Engineering Campus Development

COME TOGETHER

MEC Hall is clad in black steel and dark glass with a transparent plinth that allows for views inside.

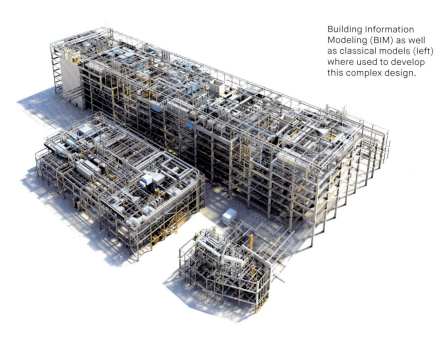

Building Information Modeling (BIM) as well as classical models (left) where used to develop this complex design.

2014-2023 Manchester, United Kingdom

6

Bachelor students spend much of their time on the lively ground and first floors of MEC Hall.

The internal street is a great social as well as spatial connector

276   Manchester Engineering Campus Development

COME TOGETHER

A triple-height Event Space with tiered seating steps and staircases to the first floor can be used for meetings, exhibitions and celebrations.

COME TOGETHER

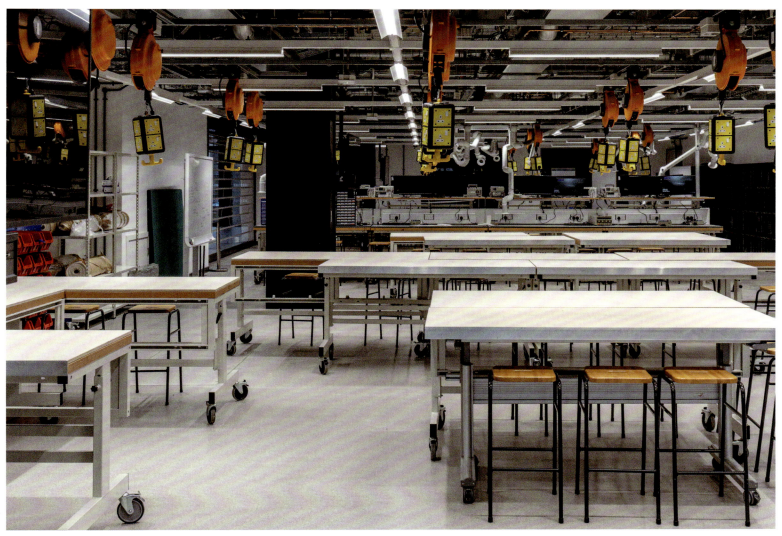

The university hosts a large variety of labs such as makerspaces and electronic labs.

← The four MEC Hall cores connect the third floor to upper levels, offering quiet study areas for master students, labs, and offices, with roof openings providing daylight to adjacent laboratories.

The first core allows for views into the Mechanical Workshop. Left and right from the staircase are computer clusters where students are being taught how to program the Mechanical Workshop equipment.

Learning by doing is on display, to inspire students and promote a multidisciplinary approach

COME TOGETHER

↑ The new York Street Building hosts the Large Extra High Voltage Lab, where generator structures rise towards the ceiling 20 metres above and discharges of up to two million volts flash like lightning.

The Medium Extra High Voltage Lab has cages which provide safety for experiments. →

It is a place where Chemical, Material, Electrical and Mechanical engineering students collaborate, innovate, and make their mark on the world

A bridge connects MEC Hall to the Upper Brook Street Building with lecture halls and labs.

7

Touch Me, Feel Me

We mainly engage with architecture's surfaces via the sense of sight. Seeing a building exterior, we read information about it such as its style and form, which suggests its function. Inside, we construct a mental map of a building from what we see. But light is not the only medium that tells us of buildings and their surfaces. Other senses — sound, touch, smell, and temperature — have a role in architecture. Francine Houben has said that 'architecture must appeal to all the senses and is never a purely intellectual, conceptual and visual game alone'. Take sound, for example. An auditorium where sounds dissolve into noise, or a room where you could hear everything going on next door, would be unacceptable, so architects design for sound. They also design for temperature to make a fresh, comfortable internal climate.

A particularly rich sense to address is touch. The difference between metal and stone, or wood and glass, or a plant and a pond, are so clear to the touch that we could know a place where such elements are with our eyes closed. Architecture can incorporate all these elements so it's the tactile dimension is a fundamental element in Mecanoo's architecture, which Houben once even summarized as 'human, it's tactile, it's multi-disciplinary'. Even bricks have their place in the adventure of texture that we find in Mecanoo's works.

The Art of Brick Laying

Bricks have been in use for at least 9,500 years, when earth was shaped and dried at Tell Aswad in modern-day Syria. They are so common we may not give them a second glance. But their surfaces are uniquely tactile, and they can bring an authenticity that contemporary buildings with anodyne cladding so often lack. An under-exploited advantage of bricks is how they vary widely in colour and texture.

In Arnhem, Mecanoo celebrates the diverse possibilities of brick in the **Netherlands Open Air Museum**, opened in 2000. It has an outside wall 143 metres long and 7.3 metres high, clad with a linear quilt of patches of different bricks. A wide range of bricklaying techniques is also on show, some developed by great Dutch architects such as Hendrik Petrus Berlage whose journey from neo-Romanesque style towards early-twentieth-century modernism was informed by materiality, and Willem Dudok, the master of pre-war modernism, while other techniques are timeless and their origins anonymous. Mecanoo themselves bring new techniques into the mix. The brick colours go from yellow through reds to grey, with a few that are actually blue. Some are smooth and regular, some laid rough in warped lines as if the bricklayers were drunk, leaving the putty to ooze out. This is a wall that calls out 'come over and feel me!'

Bricks also pave the path through the gardens which continues through the building to the outdoor museum with historical farm houses, mills, gardens and even trams. Brick surfaces are not the only ones the museum offers that talk in textures. In front of the wall is a copper-skinned pavilion shaped like a vast egg. It was originally a panoramic theatre, but in 2017 Mecanoo created a new interior for the whole building including the theatre to host the Canon of Dutch History gallery. The copper has weathered from a shiny polished look to a rich brown patina, telling of the passage of time. In 2017, a new ticketing pavilion also was added across the brick path. It is boomerang in plan and has an extraordinary 15-tonne, 14-metre-long roof of Corten steel plate, which has a strong metallic materiality that seems almost organic. The roof was crafted and welded by Dutch shipbuilders — not the only instance of Mecanoo calling on their skills, as we shall see later in the spectacular National Kaohsiung Center for the Arts in Taiwan (see p. 440).

Catalyst for the Community

In Roxbury, an inner-city neighbourhood in Boston, Massachusetts, we find a very different play of brickwork in a project that Houben proudly calls 'a catalyst for the community'. The **Bruce C. Bolling Municipal Building**, completed in 2015, houses Boston's public school administration and a community centre in a 20,000 m² building all wrapped up in a mix of facades that includes those of three restored from heritage buildings. There's a beautiful switch from a nineteenth-century red-brick facade to the new mid-rise main volume's oxblood-red glazed bricks, which have been laid in different ways to create jazzy rhythms across its facades. Bands of bricks, laid vertically in 'soldier bond', snake horizontally across the facades and around the elegantly curving corners of the new volume. The triangular Ferdinand Building that is part of the site has a pale terracotta facade from 1895, with its ornate window features and cornice. Once again it stands proud, and behind its leading corner is a roof terrace. On Washington Street, it thrusts forward as if introducing the whole block, like the prow of a great ship cutting through water.

A Country Estate

The location and functions of Boston's proud new municipal centre are a great contrast to the rural **St. Gerlach Pavilion & Manor Farm**, but the latter is another project bringing old and new together. They are part of the grand seventeenth-century country estate Chateau St. Gerlach which is now a luxury spa hotel in the slightly hilly Dutch south. In 2017, Mecanoo made a sympathetic addition to its facilities. A new pavilion with three large multifunctional meeting rooms gives the estate a roadside entrance, and a very contemporary presence. It has a wide elegant roof sheltering a long volume whose partially-glazed facade is a continuous run of larch wood columns.

While lark, with its sturdy resilience to weather, is used in facades, oak, a local material, is used in the interiors. The roof's expressive cantilevered corners are a counterpoint to the curved corners beneath it. Inspiration came from local materials such as marl and bluestone, each with their own distinct surfaces, as well as local wood. They are all found in the rich materiality that runs through the project. Between the pavilion and a 1688 manor farm building, there is now a newly-cobbled patio with seating, evoking a village square. Inside the rustic old farm building, its richly organic space of old brick walls and wooden rafters has been adapted to accommodate a restaurant. The intervention is light, letting history define the ambience.

All these buildings are compositions that succeed in creating a Poetry with their sensual surfaces that step beyond the narrow variations of standard building materials. But Nature, too, provides a palette of materials for our built environment, which brings us to parks and landscaping that engage multiple senses, including touch, smell and sound.

Urban Park

In Amsterdam, Mecanoo have created two great urban parks where landscape and built facilities come together to play very different roles in the city, but both bringing a revolution of recreation for its citizens. The ground of the 32-hectare **Nelson Mandela Park**, completed in 2011 in the southern Bijlmer quarter of Amsterdam, had to be raised in the Netherlands' constant struggle against water levels, resulting in tree loss. But the result is that the local high-density neighbourhood now has access to nature and a constellation of lakes, which are crossed by bridges with bespoke metalwork and curving boardwalks. They connect to paths through parkland brimming with an abundance of biodiversity. There is also a wealth of new sports facilities, including a running track and skateboard park. Such specialized surfaces are designed to deliver fitness, fuel ambition, and not least, generate camaraderie — things that make a community feel good. Locals of all ages can enjoy sports, events, and nature. Nelson Mandela Park is truly a project for the People.

Transformation of a Brownfield Site

Nearer to Amsterdam's city centre, Mecanoo have created a whole quarter dedicated to diverse culture, embedded in parkland. The 13.5-hectare **Westergasfabriek Terrain** site lies between a canal and a railway line on a site where the gas company powered Amsterdam's street lighting, established in the 1880s. It includes three massive gas holders and a complex of monumental brick industrial buildings by renowned architect Isaac Gosschalk, the largest of these with a similar style and scale as the iconic Amsterdam Central Station, designed by his contemporary, Pierre Cuypers. A century later, gas production had ceased and contamination with industrial pollutants had ruined the grounds.

In 1997, a collaboration between Mecanoo and landscape architect Kathryn Gustafson of London-based Gustafson Porter + Bowman won a competition to transform this brownfield site. When the Westergasfabriek and Cultuurpark (West Gas Plant and Culture Park) opened in 2003, the ground had been decontaminated, and great trees that had survived were joined by new ones in woodlands, part of a mix of parkland peppered with biodiversity, including circular ponds in the footprints of two demolished gas holders.

Diverse features such as an orchard and a water park are to be found in this parkland, which is crossed by a long, straight promenade that links the buildings and new plazas. 8,000 m² of repurposed old industrial building, whose heritage gives them an instant authenticity, along with new structures, now host a colourful, eclectic mix of alternative cultural activities and independent enterprise.

The new masterplan respects the monumental buildings and places them into a new context. The area becomes a unity where the transition from city to nature, from politics to art, and from old to new, can be experienced. Two different routes, a straight axis and a 'Path of Dreams', take the visitor to various places and landscapes in the park, to the Westerpark, the flower field, the forest, the area for public events that can host up to 10,000 people, the village, the orchard, the beach, the 'Cité des Arts', the water and wild garden and finally to the landscape outside the city.

Westergasfabriek and its parkland are alive with markets, eateries, exhibitions, performances, nightlife and more. The largest gas holder is now a venue that hosts events for up to 3,500 and is just one of several venues in the complex. From the outset, sustainability underlines the project, which is powered by photovoltaics installed on the old structures. And what a variety of surfaces there is to touch — Gosschalk's brickwork, wood in buildings and wood that is alive, water to splash in and water that flows, and all sorts of vegetation from grass and trees to waterside meadows and flowers!

World-famous Flower Garden

Flowers play a major part in the story of the Netherlands. They are responsible for the world's first speculative market crash due to 'tulip mania' in 1637 but also for the international impact of its exquisite floral paintings from the seventeenth and eighteenth centuries. Nowadays the Netherlands is Europe's largest producer of flowers. One of the world's greatest flower gardens is the

32-hectare **Keukenhof**, and it has a new gateway designed by Mecanoo. Annual visitor numbers had reached a million in 2014 during its eight weeks opening season, so these tulip gardens needed something big to channel them. Since Mecanoo's 116-metre-wide gatehouse opened in 2016, even more visitors have come — 1.5 million in 2019. What the crowds encounter takes the form of a gentle flight of giant stairs floating across one side of the plaza outside, rising in five steps from one storey above the ground to two. Each step is a rectangular canopy, sheltering facilities recessed beneath it, with the middle step covering the gateway to the park. These canopies are not solid like the great canopy for the Netherlands Open Air Museum, but diamond lattices of timber, letting visitors see the Dutch sky above and the beauty of the shadows the structure casts at their feet. Their double-isosceles triangles also act as skylights for the buildings, which include a restaurant, shop, and offices. The diamond and triangle planters across the outside plaza resonate with the latticework.

Linear Park

We have already seen that when the Library Delft University of Technology opened in 1998 (see p. 140), its grassed roof presented a small landscape. But much more would follow when Mecanoo transformed the road running through the heart of the Delft University of Technology campus (designed in the sixties) into a landscaped linear spine that connects the faculties of the university. It is called the **Mekel Park**. Students stroll, sit, eat, meet, meditate and do all the things that would have not been possible before, when it was a surface of asphalt for road and parking. Now, it's an 800-metre-long strip of gently rolling grass with trees, crossed by diagonal paths. The main path is paved with bluestone cobbles and zig-zags between knee-high granite walls, which creates a bench 1,547 metres long (excluding gaps)! A tram and bus line are integrated into the park. This project, realized in stages up to 2013, was Mecanoo's first linear park to reclaim territory with Nature's help. More would follow, as far afield as Taichung Green Corridor in Taiwan (see p. 426).

Mecanoo's architecture switches our senses on in many other places around the world too, from the interplay of different building textures all around you at Kampus in Manchester (see p. 68) to the unexpected biodiversity on the roof of the Martin Luther King Jr. Memorial Library in Washington (see p. 178). But let us take a look at one final example that is barely a minute's walk from Mecanoo's head office along the beautiful, leafy Delft canal that connects them.

A View of Delft

The **Delfland Water Authority** took over a canal-side house built in 1505, and gradually expanded their offices into adjacent historical buildings all the way to the street behind, from where a modern entrance added in 1975 is accessible. The offices were a fragmented jumble, and Mecanoo's challenge was to upgrade their 'fitness for purpose' by unifying them and bringing them up to contemporary standards. The approach they took was poetic. Themed as 'A View of Delft', it proposed transforming the experience of the headquarters by creating views within it and out to the picture-perfect historical city around it. It would respect the heritage and give visitors clear orientation. Since the 8,800 m^2 project was completed in 2017, visitors enter a double-height lobby through a new glazed facade in front of the old brick facade, and the space is crossed by an oak bridge connecting offices upstairs. New spaces inside include flexible offices and meeting points, the greatest of which is a three-storey skylit atrium, where a 52 m^2 water-themed tapestry hangs, designed by Silo Agency and manufactured at the Textile Museum in Tilburg. Silo also made the historical Delft map graphics on glass that line corridor walls to further underline the organization's identity. Historical rooms in the protected historical building parts have been restored, including furniture and fixtures. You can feel the inner history of the buildings that have been joined up, and see around the historical cityscape revealed through windows. In the yard, there is an additional feeling. What had been a car park is now a public garden, where islands planted for biodiversity thrive behind knee-high stone borders and benches, like at the Mekel Park. Sit there, and nature touches you. The paths are paved with historical brick, which extends to the entrance and into the lobby.

Poetry works by resonating with imagination and emotion. We forget that both are formed and stimulated by the diversity of our senses, but Mecanoo designs with exactly that in mind. You can literally feel the difference that makes!

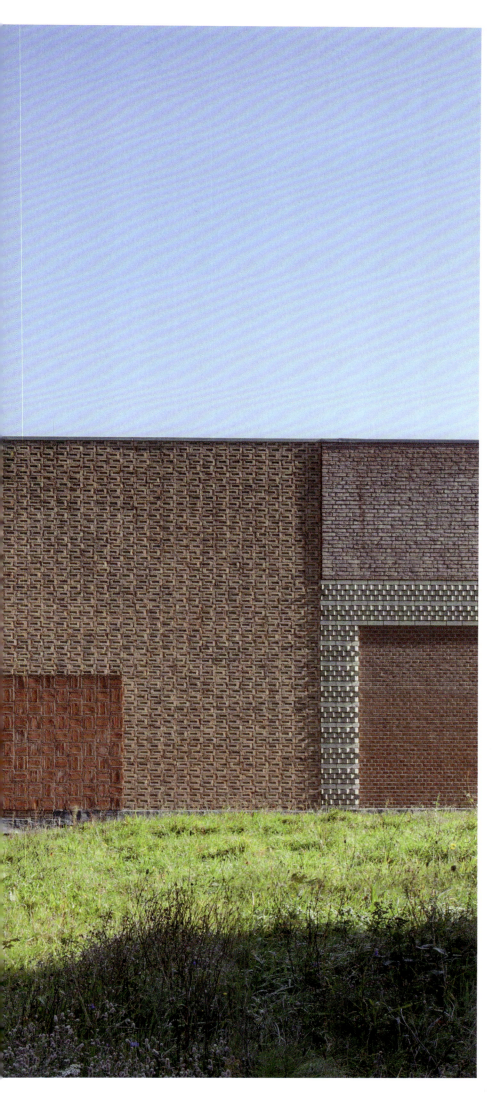

Netherlands Open Air Museum

Arnhem, the Netherlands

Discipline:

Architecture, Landscape, Interior

Typology:

Museum/Exhibition   Link

Size: 3,300 m²
Design: project 1: 1995-1998,
project 2: 2015-2015
Realization project 1: 1999-2000,
project 2: 2016-2017
Client: Nederlands Openluchtmuseum

Design team: Mecanoo

Programme: Project 1: 3,185 m² museum and panoramic theatre with 'HollandRama', including landscape design. Project 2: Museum extension with integration of the permanent national exhibition 'Canon of Dutch History', new entrance pavilion for ticketing and information, update of restaurant and museum shop, including landscape design, totalling 3,300 m².

7
CRAFTMANSHIP

The rolling landscape was taken as the starting point for the design. The 143-metre-long wall cuts through it and forms a composition with the mysterious egg-shaped building that lies in front of it.

Behind the entrance pavilion, the 44 hectare museum park unfolds

The 15 by 60-metre pavilion follows the gradient of the site and has a large overhang preventing direct sunlight entering the building.

Netherlands Open Air Museum

TOUCH ME   FEEL ME

In 2017, Mecanoo re-designed the museum's interior and added a ticketing pavilion with a 14-meter-long Corten steel roof crafted by Dutch shipbuilders.

The entrance of the museum is in a 143-metre-long and 7.3-metre-high wall clad with bricks in a range of bricklaying techniques.

1995-2017   Arnhem, the Netherlands   291

Natural materials define the pavilion such as a wooden ceiling and a wall plastered with clay.

Revisiting the museum to integrate the 'Canon of Dutch History' exhibition

Netherlands Open Air Museum

TOUCH ME   FEEL ME

Stairs lead to the below grade exhibition halls and connect to the underground corridor leading to the copper egg.

1995-2017   Arnhem, the Netherlands

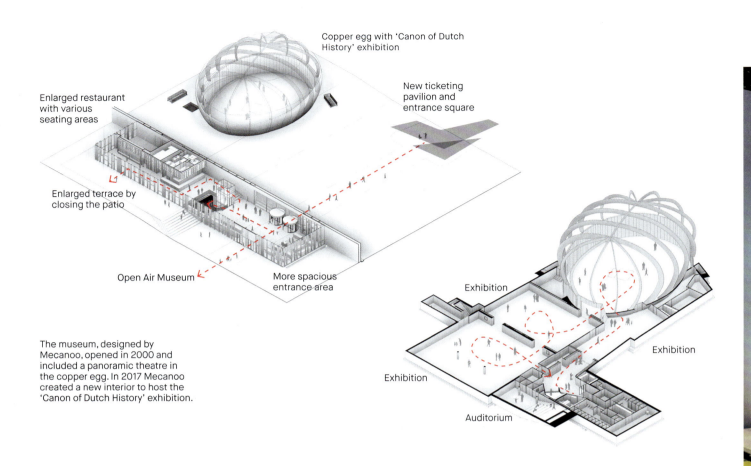

Copper egg with 'Canon of Dutch History' exhibition

New ticketing pavilion and entrance square

Enlarged restaurant with various seating areas

Enlarged terrace by closing the patio

Open Air Museum

More spacious entrance area

Exhibition

Exhibition

Exhibition

Auditorium

The museum, designed by Mecanoo, opened in 2000 and included a panoramic theatre in the copper egg. In 2017 Mecanoo created a new interior to host the 'Canon of Dutch History' exhibition.

HISTORY

Netherlands Open Air Museum

TOUCH ME   FEEL ME

In the copper egg, digital techniques showcase important moments in Dutch history. Visitors are challenged to actively seek information through a mix of media, hands-on elements and interactive games. The exhibition has been designed by Kossmanndejong.

The copper egg has been transformed from a theatre to an interactive museum hall

PLAYING

1995-2017 　　　Arnhem, the Netherlands　　　295

Bruce C. Bolling Municipal Building

Boston,
United States of America

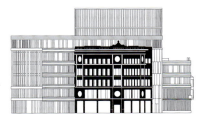

Discipline:

Architecture, Restoration

Typology:

Transformation, Office, Government/Civic

Link

Size: 16,700 m²
Design: 2011-2012
Realization: 2012-2014
Client: City of Boston, MA

Design team: Mecanoo and Sasaki Associates.

Programme: 16,700 m² office and community building for the Boston Public Schools Department with community spaces and retail, integrating three listed historical buildings, LEED Gold certified.

297

COMBINING & MERGING

Boston's late Mayor Thomas M. Menino decided to redevelop this site and create a municipal building for the Boston Public Schools Division. Three existing buildings have been integrated into the Bruce C. Bolling Municipal Building.

The 1888 Curtis Building, a Queen Ann-style red brick building (middle), and the 1890 Waterman Building (right), a Boston Cranite-style building.

Dudley Square (here pictured in 1955) has been a centre of mobility since 1901, when trains served it. Now a bus hub, it was renamed Nubian Square in 2019.

The abandoned 1895 limestone and terracotta Ferdinand Building is a symbol for what was once the vibrant heart of Roxbury with shops and jazz cafés.

TOUCH ME   FEEL ME

JAZZY

RYTHM

The three existing buildings have been stitched together with oxblood-red bricks that have been laid in different ways to create jazzy rhythms across its facades. The facade is a showcase of craftmanship.

Boston bricks with a Dutch touch: different masonry techniques from running bond to stack bond to soldier bond

There's a beautiful switch from the redbrick facade of the Curtis Building to the new main volume's oxblood-red glazed bricks.

The oxblood-red brick facade connects to the rhythm of the historic limestone facade of the Ferdinand Building.

TOUCH ME   FEEL ME

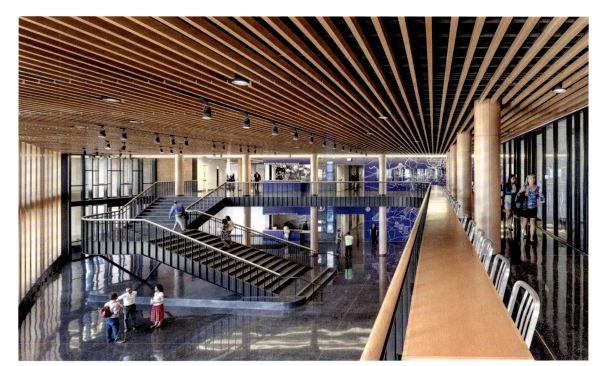

The main lobby is a public zone and community gathering space.

On the second* floor parents, students and staff can interface; higher up flexible work spaces of the Boston Public Schools department can be found. (*US floor numbering)

The rooftop space, uniquely, is free and accesible to all.

2011-2014   Boston, United States of America

St. Gerlach Pavilion & Manor Farm

Valkenburg, the Netherlands

Discipline:

Architecture, Landscape, Interior, Restoration

Typology:

Transformation, Hotel/Leisure

Size: 1,795 m²
Design 2013-2015
Realization 2015-2017
Client: Landgoed Corneli II

Design team: Mecanoo (lead architect) and HVN architecten (restoration architect).

Programme: 1,300 m² conference and event pavilion with three multifunctional meeting rooms, lobby, and catering kitchen; 500 m² renovation of the historical Manor Farm, a listed building from 1668, and landscape design of surrounding gardens.

7

ELEGANT

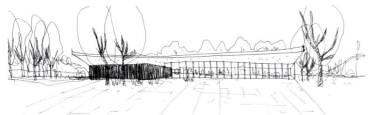

Bringing together old and new

St. Gerlach Pavilion & Manor Farm

TOUCH ME   FEEL ME

The new pavilion with three large multi-functional meeting rooms gives the 17th-century country estate a contemporary presence

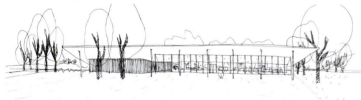

BALANCE

The materials used are inspired by the natural surroundings of Limburg: marlstone, bluestone and oak.

2013-2017   Valkenburg, the Netherlands

TOUCH ME FEEL ME

FARMSTEAD

The 1720 farmstead 'Hoeve Broers' has been built from local merle. Its courtyard can be used as a terrace for the lunch restaurant and coffee bar.

2013-2017 Valkenburg, the Netherlands

INTIMATE

St. Gerlach Pavilion & Manor Farm

TOUCH ME   FEEL ME

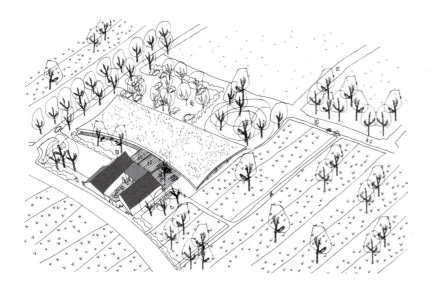

The intervention is light, allowing history to define the ambience

VILLAGE SQUARE

Between the 2017 pavilion and the 1668 Manor Farm is a newly cobbled patio that evokes a village square.

2013-2017 · Valkenburg, the Netherlands

Nelson Mandela Park

Amsterdam, the Netherlands

Discipline:

Landscape

Typology:

Leisure, Masterplan

Size: 32-ha
Design: 2003-2004
Realization: 2009-2011
Client: District Amsterdam-Zuidoost
Design team: Mecanoo

Programme: Urban masterplan with 700 dwellings and landscape design for a 32-ha urban and nature park and 8-ha sports programme, including gates and bridges.

Meandering through the park are footpaths that connect the cultural northern end with the natural, ecological southern end.

→ The park has eight entrance gates with Bijlmerpark (in 2014 the name was changed into Nelson Mandela Park) in the handwriting of Francine Houben.

A seven-metre high hill with viewpoint is covered with butterfly bushes.

The park includes a festival terrain for the annual multicultural Kwaku Festival and other events.

→ The constellation of lakes is crossed by bridges and curving boardwalks.

The wealth of new sports facilities delivers fitness, fuels ambition and generates cameraderie

SPORTS

Nelson Mandela Park

TOUCH ME   FEEL ME

The skate park is one of the largest in the Amsterdam area.

& ADVENTURE

2003-2011   Amsterdam, the Netherlands

Westergas-fabriek Terrain

Amsterdam, the Netherlands

Discipline:

Architecture, Landscape, Restoration

Typology:

Transformation, Leisure, Masterplan

Size: 13.5-ha / 11,500 m²
Design: 1997-2000
Realization: 2000-2001
Client: Stadsdeel Westerpark, Amsterdam; Projectgroep Westergasfabriek; MAB.

Design team: Mecanoo and Gustafson Porter + Bowman.

Programme: Transformation of the former 13.5-ha Westergasfabriek gasworks in a cultural park, with re-development of 8,000 m² historical industrial buildings and 3,500 m² new development.

GAS PLANT

The Westergasfabriek gas plant, designed by architect Isaac Gosschalk in the Dutch neo-Renaissance style, was built in 1883. The plant closed in the 1960s. In 1997, Francine Houben together with Kathryn Gustafson won the competition to transform this brownfield into a cultural park.

TOUCH ME   FEEL ME

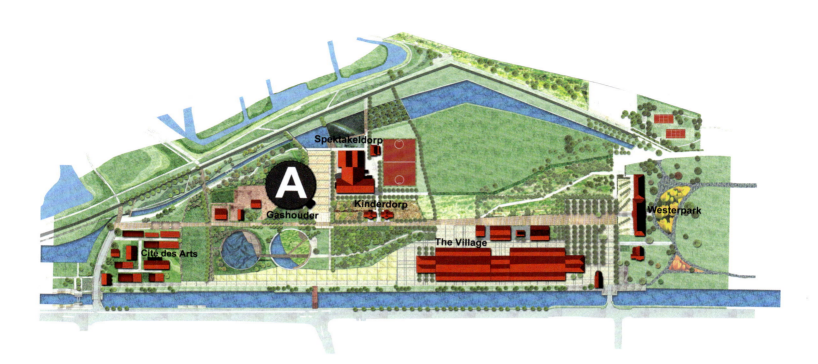

The masterplan respects the monumental buildings and places them into a new landscaped context.

Hand sketches envision new functions for the gas holder and other buildings.

TOUCH ME   FEEL ME

Two routes, a straight axis and a 'Path of Dreams', take the visitor to various places and landscapes. The area for public events can host up to 10,000 people.

The area has become a unity where the transitions from city to nature, from politics to art, and from old to new can be experienced

1997–2001   Amsterdam, the Netherlands   323

7

TRANSITION

The largest gas holder is now a venue that hosts events for up to 3,500, varying from music concerts to theatre performances and dinners.

TOUCH ME   FEEL ME

PARKLAND

The park has various places and landscapes including a forest, an orchard, a flower-field, and a wild garden interspersed with water features.

1997-2001   Amsterdam, the Netherlands   325

Keukenhof

Lisse, the Netherlands

Discipline:

Architecture, Landscape

Typology:

Leisure, Museum/Exhibition

Link

Size: 1.35-ha / 3,200 m²
Design: 2013-2015
Realization: 2015-2016
Client: Stichting Internationale
Bloemententoonstelling Keukenhof

Design team: Mecanoo

Programme: 3,200 m² entrance building of the world-famous Keukenhof flower gardens, including ticketing, restaurant, retail, visitor facilities and offices, and 1.35-ha landscape design including entrance square with two plazas and combined landscaping and furniture elements.

7

STEPPED

The canopy of the 116-metre-wide gatehouse has diamond lattices of timber, letting visitors see the Dutch sky above and the shadows that the structure casts at their feet.

A new gateway for the 32-hectare tulip gardens of the world-famous Keukenhof

TOUCH ME   FEEL ME

CANOPY

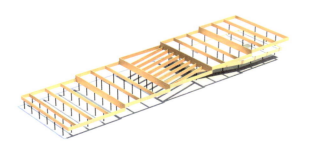
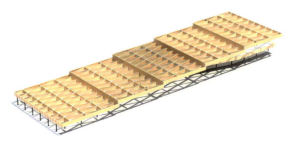

2013-2016 — Lisse, the Netherlands

The diamond and triangle shapes of the planters across the plaza resonate with the wooden lattice work.

During its yearly six weeks of opening, over 1 million people visit the 32-hectare tulip gardens of the Keukenhof.

Mekel Park, Delft University of Technology

Delft, the Netherlands

Discipline:

Urbanism, Landscape

Typology:

Masterplan, University/Campus, Mobility

Link

Size: 10-ha
Design: 2004-2006
Realization: 2007-2009
Client: TU Delft Vastgoed

Design team: Mecanoo

Programme: Masterplan and landscape design for the 10-ha university campus preparing it for the future: pedestrians-, cyclists- and community-focused, adding biodiversity and water management, and integration of bus and tram lines.

7

The Delft University of Technology campus was designed in the sixties with a two-way road running through its heart, lined with parking lots and faculty buildings.

334　　　　　　　　　　　　　　　　　　　　　　　　Mekel Park, Delft University of Technology

TOUCH ME   FEEL ME

Mecanoo transformed the road into a landscaped spine that connects the faculties of the Delft University of Technology in order to facilitate collaboration and innovation.

An 800m-long strip of gently rolling grass with trees, crossed by diagonal paths connects faculties and people

2004-2009   Delft, the Netherlands   335

7

The main path is paved with bluestone cobbles and zig-zags between knee-high granite walls, which creates a bench 1,547 metres long!

The park, with its rolling lawns and colourful trees, is an informal meeting place where students and staff can stroll, read, eat and celebrate.

Mekel Park, Delft University of Technology

Mekel Park, Delft University of Technology

TOUCH ME   FEEL ME

Mekel Park lends a grandeur to the university and provides a meeting place for the international community of staff and students

2004–2009   Delft, the Netherlands

Delfland Water Authority

Delft, the Netherlands

Discipline:

Architecture, Interior, Landscape, Restoration

Typology:

Transformation, Office, Government/Civic

Size: 8,800 m²
Design: 2014-2015
Realization: 2016-2017
Client: Hoogheemraadschap van Delfland

Design team: Mecanoo

Programme: 8,800 m² renovation and restoration of a partly fifteenth-century listed building complex, including a variety of workplaces, restaurant, conference rooms, archive and landscape design of the patios and garden.

IDENTITY

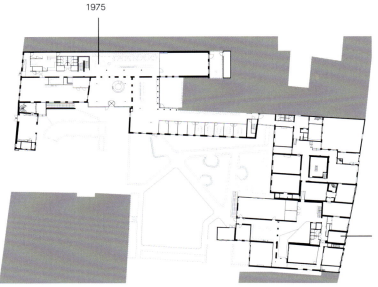

1975

1505

Since 1645, a sixteenth-century city palace has been the seat of the Delfland Water Authority, one of the oldest water authorities in the country.

Over the centuries, the city palace expanded into adjacent historic buildings including a new extension in 1975.

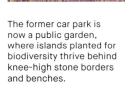

The former car park is now a public garden, where islands planted for biodiversity thrive behind knee-high stone borders and benches.

The challenge was to unify the buildings and bring them up to contemporary standards

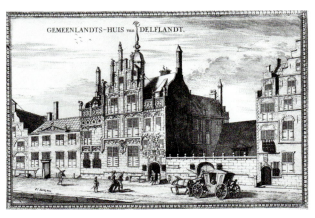

342   Delfland Water Authority

TOUCH ME   FEEL ME

2014–2017   Delft, the Netherlands

Visitors enter a double-height lobby integrating the old brick facades. An oak bridge connects the upstairs offices.

An 'honorary gallery' showcases objects and gifts received by the Water Authority.

A conference centre has been integrated in the building complex.

Views to the historical city were created while respecting the heritage.

TOUCH ME   FEEL ME

Historic rooms have been restored, including furniture and fixtures.

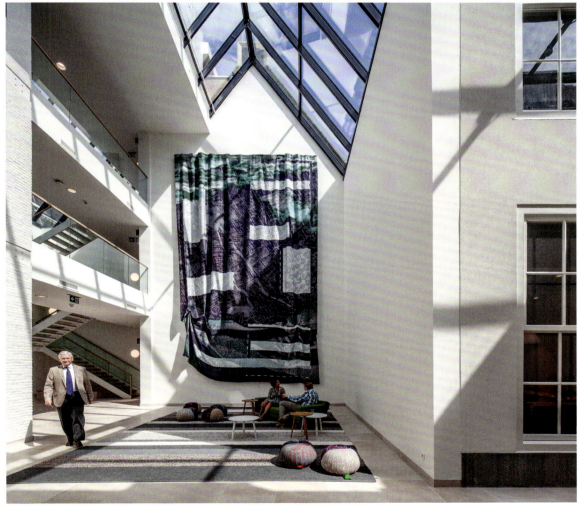

A patio transformed into an indoor space with a skylight and a water-themed tapestry made by Silo and the Tilburg Textile Museum.

8

Things are
Looking Up

Skyscrapers can be inspirational, distinguished and elegant, but they can also be monotonous, repetitious, formulaic and even ominous. In 1900 — a whole 27 years before Le Corbusier famously said 'a house is a machine for living in' — American architect Cass Gilbert declared that 'a skyscraper is a machine for making the land pay'. That was hard capitalist logic — stacking floors maximizes gross floor area, and therefore commercial returns per square metre of plot. Replace 'commercial returns' with 'population' and you have the socialist logic behind the worldwide spread of post-war high-rise social housing. Naturally, architects in the Netherlands — a country which, as Francine Houben points out, has 'a shortage of land' — will instinctively understand what drives high-rise.

What About Place?

But surely a skyscraper should be more than a machine? The people living or working inside are not just population statistics or productivity units, they are all individuals. What about place? If buildings are endlessly replicated, they and their location become 'non-places' (which is the title of a 1992 book by Marc Augé exploring the anonymity of 'super-modern' spaces). A tower should enhance the lives of people in and around it, and even the whole city across which it will be visible. It should make the place better by 'place-making' — bringing space and life to the public realm. A skyscraper may stand with its head in the clouds, but its feet are on the street. Nowadays, it has almost become a mantra with architects and urbanists to say that how a skyscraper hits the ground is at least as important as the shape it cuts on the skyline. When People and the Place where it stands are considered, we can hope for an emotional, intuitive bonus in a tower — some Poetry. We find it first in two European residential tower projects by Mecanoo.

A Huge M

Mecanoo's **Montevideo**-project in Rotterdam was not its first high-rise. In 1989, an 18-storey curved social housing block was built in the Hillekop urban renewal project, also in Rotterdam. But in 2005, Montevideo was Mecanoo's first tower to show off refreshing design ideas from a prime city stage, in this case a sliver of disused Rotterdam dockland called Wilhelmina Pier. Mecanoo's slender 143-metre-high tower is like a stack of different parts that change structurally (from steel to concrete to steel again) and in appearance over half-way up. Window arrangements in the mainly solid facades vary, in complete contrast to the anonymous glass curtain walls in the prevailing 'Big Glass' style of Montevideo's bulky neighbour, De Rotterdam (designed by OMA). A huge letter M mounted above Montevideo is actually a weather vane, its orientation changing by how the wind blows. It evokes the shipping line logos like those on the big liners bound for New York from the pier, and commercial lettering mounted on rooftop trusses in downtown pre-war American cities. The M reaches 152 metres up, visible from far across city and water. But Montevideo is not all about external appearances. The sense of freedom and voyage comes right into the apartments, with low windows revealing the waterside below, and even circular windows, like port-holes. Below the tower, a long plinth element is transparent at street level and restaurants attract street life. Rotterdam's High Rise Vision 2019 called for exactly such contributions to activate city life in all new towers — 14 years after Mecanoo'sexample! A nine-storey element reaching 16 metres out towards the water's edge even shelters outdoor café seating. From top to bottom, inside and out, Montevideo's spatial composition is unique and logical. It is poetic, as is the romance of ocean travel it evokes.

Gateway Marker

Wilhelmina Pier is central in the geography and collective memory of Rotterdam. So too is a different transport infrastructure location in Frankfurt — the swathe of railway lines into its central terminus. How many remember the view from a train of the station's great arched roofs and the skyscrapers behind them, as the tracks curve into this last straight stretch of the journey? As in many cities, Frankfurt's railway lands nowadays present development opportunities. There, Mecanoo have the winning design for a 140-metre-high residential tower called **Icoon**. Its form and finish make it a gateway marker for the city, and differentiate it from the office towers that dominate the city. Frankfurt has more iconic skyscrapers than many other high-rise cities several times its size. They include the Norman Foster-designed Commerzbank, the Messeturm by Helmut Jahn and the European Central Bank by Coop-Himmelb(l)au, but Icoon brings a whole new look.

Above ground floor amenities, there are two volumes with copper-coloured exteriors. Copper is warm and a bit ritzy, but not like the bling of gold, and its metal materiality resonates with the adjacent rails. Both volumes have seven floors of social housing, but one continues upwards to level 40 with apartments for sale. Balconies curve around the corners, but in the tower, the floors gradually widen, and the corner curvature reduces, until at the top (where balconies enclose winter gardens) the corners are sharp. The whole building is a shape shifter, yet it stands smartly to attention with style.

A Spectrum of Residents

Not all residential towers are designed to make a big impression on a city skyline. There are thousands of standardized post-war social housing towers across the world, many of them not happy places to live in. On the other hand, the Dutch have a reputation for good social housing, which goes back to the 1920s. That reputation, updated with Mecanoo's humanistic approach, now comes to Taiwan in **Kaohsiung Social Housing**, the first social housing project ever in Taiwan's third largest city, Kaohsiung. This development brings 245 apartments in two bright white towers with roof gardens, 45-metre and 42-metre-high, which mix apartments and collective space. Windows and balconies are set back from the building envelopes for shade. Cut-away garden terraces in the western tower create a vertical garden that visually links with the green corridor that starts at the new Kaohsiung Station (see p. 416) to the west. A garden plaza nestles between the towers, which together make the front end of a future new linear development that will extend eastwards. For now, the first two towers are about to welcome a whole spectrum of residents — students, families, the elderly, and those in the community with special needs. A new vision of community and urban greenery in Kaohsiung has begun.

Connecting Visually and Socially

A 'brink' is an old Dutch word for a green open space, a village green, where people meet. Bringing people together in a healthy, plant-filled project is also at the heart of the **Brink Tower** in Amsterdam, which started construction in 2022. The location is north Amsterdam, an area that is separated from the rest of the city by the waters of the IJ. Since 2018 it is connected not just by ferries but also by a new metro line, and change has been rapid. The Brink Tower lies at the edge of the neighbourhood of Overhoeks, which has seen an explosion of new residential development, but just across a canal lies the low-rise Van der Pek neighbourhood. Despite a bridge between them, there is a great mental distance between the two. The Brink Tower will connect them visually and socially.

The 28-storey tower contains 408 apartments of which 266 are rental homes in the middle segment, 120 at affordable rent and a residential care facility combined with a neighbourhood centre. The architecture is stunning and exceptionally sustainable. A wide base with double-level retail turns the corner by the canal bridge, and above it, a series of step-backs with soft, elegantly curved corner edges gradually cut back the floors, with a final vertical stretch reaching a height of 90 metres. This side presents a slim form with a cascade of green terraces overlooking Van der Pek. On the other side, the tower is wider, like the massive neighbouring towers that march in a line across Overhoeks towards the IJ. Unlike them, the Brink Tower's cladding is done in warm red brick, referencing the 'Amsterdam School' style of architecture of the 1920s that characterizes much of the city, including Van der Pek. The beautiful brickwork is integrated with concrete bands and detailing in the facades, which frame full-height windows all the way to the top on all sides.

Just as remarkable as its transformative social role and visual presence is its sustainable ambition. The Brink Tower is designed to become an energy-positive residential tower and generates more energy than it consumes, thanks to photovoltaics on terraces and facades, wind and more solar energy harvesting on the top roof, and various energy-saving measures, including an aquifer thermal energy storage (ATES) system. It also takes biodiversity to new levels, not just with its choice of vegetation, but with nests and nooks for birds and insects. Both plants and creatures find homes according to height — for example conifer trees on the highest terrace and falcon nests even higher, and wild grasses at the very top. The Brink Tower shows that even in the city, humanity and Nature can co-exist in harmony, and its visibility advertises the message across Amsterdam.

Jazzy Rythms

In Seoul, South Korea, the slender 14-storey **Heungkuk Tower Namdaemun** (2016) isn't tall enough to be seen across the city, but it reminds us that, as with other matters, it's not size that matters. This office tower, built for financial company Heungkuk, has an echo of the minimalistic modernist skyscrapers by Mies van der Rohe in Chicago, New York and Toronto in its straight-up vertical extrusion, rectangular facades, and especially colour. Black is back, in the solid lines of its dark exterior metal frame, and it contrasts with the visual noise of nearby Namdaemun Market. Within this frame are seven variations of diagonals, repeated horizontally across floors and around the enclosed green roof. This is a building of jazzy but dignified rhythms. Since 2021, the tower has had a sister in Busan, the second vast metropolis of Korea. However, the younger **Heungkuk Tower Busan** is not a little sister, but a big one, with over three times the floor area over the same number of floors. Its black facades carry rows of curved steel elements creating different rhythms of light inside and out that subtly change over the day. This tower is just a little more colourful than her older sister. She dresses with a vertical facade band in a shade of pink that brands Heungkuk's insurance business. A professional women's volleyball team sponsored by Heungkuk wears the same colour!

It's said that this is the century of China, and it has already eclipsed the USA in one very visible indicator of economic success — skyscrapers. In 2020, 13 of the world's 25 tallest buildings were in China (excluding Hong Kong). Reforms in the 1980s kickstarted China's rapid economic climb and urbanization on a staggering scale, and they started in Shenzhen. This megacity of 12 million inhabitants has been at the leading edge of China's advance ever since. What is Mecanoo bringing to a place where, perhaps more than anywhere else, today is already tomorrow?

Dynamic Drama

Shenzhen already has three Central Business Districts, but the restless city is now building the next, located near the high-speed railway station at Shenzhen North. The **Shenzhen North Station Urban Design** was begun by Mecanoo in 2017. Here we see no less than twelve skyscrapers, rising as high as 428 metres (a height only exceeded twice in Shenzhen as of 2022). The final architecture of individual towers is the responsibility of architects assigned to them, but the masterplan encourages angular, stepped-back forms and specifies a range of cladding. That will make a family of towers 'sharing' the same aesthetics (an approach pioneered by Raymond Hood at New York's Rockefeller Center in the 1930s), rather than the style mix that comes with changing times and architects in planned business zones such as London's Canary Wharf (which Shenzhen North will almost equal in total office space). Development is so rapid that the first great skyscraper, the 78-metres-high Huide Tower, designed by German architects HPP, was completed on the north side of this new Central Business District in 2019.

At Shenzhen North, hitting the ground is complex because the station itself and its plaza are raised above it. The plan creates a network of raised paths woven above gardens and water features. Despite the frenzy of Shenzhen and the dynamic drama of these towers, Shenzhen North will be a tranquil place. It was intuitive to make this so, to bring Poetry to the People and Place.

Worldwide, urbanization will continue throughout the twenty-first century. Land shortage, the profit motive (which Gilbert understood 120 years ago), and the wish to create spectacle from scale mean that inevitably cities will build upwards. Skyscrapers are too big to ignore, and they generate emotional response. The repetitive, dehumanized excesses of modernism did not always make that response a positive one, but Mecanoo's humanistic, localized approach to high-rise brings forward far warmer feelings. Things are looking up!

Montevideo

Rotterdam, the Netherlands

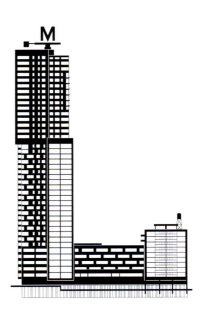

Discipline:

Architecture

Typology:

Residential, Office, Leisure

Size: 57,500 m²
Design: 1999-2002
Realization: 2003-2005
Client: ING Real Estate

Design team: Mecanoo

Programme: 152 metres mixed-use high-rise tower of 57,500 m², including 192 apartments (37,000 m²), 900 m² pool, fitness and service spaces, 6,000 m² offices, 1,600 m² retail and a 8,400 m² parking garage.

351

8

The Wilhelmina Pier was once a bridge to the new world, where ocean liners departed for New York

Montevideo was the third high-rise building on the pier with the former Holland-America Line offices at its feet.

THINGS ARE LOOKING UP

In 1999 Mecanoo made a masterplan for the Wilhelmina Pier with Montevideo (in blue) as a prototype for the buildings on the pier.

The low-rise buildings form a counterweight to the tall buildings, creating sight lines to the city centre

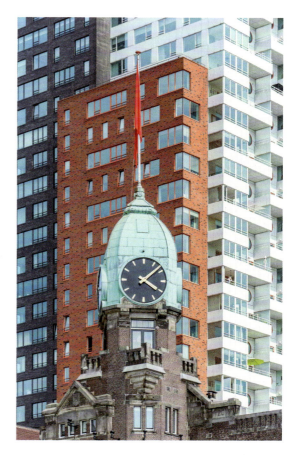

↑ The M on top of Montevideo reaches 152 metres up and is visible from far across the city.

The tower is clad in brick, just → as the former Holland-America Line office building is.

VERTICAL CITY

1999-2005 — Rotterdam, the Netherlands

Montevideo has 192 dwellings of 54 different types and floor heights amongst Loft, City, Sky and Water apartments. (Photo 2022)

The first two floors are built of steel and carry the tower and the Water apartments block, which juts 16 metres out. In the transparent plinth are restaurants, with their terraces along the quay.

THINGS ARE LOOKING UP

Lying in your bed, a large porthole provides a view of the ships passing on the Nieuwe Maas River.

Montevideo is a composition of intersecting volumes and refers to the history and romance of the site from where the ships of Holland-America sailed. (Photo 2015)

1999-2005   Rotterdam, the Netherlands   355

The slender tower is a stack of different volumes and facades

Montevideo refers to early twentieth-century high-rise buildings of New York, Chicago and Boston: brick-clad, with refined detailing and use of colour, roof terraces and loggias.

Icoon

Frankfurt, Germany

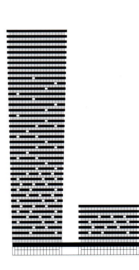

Discipline:

Architecture, Landscape

Typology:

Residential

Size: 58,000 m²
Design: 2018-2019
Realization: to be planned
Client: Groß & Partner; PHOENIX Real Estate Development.

Design team: Mecanoo

Programme: Mixed-use complex totalling 58,000 m², with 55,000 m² residential programme of which 16,500 m² social housing, two underground garage levels, 1,300 m² kindergarten and 1,700 m² commercial functions, 1st prize competition.

Icoon is located close to Frankfurt Central Station. Its form and finish make it a gateway marker for the city.

The 140-metre-high tower has a dynamic shape. As the tower rises, the floors gradually widen, and the corner curvature reduces, until at the top the corners are sharp.

The building is a shape shifter, yet it stands smartly to attention with style

THINGS ARE LOOKING UP

The two buildings are connected by a transparent plinth, which is enlivened by residential entrances and facilities such as a kindergarten.

2018–2019   Frankfurt, Germany   361

DYNAMIC & CONTEXTUAL

THINGS ARE LOOKING UP

The tower contains social housing up to the seventh floor and owner-occupied units and penthouses on the higher levels. The lower volume consists of social housing.

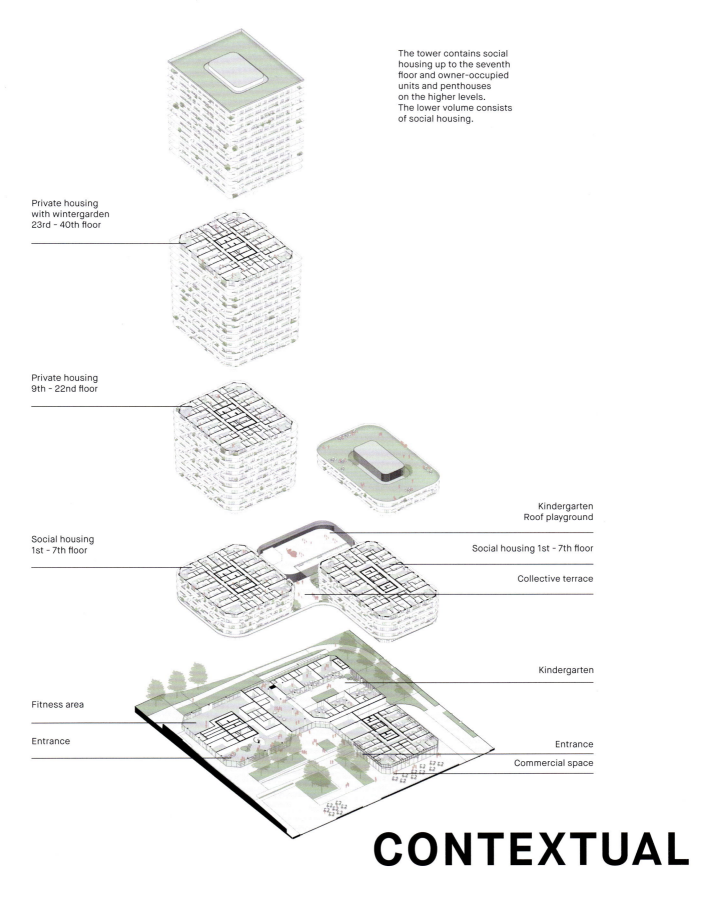

Private housing with wintergarden
23rd - 40th floor

Private housing
9th - 22nd floor

Social housing
1st - 7th floor

Fitness area

Entrance

Kindergarten
Roof playground

Social housing 1st - 7th floor

Collective terrace

Kindergarten

Entrance

Commercial space

2018-2019   Frankfurt, Germany

Kaohsiung Social Housing

Kaohsiung, Taiwan

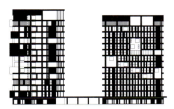

Discipline:

Architecture, Urbanism, Landscape

Typology:

Residential, Masterplan

Size: 15,840 m²
Design: 2016
Realization: 2018-2023
Client: Urban Development Bureau, Kaohsiung City Government.

Link

Design team: Mecanoo (lead architect) and
C.M. Chao Architect & Planners (executive architect).

Programme: Two residential towers, 45-metre and 42-metre-high, totalling 15,840 m² with 245 units, 870 m² of commercial spaces, 4,050 m² of shared facilities (gym, shared kitchen, reading room and outdoor spaces), kindergarten, parking garage for 130 cars and 280 scooters, and roof gardens and public square.

This pioneering social housing project brings 245 apartments in two bright white towers, 45-metre and 42-metre-high, with roof gardens, collective space, a courtyard and a mix of apartments.

The units, between 25 and 75 m², have been designed for a large variety of users, from students or young couples to families with children, as well as for the elderly and people with special needs.

Kaohsiung's first social housing project is designed to create a community

A public Sky Park of green terraces brings residents and local community together

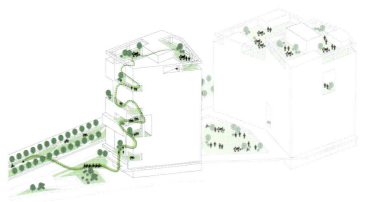

This social housing development heralds a new vision on community and urban green space in Kaohsiung

The two towers make the front end of a future linear development that is part of the green corridor, which also includes Mecanoo's Kaohsiung Station. Mecanoo's National Kaohsiung Center for the Arts can be seen in the background.

THINGS ARE LOOKING UP

Brink Tower

Amsterdam, the Netherlands

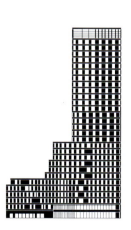

Discipline:

Architecture, Landscape

Typology:

Residential

Size: 30,184 m²
Design: 2019-2020
Realization: 2022-2025
Client: Xior Student Housing; DubbeLL-neighbourhood developers.

Design team: Mecanoo

Programme: 90-metre-high, energy-positive residential tower of 30,184 m² including 408 homes (266 rental homes in the middle segment, 120 at affordable rent), a residential care facility, community centre, a communal roof, inner garden, and commercial functions including co-working, a bowling centre with restaurant, and various retail and catering venues.

A brickwork tower with
a strong visual presence,
a transformative
social role and high
sustainability ambitions

THINGS ARE LOOKING UP

The stepped tower reaches 90 metres high with a cascade of green, collective roof terraces and gardens where residents can meet.

The Brink Tower lies at the edge of the neighbourhood of Overhoeks. The tower's warm red brick cladding references the Amsterdam School style of architecture of the 1920s that characterizes the nearby Van der Pek neighbourhood.

Heungkuk Tower Namdaemun and Busan

Seoul and Busan, South Korea

Discipline:

Architecture

Typology:

Office

Link

Size: 5,900 m²
Design: 2014-2015 Namdaemun, 2016 Busan
Realization: 2015-2017 Namdaemun,
2017-2021 Busan
Client: Heungkuk Life Insurance Co.

Design team Namdaemun: Mecanoo (lead architect) and Hanlim Architecture Group (architect of record). Design team Busan: Mecanoo (lead architect) and DA Group (executive architect).

Programme: Namdaemun is a 14-floor building of 5,900 m² with offices and retail; Busan is a 20,000 m² office building.

The elegant building in Seoul has a jazzy but dignified rhythm. Seven variations of diagonals are repeated horizontally across floors and around the enclosed green roof.

THINGS ARE LOOKING UP

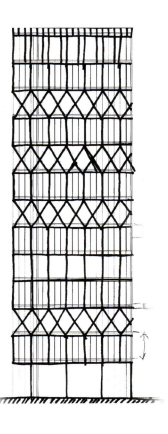

The solid lines of its dark exterior metal frame contrast with the visual noise of nearby Namdaemun Market.

NAMDAEMUN

2014–2017　　Seoul, South Korea

8

BUSAN

Heungkuk Tower Busan

The Busan tower is a big sister of the Namdaemun tower. The building's distinguishing feature is its stark black and fuchsia facade of various linear patterns.

Shenzhen North Station Urban Design

Shenzhen, China

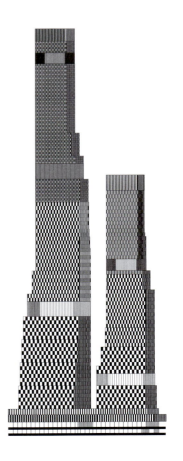

Discipline:

Architecture, Urbanism, Landscape

Typology:

Residential, Office, Masterplan/Mobility

Link

Size: 1.36 million m²
Design: 2017
Client: Government of Longhua District / Urban Planning, Land & Resources Commission of Shenzhen Municipality.

Design team: Mecanoo (lead architect) and HSA Architects (local architect).

Programme: Urban design for 1.36 million m² development with offices, retail, apartments and hotel, underground parking, connection to public transport hub, design public space, 1st prize competition.

THINGS ARE LOOKING UP

URBAN PARK

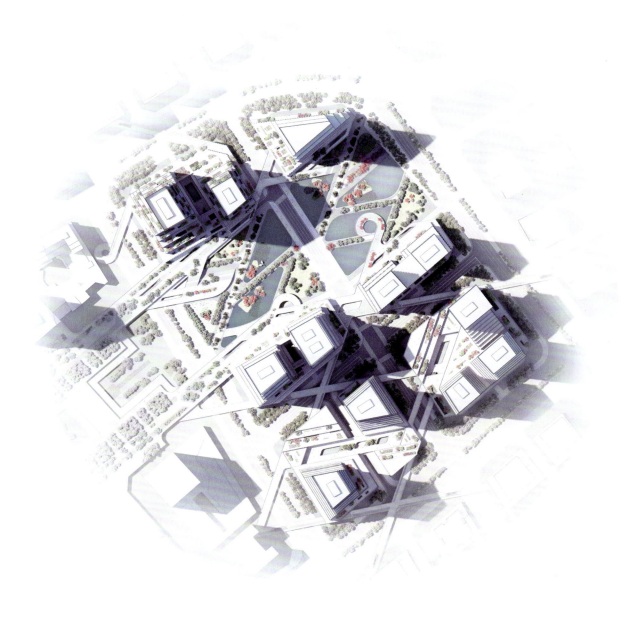

Twelve skyscrapers, rising as high as 428 metres share the same aesthetics, with angular, stepped-back forms. A network of raised paths are woven above gardens and water features.

2017 — Shenzhen, China

The buildings vary in height between 278 and 428 metres. Transportation nodes are located on subterranean levels. The public park is an open green space, something the area currently lacks.

A contextual approach to high-rise, with a family of skyscrapers around a central urban park

Shenzhen North Station Urban Design

THINGS ARE LOOKING UP

2017 — Shenzhen, China

9

On the
Move

Architecture stands still, but people move. Architectural design has to consider two totally different timescales — that of the structure that will emerge on site, which may last decades or even centuries, and that of its users, who move through, to or from it hour by hour in a never-ending succession of motions that last mere minutes or seconds. It is in the latter timescale that our experience of Place lies. Nowhere is this more obvious than with a building whose Purpose is to facilitate mobility, such as a busy railway station, but it is equally important to projects where movement is more leisurely, such as an urban park. In different ways and with different agendas, everyone moves through the built environment — even the dead.

The Last Journey

The **St. Mary of the Angels Chapel** (2001) in Rotterdam is one of the most poetic buildings in Mecanoo's portfolio. A thin rectangular roof, bending like a piece of paper aloft in the air, floats over an enclosure that is like two metallic drums joined together. Inside, you find yourself in an almost abstract space of colour and light, which creates an unusual, profound sense of tranquillity. Light enters above and below the walls, and through an opening in the golden ceiling above the altar. A curving wall of the vivid blue that recurs in different Mecanoo projects wraps around you, interrupted by curving doors which swing out, opening the space to the sight and sound of the surrounding cemetery. All is still.

It is funeral services that bring life inside and give the dead mobility, on their last physical journey. The coffin enters through the opened wall, and a little later, exits through the other side. From the chapel, those attending can visually follow this journey, which is a poetic metaphor for the journey of life. Whether or not a spirit also embarks on a journey after death, the body's journey is already in a heavenly place — through the surrounding cemetery, which those attending can see, hear and feel even inside the chapel.

A Dynamic Identity

The spirit may fly to heaven when the departed are laid to rest, but for the living who fly, a place of rest before or after flight can be an airport hotel. Too often, airports are anodyne transit environments that could be anywhere, a feeling that permeates many terminals, banal multi-storey car parks, support buildings and boxy airport hotels. Amsterdam's Schiphol Airport is one of the busiest airports in the world, and at the **Hilton Amsterdam Airport Schiphol** (2015), Mecanoo decided to break the 'non-place' paradigm and make a place that was a Place.

Between the repetitive rectilinear slabs of Schiphol's World Trade Center and a loop of road flyover, the 433-room hotel instantly signals a unique, dynamic identity in its form and facades. A cube volume rises from an extended plinth, softened with fluidic rounded corners and gently curved sides. It is wrapped in a diamond grid geometry of windows and white and black panels that makes a crisp, abstract pattern. Diamond shapes in the steel diagrid side of the bridge from the terminals introduce an experience that's not just another airport passageway.

But the big thrill is stepping into the heart of the hotel itself. Rooms and passage balconies surround a 42m-high atrium, flooded by natural light through the glazed oculus 30 metres wide and 32 metres long. It was the American architect John Portman who introduced the great central atrium into hotel architecture in the 1960s, but at Schiphol, Mecanoo's atrium has echoes of another great American architect. Around the inside, white ribbons of balustrade on each floor create an effect not unlike the spiral ramp inside Frank Lloyd Wright's New York Guggenheim Museum (1959). From these balustrades, and also from the rooms directly facing inwards, you can look down at the guests riding the white escalators from the ground to the first floor with its amenities, cabin staff gathering to check in or out, friends or family perched on stools at the bar, or meeting and sitting in the lobby with lounge area islands across the floor. Awe-inspiring enclosed voids under an oculus date back 1,900 years to Rome's Pantheon, but the Romans never had the chance to look down from higher floors and watch the Poetry of People coming together below.

A Daily Pursuit

Designing for people on the move is something that runs deep in Mecanoo's DNA. As professor of aesthetics of mobility at the Delft University of Technology, Francine Houben has taught and researched the subject. She says that mobility 'is a daily pursuit, just like housing, work and recreation' and that 'designing for mobility must be about people deriving a sensory experience from their everyday mobility'. The personal experience is always central to Mecanoo's designs, and when Houben's journey with mobility began in 1998, she proposed that the motorway should be viewed as a design brief. Millions of people experience the changes of the city and countryside — the 'landscape of the road' — through the windscreen of a car. They are in a built structure that happens to be mobile but, like a room, offers a view.

Houben made 'Mobility: A Room with a View' the theme of the 2003 Rotterdam International Architecture Biennale which she curated, and the title of a book she produced. The project took her audience on journeys far beyond the Netherlands, from Hong Kong and Tokyo to Los Angeles and Mexico. But as Houben notes, 'the motorist seems (to have become) politically incorrect and designers must see to it that everyone makes use of public transport'. Moreover, she sees the expansion of multi-modal mobility, in which the mix of train, tram, bus, bicycle and walking is now joined by e-bikes, e-scooters and mobility scooters. She observes that 'the architects' task is to produce designs that answer the steadily growing demand for mobility in all its modalities'. Crucially, she notes that 'the provision of mobility infrastructure has city-scale effects. So, we should consider mobility as a tool for connecting communities, facilitating new opportunities and creating conditions for economies to flourish'.

Re-uniting Delft

An excellent example of the urban effect of mobility infrastructure is Mecanoo's **Delft Railway Station and City Hall**. Since 2015, it has not just replaced an ornate 1885 brick station (designed by the elder Christiaan Meyjes and modest in size but with a fanciful spire), it has also transformed the city. As at Dordrecht (see p. 120), the main rail line had been a physical barrier between the old town and its eastern part. Since Delft buried the line in a 2.3-kilometre tunnel, the town has been re-united, and the station is the connector. Delft's population is modest — only 100,000 — but it is busy. Its quintessentially Dutch historical streets, canals and architecture draw international tourists, and the Delft University of Technology also makes it a student town. The new transport facility has to accommodate large people flows. It feels like a big-city, downtown station — 11 million journeys start or end here every year. Riding the escalators from the platforms up through a double-height void to the station hall, travellers see an 1877 map of the city printed on louvre strips curving across a vast 70-metre-wide ceiling, which extends up to 110m deep. This fabulous feature is a collaboration with wayfinding specialists Geerdes Ontwerpen, and a circular skylight — an oculus — is discretely set in it. The ceiling is not the only feature that celebrates Delft. The new 2,450 m^2 public hall is also lined with blue mosaics which refer to the town's famous blue tiles, and through the station's all-round glazing, the historic skyline is revealed, still recognizable as when it was painted by Vermeer around 1660.

The station has a free bicycle parking facility with a capacity of 5,000 cycles built in, and just outside are a bus station and tram stops. But the project is more than a multi-mode transport hub. In fact, most of the new structure floats directly above the station in a three-storey angular glass building completed in 2016, which hosts Delft City Hall. Covering 19,430 m^2, it is one of Delft's largest buildings, but its scale is tempered by its long, low form with sloping roofs. On the top floor, incisions in the glass volume create alleys and courtyards with the same scale as those in the old town. Like the similar patio incisions in the block volume of Palace of Justice in Córdoba (see p. 34), they create shady spaces for those working there. Meanwhile, adjacent to the whole new project, the old station is still in use — but as an Italian restaurant. Switching between transport modes in Delft offers many pleasures!

Gently Domed Canopy

In the Taiwanese city of Kaohsiung, home of Mecanoo's vast National Kaohsiung Center for the Arts (see p. 440) and with a population of 2.7 million — 27 times larger than Delft — the main railway has also been recently buried underground. At Mecanoo's new **Kaohsiung Station**, which partially opened in 2018, travellers surface from the train platforms, or from the even deeper metro lines, into open space beneath a breathtaking field of pearl-grey shapes like flat, rounded pebbles. This is the underside of a gently domed canopy 72 metres across. The station hall is centred in a vast 13,000 m^2 sunken plaza, below an off-centre opening in the canopy — another oculus to the sky, wider than in Delft and large enough to flood the station with natural light. This level is overlooked from a wide circle cut into a wider, ground level plaza, which has shelters with the same ceiling motif as the sunken plaza. It is open to the city around it, including a bus station, an intercity bus terminal and the original small station built by the Japanese colonial occupiers in 1941, which is now a local rail history museum.

The whole project extends out from the station canopy into the city, and is set for completion in 2025. It brings new public space far beyond the station, whose landscaped green roof already rises like a gentle hill with round openings to the plaza, the station and more green space below. A cycle and pedestrian highway meanders across the central dome and descends gradually down to ground level, into green corridors that stretch outwards like dendrites extending from a neuron. As Houben comments, the long and winding pathway reaches 'out into the neighbourhoods'. That reach is long — to the west, it stretches 270 metres from the station as well as to the east. Back at the station, the green canopy also spreads north and south into elevated organically-shaped wings around the station. Because this project creates adjacent sites for four new landmark buildings around the new landscape, it has parallels with what Americans call Transport Orientated Development (TOD), a term for walkable, car-free urban growth around a new station. The difference in Kaohsiung is that there already was a station, and the area has long had urban density. Gritty mid-twentieth-century buildings crowded around the old station area, dominated by traffic and a highway flyover. Now, the emerging new buildings have gentle curves, the air is fresh and the ground is green. The new Kaohsiung Station gives the city a green, urban heart, woven together by a Poetry of layers, openings, and flow.

Linear Park

Between Kaohsiung and Taiwan's capital Taipei, the railway crosses Taichung, another large city, at a high level. Elsewhere, tracks above the city streets are abandoned, and have become linear parks — New York's High Line (opened from 2009) is the most famous, although the similar Coulée Verte in Paris was the first in 1993. Despite a new high-speed rail line and a new HSR Taichung Station south-west of the centre, the original route made in 1908 and the downtown Taichung Station on it remain very active. The tracks were raised up on high concrete columns in 2016. Even so, Mecanoo have created a linear park, the **Taichung Green Corridor** — but below the active rail line. This 1.7-kilometre-long project is about breathing urban life, biodiversity and connectivity into a strip of the central city that was literally overshadowed.

At its eastern end, a bike path starts in parkland shaded by trees and leads to the station, a large contemporary structure besides which, as in Kaohsiung, the old Japanese-era station has been retained. The path crosses a wide plaza in front of it to the western stretch of the green corridor that follows the disused 1908 rail line, which was on an embankment. Its route is landscaped on either side of the path, which is paved with stone but embeds the old rails as a visible reminder of its heritage. Old steel bridges are re-used to cross streets, and the path over them is boardwalk, while new, smaller sculptural bridges allow corten-steel-lined pedestrian passages to cut through underneath. Alongside the old line at street level, the green corridor is tree-lined, and one side is directly below the high concrete rail structure. There is a succession of amenities, including an open-air fitness facility, big steps providing tiered seating, a playground, a herb garden and a viewing platform. The Lyu-Chuan canal, a once polluted and neglected narrow waterway, meets the route and turns to run alongside it, and the green corridor provides a lower path beside its waters, which are now fresh and its embankments green. The Taichung Green Corridor brings Nature into the very heart of the city, and a tranquillity and charm that would have been unthinkable just a few years ago.

The Adventure of Travel

When Francine Houben was a student at Delft, looking out from her room on the now-demolished railway viaduct there, she imagined the adventure of travel as trains passed by on their way to great cities like Paris or Amsterdam. Mecanoo's multi-modal transport hubs and new rail stations are portals to the romance of travel but also bring beauty to the everyday commute. For those crossing the city by foot and bike, Mecanoo's green urban corridors cut through dense downtown urban fabric, yet have the peace and beauty of a magical place. There are other projects where this transformation of everyday mobility transforms urban experience, benefits communities and improves health and wellbeing, such as A New Perspective for Rotterdam South (see p. 110). All facilitate journeys, and all of them are journeys towards the greener, barrier-free humanistic city we need for the future. As you rise into a wonderful station or go along a new, living green corridor, anyone and everyone can feel the fresh, free new spirit of that better future, and that optimistic feeling is Poetry.

St. Mary of the Angels Chapel

Rotterdam, the Netherlands

Discipline:

Architecture, Interior

Typology:

Religious

Size: 120 m²
Design: 1998-1999
Realization: 2000-2001
Client: Roman Catholic Cemetary St. Laurentius

Design team: Mecanoo

Programme: Chapel of 120 m² on a cemetery.

Link

9
CAMPO SANTO

The first chapel subsided because of the poor quality of the subsoil. The second chapel, built in 1963, had the shape of a pyramid, and it was also affected by foundation problems.

Mecanoo's chapel is the third for the St. Laurentius Cemetery in Rotterdam. It sits within the perimeter of the first chapel from 1869, the outline of which is visible from the exposed ruins of the original wall.

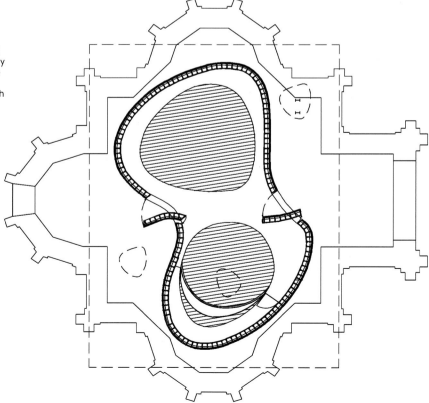

St. Mary of the Angels Chapel

The cemetery was designed by Herman Jan van den Brink and opened in 1869. It was designed as an Italian 'campo santo' with a Neo-Gothic chapel in its centre.

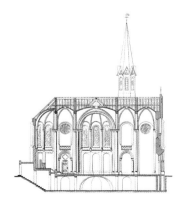

A new chapel for St. Laurentius Cemetery

1998-2001 — Rotterdam, the Netherlands

The chapel has a continuous curving wall, suspended seventy centimetres above the ground. Its thin rectangular roof bends like a piece of paper aloft in the air.

An opening in the ceiling allows a beam of light to enter the chapel, which is highlighted when incense is burned.

The almost abstract space of colour and light creates a sense of tranquility

St. Mary of the Angels Chapel

The routing is a poetic metaphor for the journey of life

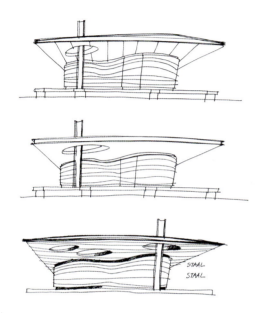

The chapel facilitates the ceremony of entering, standing still, reflecting and then moving on again, symbolizing that life continues.

UNDULATING WALL

On the wall, sentences from the 'Requiem' and 'In Paradisum' are written in the seven languages of Rotterdam's multicultural Roman Catholic community.

1998-2001 — Rotterdam, the Netherlands

St. Mary of the Angels Chapel

ON THE MOVE

A curving wall in vivid blue is interrupted by oversized pivot doors that swing out to reveal the surrounding cemetery.

30 May 2001, the bishop of Rotterdam rededicates the chapel to St. Mary of the Angels.

1998–2001   Rotterdam, the Netherlands   397

Hilton Amsterdam Airport Schiphol

Schiphol, the Netherlands

Discipline:

Architecture

Typology:

Hotel/Leisure

Link

Size: 40,150 m²
Design: 2009-2012
Realization: 2013-2015
Client: Schiphol Real Estate

Design team: Mecanoo (lead architect), Hirsch Bedner and Merx+Girod (interior design lobby, restaurants, meeting centre, health club and guest rooms).

Programme: Hilton hotel with 433 rooms, 4,100 m² meeting and conference centre with 23 meeting rooms, restaurants, health club, swimming pool, company rooms, lounge areas, a banquet hall for 600 guests and a parking garage for 135 cars, totalling 40,150 m².

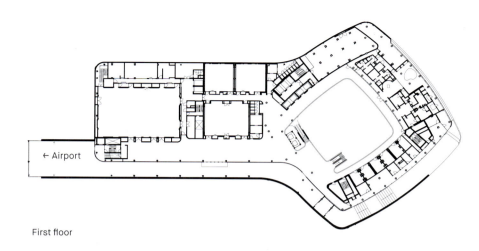

First floor

The 42m-high atrium, with its glazed oculus forms the spectacular heart of the hotel

The oculus is 30 metres wide and 32 metres long. Sculptural balconies circle around the atrium.

With its diagonally patterned facade, curved corners and strategic location, the building is a recognizable icon at the airport and prominently visible from the motorway

ON THE MOVE

The hotel's conference centre on the first and second floors is connected to the airport by a passageway.

Delft Railway Station and City Hall

Delft, the Netherlands

Discipline:

Architecture, Interior

Typology:

Office, Government/Civic, Mobility   Link

Size: 28,320 m²
Design: 2006-2010
Realization: 2012-2016
Client: Ontwikkelingsbedrijf Spoorzone

Design team: Mecanoo

Programme: 28,320 m² railway station and city hall, including a 3,550 m² station hall with 850 m² retail spaces; 19,430 m² municipal offices and a 2,230 m² public hall with counters on the ground floor; an archive and loading dock.

405

VIEW OF DELFT

When Vermeer painted his hometown (1660-1661), he captured not only the interplay of light, shadows, sky and cityscape, but also mobility: citizens stand by a passenger barge.

The skies in Johannes Vermeer's 'View of Delft' gave the insight to treat light as a design material

Inspired by the narrow streets and alleyways of the historic city centre of Delft, the building's form is incised by pocket courtyards and lightwells.

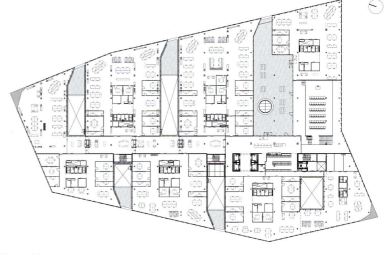

Second floor

406

Delft Railway Station and City Hall

ON THE MOVE

Before the railway was buried in a tunnel in 2015, Delft's historical centre and its east were divided. Now the City Hall and Railway Station are a connector between them.

The building's allround glazing reveals and reflects the historic skyline. The glazed skin is reminiscent of the bottled glass produced in the sixteenth and seventeenth century in Holland.

The light filled space above ground dramatically reveals itself as you ascend to the above ground station hall that is connected to the City Hall.

An 1877 map of Delft was redrawn and enlarged by graphic designer Martijn Geerdes, and printed onto the 1,800 lamella-fins of the roofscape.

Arriving in Delft has become an unforgettable experience

- ① Train station Hall
- ② City Hall
- ○ Public Area
- ● Commercial/Private Area

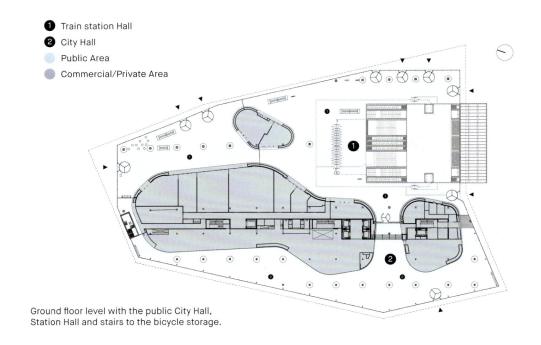

Ground floor level with the public City Hall, Station Hall and stairs to the bicycle storage.

The station platforms sit below ground, along with the bicycle storage rooms on mezzanine level with a capacity of 5,000 bikes. ↓

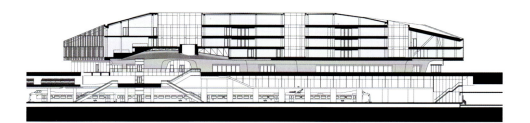

The building is welcoming on all sides and makes switching between modes of transport easy and pleasant

The walls and columns in the station hall are clad in a blue and white mosaic in a contemporary, abstract way, reimagining Delft Blue tiles.

The City Hall is clad in blue and white mosaic. The municipal offices on the upper levels are flooded with daylight, thanks to the pocket courtyards and lightwells.

ON THE MOVE

The building is a multi-modal transport hub and hosts municipal offices on its upper levels

2006-2016　　　　Delft, the Netherlands　　　　413

Kaohsiung Station

Kaohsiung, Taiwan

Discipline:

Architecture, Urbanism, Landscape

Typology:

Government/Civic, Mobility

Link

Size: 182,000 m²
Design: 2014-2016
Realization: 2014-2025
Client: Taiwan Railway Reconstruction Bureau

Design team: Mecanoo (lead design) and PECL, Pacific Engineers & Constructors (local architect).

Programme: Site of 8.5 ha with sunken station plaza (13,000 m²), green canopy (35,000 m²), multi-layered bicycle path, landscape (60,000 m²), hotel (22,000 m²), commercial buildings (52,000 m²), local and intercity bus terminal, restoration of colonial Japanese station building, and masterplanning for future developments.

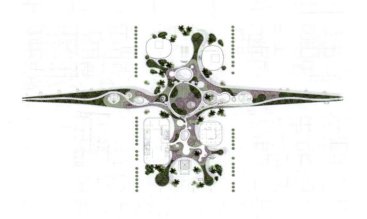

Roof plan

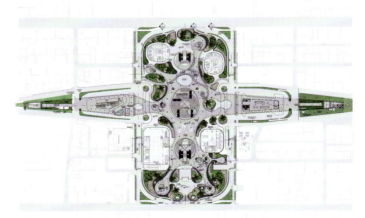

Ground floor plan

Kaohsiung Station

ON THE MOVE

LANDSCAPED MOBILITY HUB

The new station hall is covered by a spectacular landscaped green roof with cycle and pedestrian paths meandering across the dome and reaching 270 metres out into the neighbourhoods on the east and west.

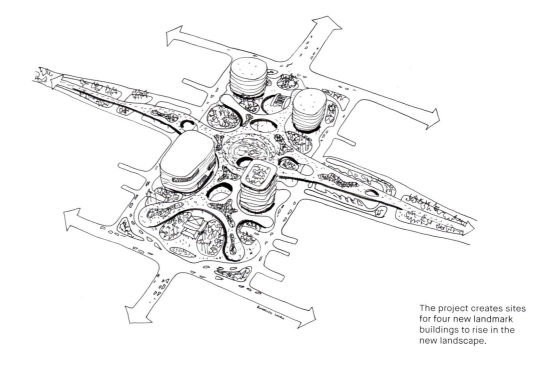

The project creates sites for four new landmark buildings to rise in the new landscape.

2014-2025 Kaohsiung, Taiwan

Kaohsiung Station

ON THE MOVE

GREEN CORRIDOR

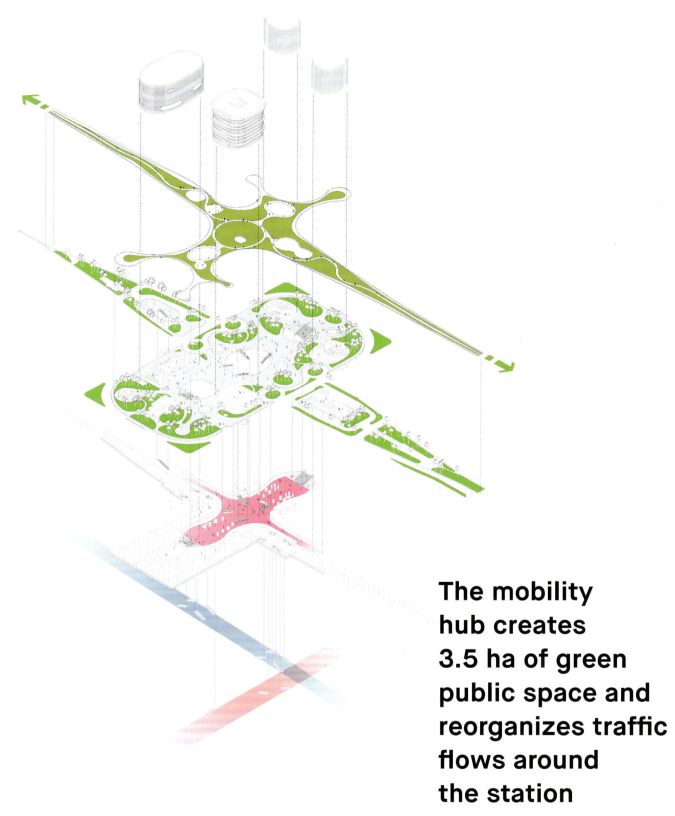

The mobility hub creates 3.5 ha of green public space and reorganizes traffic flows around the station

← The construction of the second phase of the station hall with underground connections to the trains, metro and buses, and offices and retail. (Photo 2022)

2014-2025   Kaohsiung, Taiwan

Arriving from the underground platforms, the immersive space creates a memorable experience for travellers. Here people can meet, or visit events like a farmers' market, traditional open-air opera or mobile library.

The sunken plaza unfolds underneath a bright ceiling of oval-shaped lights.

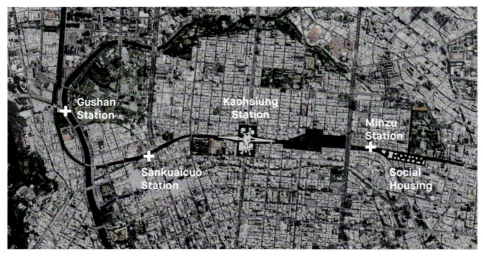

Kaohsiung Station is the crowning achievement of the Kaohsiung Metropolitan Area Underground Railway Project, which includes seven subterranean stations along a 9.75 km railway tunnel. Close to Minzu Station is Mecanoo's Social Housing project.

The station has been designed to bring green space to the heart of the city and creates new corridors for pedestrians and cyclists

ON THE MOVE

2014-2025 — Kaohsiung, Taiwan

Taichung Green Corridor

Taichung, Taiwan

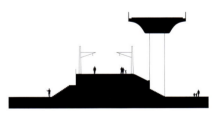

Discipline:

Urbanism, Landscape

Typology:

Leisure, Mobility

Size: 1.7 km
Design: 2017
Realization: 2018-2020
Client: Taichung City Government

Design team: Mecanoo, S.D Atelier and ARIA architect & planners.

Programme: Transformation of the 1.7 km existing dyke and former railway track into a linear park with herb gardens, street fitness, stepped seating, playground, viewpoint and waterpark.

427

9

The tracks of the 1.7 km long railway line, dating from 1908, were raised up on columns in 2016. The space underneath and along the railway line has been transformed into a green corridor with bike and pedestrian lanes, transforming this barrier into a connector.

ON THE MOVE

Old steel bridges are reused to cross streets, carrying boardwalk paths as well as paving which embeds the old rails as a visible reminder of its heritage.

GREEN CONNECTOR

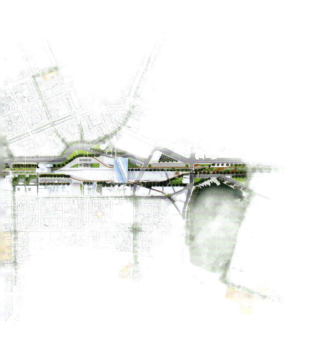

2017-2020

Taichung, Taiwan

429

The linear park breathes urban life, biodiversity and connectivity into the strip. It is designed to intensify the use of the area, while promoting a more coherent city infrastructure.

ON THE MOVE

LINEAR PARK

2017-2020 — Taichung, Taiwan — 431

10
Dear Audience

Drama, music, and art celebrate humanity's ability to share creative imagination by realizing it and presenting it to an audience, and they come from deep in humanity's history, perhaps from the very beginning of human culture. But buildings where performance and artistry are presented to an audience are more recent. In Europe, Ancient Greece created open air theatres. Later, art and performance were sheltered in churches and kept under control by religious authority. It was not until the Renaissance that dedicated public theatres were built (Italy's oldest art theatre, designed by the great architect Palladio, opened in Vicenza as late as 1585). Nowadays, theatres, concert halls and galleries are part of our cultural infrastructure, along with libraries, museums, and historic places. Venues for contemporary culture and live performance make a crucial contribution to society, both economically and socially. The twenty-first century has brought new reasons why such venues are vital — we'll come back to that.

Mecanoo have created buildings across the world in which artistry and culture meet audiences. Each has its own Poetry that makes the building itself a pleasure for People to be in, whatever they are there to see. These are often Places that are destinations in their own right, responding to but transforming their locations. In scale, they range dramatically, from a barn in the Dutch countryside to a vast sculptural object under an undulating roof of world record size, set in a Taiwanese city park. Let us start a journey with a project that is squeezed into the historic Dutch urban fabric.

From Church to Theatre

Mecanoo's first stage for performance is beside a central Amsterdam canal, in a building that had been an active church from 1793 until the 1950s. By the 1990s, the abandoned building was in poor state, but its slender neo-classical columns, which defined the rectangular central void of the church's nave, still stood strong over three floors. These columns and the walls embodied the building's history, a key part of what makes it a special place. Adapting it for an avant-garde theatre company called De Trust, Mecanoo decided to let the historical structure tell its story, and co-exist with the new theatre, which opened in 1996. The new elements are clear and contemporary, but at the same time in sympathetic dialogue with the past. This approach was quite different from modernist interventions in old buildings, which tend to extend or insert aesthetically disconnected new space to old structure.

At the **Trust Theater**, the old structure was stripped back, exposing the textures of the original wood, bricks and plasterwork. Where the church organ had been, beyond the entrance lobby, is a big new intervention. An entire full-height new slice of building has been inserted. It greets visitors with a small, open bar and has walls of red and gold. The intervention contains the services a stage production needs, and carries a new staircase leading up to it on the first floor.

Francine Houben remembered at the time that 'the protocol in restoring a painting is that you must do it in such a way that your interventions can be reversed'. She applied the idea to the church, and so the new structure was designed to be entirely demountable, anticipating the future-proofing of internal spaces that architecture would start to embrace in this century. Upstairs, above new spaces including studios and storage, the double-height theatre auditorium space is like a black box, but it can be opened up with galleries on both sides, simply by opening curtains between the columns. The cleverness and charm in spatial configuration and the interplay between old and new textures, as well as the solidity of historical structure and the ephemerality of the present, come together.

The Trust Theater is poetic, and it comes with intimate touches. As you head to the auditorium for the performance, small chandeliers hang above the stairs, signalling theatre tradition, surprise... and just a little romance.

Later, we shall come to more recent examples of warm, human-scaled Dutch projects, but what happens when Mecanoo applies its humanistic ideals to designing mega-scale cultural buildings?

Banyan Tree

The **National Kaohsiung Center for the Arts** (2018) has just three floors, but under a roof bigger than that of any other performing arts centre, ever. It covers world-class auditoria, vast technical areas, halls for conference, rehearsal, and education, an exhibition space and not least, an extraordinary public plaza. This is Mecanoo's most ambitious cultural building to date — the client compares its impact for Taiwan to that of the 1973 Sydney Opera House, conceived by the Danish architect Jørn Utzon, for Australia. As we shall see, the design of the new arts centre is inspired and shaped by things local to Kaohsiung — its evening informality, street performances and colour, the legacy and skills of its shipbuilding industry, and the extraordinary banyan tree...

Close up, the design concept of Kaohsiung's arts centre is simply too big to take in. To see it clearly, you have to get some distance, in the surrounding Wei-Wu-Ying Metropolitan Park. It is as if a metallic mothership has landed in the park, but one that brings art, not aliens. There's an echo of La Llotja (see p. 466) in the way the top floor cantilevers out to fill the edges of the building's rectangular footprint, but this floor takes a fluid form, thinning and bending, and the rectangle is a giant 225m x 160m. Four great auditoria reach up into this floor, and Mecanoo worked with Paris-based Xu-Acoustique on their acoustics throughout. Let's go inside...

The biggest auditorium is the Opera House, with a traditional interior, and a capacity of 2,236. The Playhouse seats 1,210, is flexible in what it can stage, and feels modern. The most gorgeous auditorium is the Concert Hall, an organic champagne-coloured space over which a 22-tonne acoustic canopy hangs. It seats 1,981 in tiers that surround the stage; an audience configuration called vineyard seating. The smallest is the Recital Room, with 434 seats. Features include dynamic walls that change their surface, and suspended acoustic baffles that look like elements from an Alexander Calder mobile sculpture.

In the open air, there are further performance spaces. The undulating steel roof itself curves down into a great amphitheatre, and performers on its stage can face several hundreds sitting in it — or several thousands if they turn to face the park. It is out there that you find banyan trees. They gave Francine Houben an epiphany when she first visited Kaohsiung. A banyan has multiple trunks with branches that widen and join to form a continuous crown, creating shady cave-like spaces which in Taiwan catch the cooling wind of the ocean. Why not shape the arts centre in the same way? The Banyan Plaza does just that, inside the volume of the arts centre. The auditoria lie within its trunks, and the crown is the underside of the art centre's top floor. The exterior surfaces are made of 2,320 clearly visible steel plates. Like with the canopy of the Netherlands Open Air Museum (see p. 288), they were welded by shipbuilders, here both local and Dutch. At night, suspended 3.5 metre-wide chandelier disks of LEDs can fill the space with light of different colours, just as the streets of Kaohsiung come alive with coloured light as darkness falls. The Banyan Plaza can be a performance space, and its white surfaces make a great screen for open-air cinema, but without the worry of rain. It is like a living room for the whole city. It is a democratic space, open to anyone and everyone — it is for the People.

Urbanist Mission

In Manchester, **HOME** (2015) is home to an arts centre with an urbanist mission. The three-storey building kickstarted the life that animates the new First Street mixed-use pedestrian quarter. Its downtown site is awkward, between Oxford Road (see Manchester Engineering Campus Development, (see p. 272) and Castlefield's canals and high-rise, and it is partially hidden by a railway viaduct. HOME's longest side runs parallel to the viaduct, but the building is a triangular wedge, standing beside a gently stepped terrace which transitions into First Street's central piazza, with a rounded corner cantilevering over the entrance. All three rounded corners carry the memory of The Cornerhouse, HOME's antecedent, which was in an old triangular building. Glass facades react to the weather, but as darkness falls, they reveal activity in the restaurant, bar and foyers on different floors.

There's a tangible buzz inside, but at the same time, a warmth in which you can relax. It's like being at home. The double-height first floor is as airy as a great hall, and flooded with light by day. The central oak stairs channel natural ventilation through the open labyrinth. HOME hosts a gallery, five art-house cinemas (the most intimate seating just 40), and two theatres, both with a black metal aesthetic that resonates with cutting-edge drama. The larger one leaves none of its 500 seats further than 15 metres from the stage. Intimacy infuses HOME's city lifestyle vibe. Even with all the space and spaces which the 7,600 m² building packs in, there is nothing monumental about it. The scale remains human.

Shadow and Shelter

The first Mecanoo project outside of the Netherlands, the **La Llotja de Lleida** theatre and conference centre (2010), is in Catalonia's second city, Lleida (Lérida). Its form takes some inspiration from the Netherlands — the neighbouring building to the Library Delft University of Technology called the Aula (1966) by Johannes van den Broek and Jaap Bakema, a futuristic brutalist icon. Like the Aula, La Llotja has a rectangular plan level which cantilevers above a widening base to float above the ground, but otherwise, it is shaped by what it does, and where it is. You won't find a sliced pyramid rising over the roof in Delft, but in Lleida, there is one housing the fly tower for the 1,000-capacity theatre below. The cantilever serves a purpose — shelter from the sun and rain in the extended plaza that comes in up to 16 metres beneath it (an idea Mecanoo echoed later in another Spanish town, Córdoba - (see p. 34). The floating first floor has continual glazing that exposes the bright colours of its foyer walls, and the theatre walls are patterned with luminous trees — both features reference the orchards of the region. There are also two conference halls, one separated by just glass from an exhibition space. Beside the fly tower, the roof carries an open lounge bar from which to survey the historical cathedral town. As for the materiality, it could not be more different from the heavy Dutch concrete at Delft University of Technology. The building is clad in natural stone panelling, each section a different brown or yellow to its neighbours, giving the effect of big, earthy stone blocks. Their warmth issues a gentle, seductive call.

'No Comment' Environment

Mecanoo has designed several art shows at the **Kunsthal**, Rotterdam, a modernist-style building designed by OMA. In 2015, Mecanoo partner Dick van Gameren designed the exhibition of the exclamatory, colourful art of Keith Haring, with its street political stances and bizarre cartoon-like protagonists, in a white 'no comment' environment. The exhibition design's circulation route included angled walls, and two walls with rectangular openings into the central gallery space, creating different perspectives. A black passage lit by UV hosted Haring's fluorescent works. In a 2016 show, Mecanoo created black and white spaces empathizing with the black-and-white photographs of Peter Lindbergh. On show were not only his trademark fashion portraits capturing candid moments, but also background material such as props and notes, and some blow-ups that were metres across. This called for transitions between contemplation, study, and drama across different sections. In 2021, the 'Calder Now' show brought American artist Alexander Calder's hanging mobiles and standing sculptures together with new works by ten major contemporary artists such as Olafur Eliasson and Sarah Sze. Some of these had demanding spatial needs, heightening the exhibition's design challenge. Mecanoo created a path through Calder's works, with openings and windows into the new works. Key artistic elements — time, gravity, performance, sound, material — link the old and contemporary artistic universes, creating a multi-sensory experience.

A New 'Barn'

Drama or musical ensembles also need the right physical and emotional space to develop, try out, rehearse and perform their material. In the southern Dutch village of Herpt, Mecanoo have crafted such a place from an old barn. The project is a non-profit initiative of Hans Andersson, Francine Houben's husband. It opened in 2020 as **De Nieuwe Schuur**, which means 'the new barn'. With its large pitched roof, the building's simple shape refers to the original barn that stood on the site, but its ground floor now houses a theatre hall and kitchen. Groups can sleep on different floors with windows looking out across the surrounding orchard, and the idyllic flat farmland, rivers and trees of the Brabant countryside. All floors are completely lined with wood, which makes the space feel warm and cosy. De Nieuwe Schuur is also the perfect inspiring environment for management teams as a retreat to brainstorm and plan, away from the corporate environment.

Above ground, De Nieuwe Schuur is a cross-laminated timber structure with wood cladding. With this traditional technique, originated by the Japanese in the eighteenth century, the wood is burned until the surface is charred, and then coated with natural oil. The char acts as an insulator. Colours appear on the long ground floor facades under the roof eaves, which are clad with glazed tiles in eight shades of grey, green and blue, made by Netherlands oldest ceramics company (1572), Royal Tichelaar. In the furniture we recognize the Mecanoo blue fabric of the chairs of the Playhouse, one of the halls in the National Kaohsiung Center for the Arts (see p. 440). The large concrete basement houses not only sustainable mechanical equipment and storage space – indispensable for a theatre – it also houses a jazz cellar. In one room down there, a Mecanoo Blue carpet is literally rolled out and up the wall for Houben's personal project The Blue Wall, which captures all visitors in a photograph.

Come Together

Every project we've looked at is a unique structure that offers an extraordinary experience as a Place as well as its Purpose to host culture. Nowadays, such places are more relevant than ever.

There is an emerging urgency in our world, which is precisely about People and Place. As the digital world frames experience in the screen of a phone or computer, it dissolves location and makes social interaction virtual. We are a social species, but the explosion of digital paths to connect with others increasingly separates us physically. Our identities find expression in representations held and streamed as data. Instead, we need to come together in the real world! Venues are where we can share company, as well as experiences, whether it's art, performances or gardens. Togetherness makes everything better. We need what Mecanoo has long known — Places are for People, and ultimately the Poetry they provide to keep us human.

Trust Theater

Amsterdam, the Netherlands

Discipline:

Architecture, Interior, Restoration

Typology:

Transformation, Theatre/Concert Hall

Size: 2,700 m²
Design: 1995
Realization: 1996
Client: Trusttheater

Design team: Mecanoo

Programme: Transformation and restoration of a listed former Lutheran church (1793) into a 2,700 m² theatre.

Transforming a church into a theatre

The church on Amsterdam's Kloveniersburgwal dates back to 1793 and was active until the 1950s.

The huge organ was taken out and replaced with an expressive 'piece of furniture' that defines the theatre.

DEAR AUDIENCE

The principle behind the detailing is that the existing and the new come into contact as little as possible.

The stage is situated on the first floor. The existing colonnades can be used as side stages with views out onto the canal. But when the curtains are closed, a black box is created.

National Kaohsiung Center for the Arts

Kaohsiung, Taiwan

Discipline:

Architecture, Landscape

Typology:

Theatre/Concert Hall

Link

Size: 141,000 m²
Design: 2007-2009
Realization: 2010-2018
Client: Preparatory Office of The Wei-Wu-Ying Center for the Arts of the Council for Cultural Affairs.

Design team: Mecanoo (lead architect) and Archasia Design Group (architect of record).

Programme: Theatre complex of 141,000 m² in the Wei-Wu-Ying Metropolitan Park with a total capacity of 5,861 seats (Concert Hall 1,981 seats, Opera House 2,236 seats, Playhouse 1,210 seats, Recital Hall 434 seats), exhibition space of 800 m², 1,000 m² of rehearsal/education halls for music and dance, two conference halls with 100 and 200 seats and stage building workshops, lobbies and restaurants, the grand covered public space Banyan Plaza, and 7-ha landscape design.

Kaohsiung has a tradition of informal outdoor theatre, including Chinese opera. This became an inspiration for a sheltered, outdoor public space for theatre and events.

The open, protective shape of the banyan trees becomes a springboard for the design

Our dream for Banyan Plaza is a public, protected space where people can freely make music, dance, practice Tai Chi, and where also organized events can take place.

National Kaohsiung Center for the Arts

DEAR AUDIENCE

The curved steel structure was built in cooperation between local and Dutch shipbuilders.

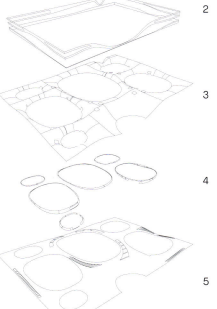

1. Roof including outdoor seating (34,843 m²)
2. Vertical facade (6,896 m²)
3. Skin (2,320 m²)
4. Fillet (2,320 m²)
5. Banyan Plaza (17,446 m²)

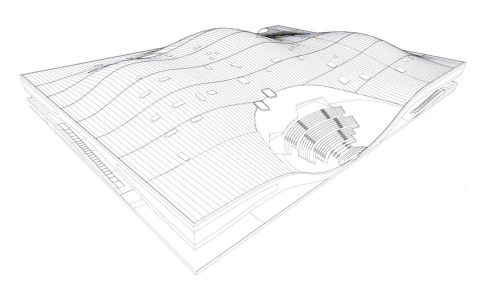

2007-2018   Kaohsiung, Taiwan

10

The undulating steel roof curves on one side, down into an amphitheatre

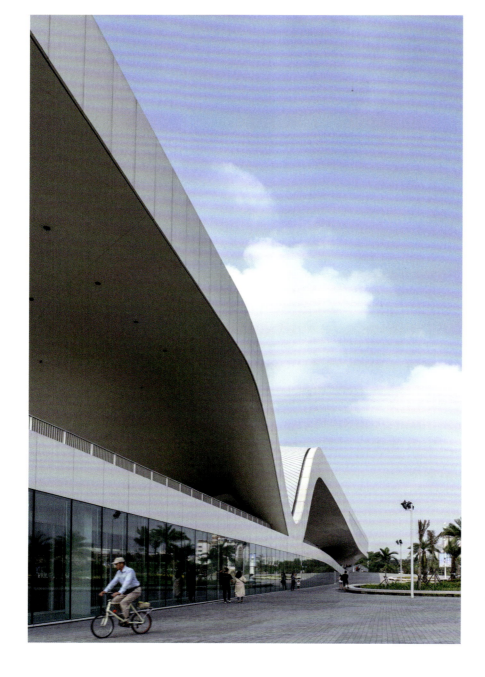

444

National Kaohsiung Center for the Arts

DEAR AUDIENCE

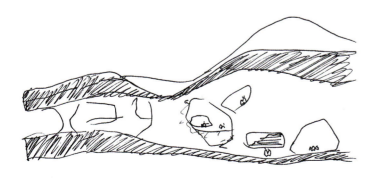

UNDULATING STRUCTURE

2007-2018   Kaohsiung, Taiwan

Four auditoria create organic forms like huge tree trunks in Banyan Plaza, reaching up to the higher floors

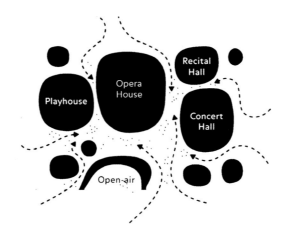

← People, as well as the cooling wind, can flow freely through the open structure.

→ The canopy is punctured by skylights bringing daylight to the plaza.

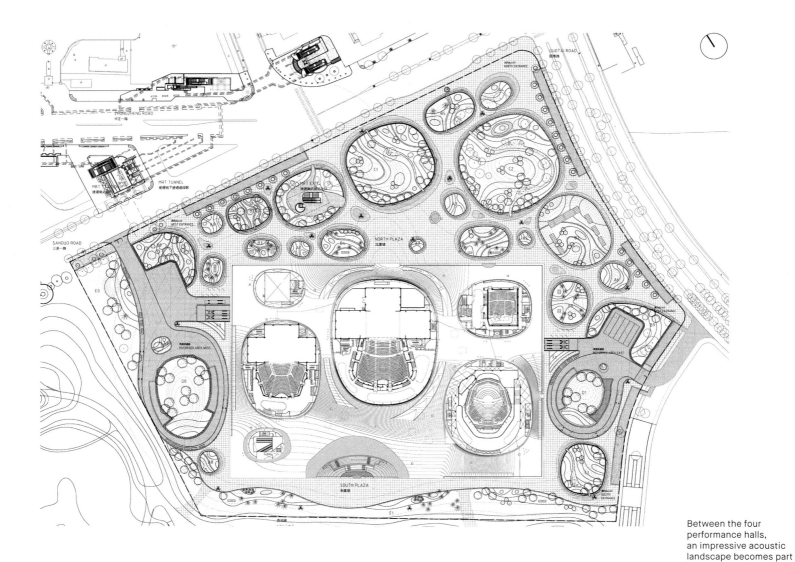

Between the four performance halls, an impressive acoustic landscape becomes part of the Banyan Plaza.

446 National Kaohsiung Center for the Arts

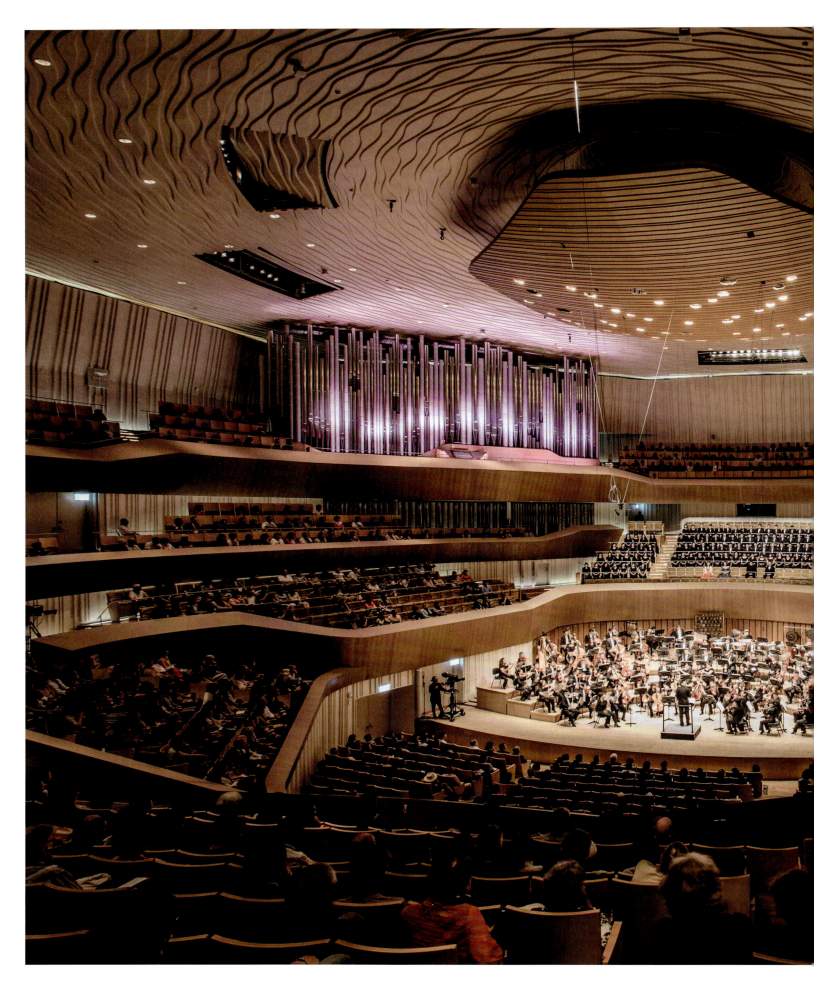

CONCERT HALL

The 1,981-seat Concert Hall is shaped like a stepped vineyard and a 22-tonne acoustic canopy floating above

The 434-seat Recital Hall has the most intimate atmosphere of the four and is designed for chamber music and recitals

Features include dynamic walls that change their surface, and suspended acoustic baffles that look like elements from an Alexander Calder mobile sculpture.

DEAR AUDIENCE

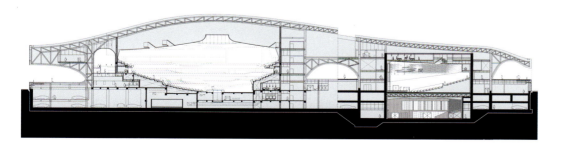

RECITAL HALL

2007–2018 Kaohsiung, Taiwan

The 1,210-seat Playhouse can host a variety of drama and dance performances

DEAR AUDIENCE

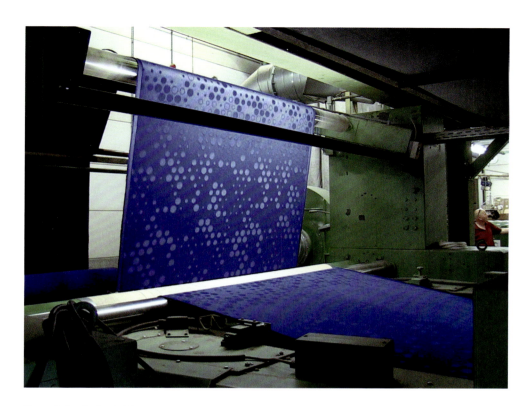

The mohair velvet upholstery fabric adorning the over 5,800 theatre chairs was crafted by Vescom, a renowned Dutch manufacturer. Employing an intricate weaving technique, they skillfully manipulated the pile's orientation, resulting in captivating shadow effects.

PLAYHOUSE

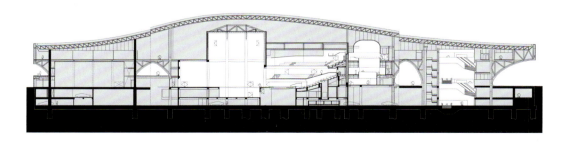

2007-2018   Kaohsiung, Taiwan

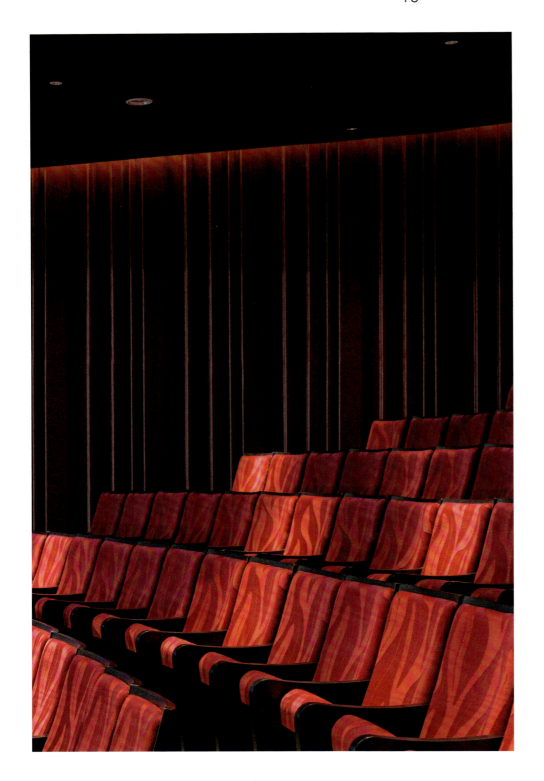

The 2,236-seat Opera House is well suited for Western opera with orchestras of over seventy musicians

DEAR AUDIENCE

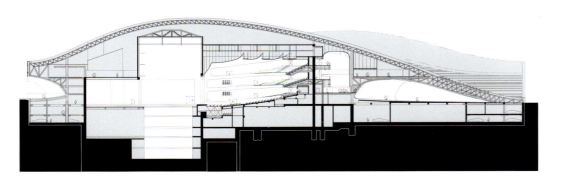

OPERA HOUSE

2007–2018   Kaohsiung, Taiwan   455

Banyan Plaza is like a living room for the city, open to anyone and everyone – it is for the People

The skin of the Banyan Plaza has the character of a cargo ship, with visible welding joints, integrating hoist points for hanging lights, flags and banners.

DEAR AUDIENCE

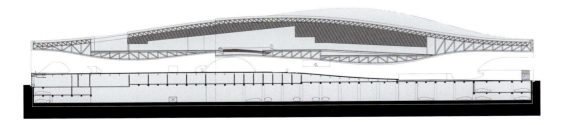

BANYAN PLAZA

2007-2018 — Kaohsiung, Taiwan

HOME Arts Centre

Manchester, United Kingdom

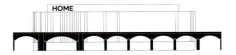

Discipline:

Architecture, Interior

Typology:

Theatre/Concert Hall, Museum/Exhibition   Link

Size: 7,600 m²
Design: 2011-2012
Realization: 2013-2015
Client: Manchester City Council

Design team: Mecanoo (lead architect), Concrete (interior consultant) and Planit-IE (landscape design).

Programme: Art house of 7,600 m² with two theatre halls (500 and 150 seats), five cinemas (250, 150, 60, 40 and 40 seats), a restaurant, café, roof terrace, gallery, three foyers, bookshop, sponsor's room, offices, rehearsal room, work places, educational spaces, dressing rooms, expedition rooms and a public square, BREEAM Very Good.

461

10

CULTURAL

↑ The arts centre is a triangular wedge, and its terrace gently transitions into First Street's central piazza, bringing buzz to this mixed-use pedestrian quarter.

The four-metre-high flexible gallery for modern art is located on the ground floor. ↓

The central stairwell acts as an informal social space, connecting the theatre halls, cinemas and gallery.

HOME Arts Centre

DEAR AUDIENCE

HOME's warm, busy restaurant has a characteristic logo that can be seen from the outside.

A new home for arts, cinema and theatre

HOTSPOT

2011–2015 — Manchester, United Kingdom

10

HOME produces, co-produces, commissions and presents small- and mid-scale theatre

The main theatre on the first floor leaves none of its 500 colourful seats further than 15 metres from the stage.

464 HOME Arts Centre

La Llotja de Lleida

Lérida, Spain

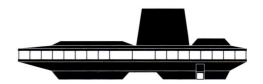

Discipline:

Architecture, Landscape, Interior

Typology:

Theatre/Concert Hall, Exhibition

Link

Size: 37,500 m²
Design: 2004-2006
Realization: 2006-2010
Client: Centre de Negocis i de Convencions S.A.

Design team: Mecanoo (lead architect) and Labb arquitectura (executive architect).

Programme: Multifunctional theatre and conference centre of 37,500 m² with a 1,000-seat theatre/conference hall, two conference halls (400 and 200 seats), a multifunctional exhibition hall, two foyers, a lounge, roof terraces, Mercolleida office, 2,600 m² of retail, 9,500 m² of parking, and a public square of 15,000 m².

10
SHADOW

The foyer was raised to capture the view to the thirteenth century Seu Vella Cathedral.

La Llotja is positioned between the river and the old city on the hill.

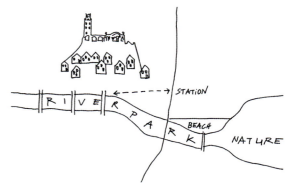

La Llotja de Lleida

DEAR AUDIENCE

The multifunctional hall on the first floor can host exhibitions and events.

The cantilever reaching out over a public square provides shelter, also for performers at city events

SHELTER

Shadow and Shelter

2004–2010 Lérida, Spain

10

COLOUR RHYTHM

The lobby is bathed in light by the changing colour schemes of the LED lights integrated in the ramp to the second floor.

A gently ascending staircase coupled with a grand ramp weaves all the functions together.

DEAR AUDIENCE

The long foyer wall has a colour scheme inspired by the fruit production of the region and a panoramic view to the old city.

Fruit leaves – apple, pear, plumb and peach – have been carved into wooden panels.

Silhouettes of fruit trees on the walls, combined with thousands of leaves in the ceiling, gently illuminate the auditorium

The 1,000-seat theatre hall evokes the atmosphere of an orchard. During daytime it serves as a conference hall, while in the evening it transforms into a festive theatre.

La Llotja de Lleida

DEAR AUDIENCE

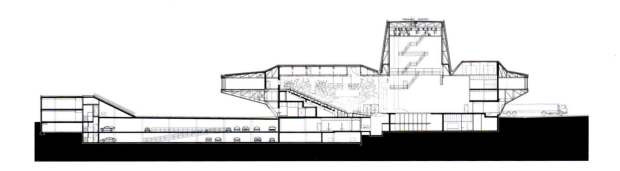

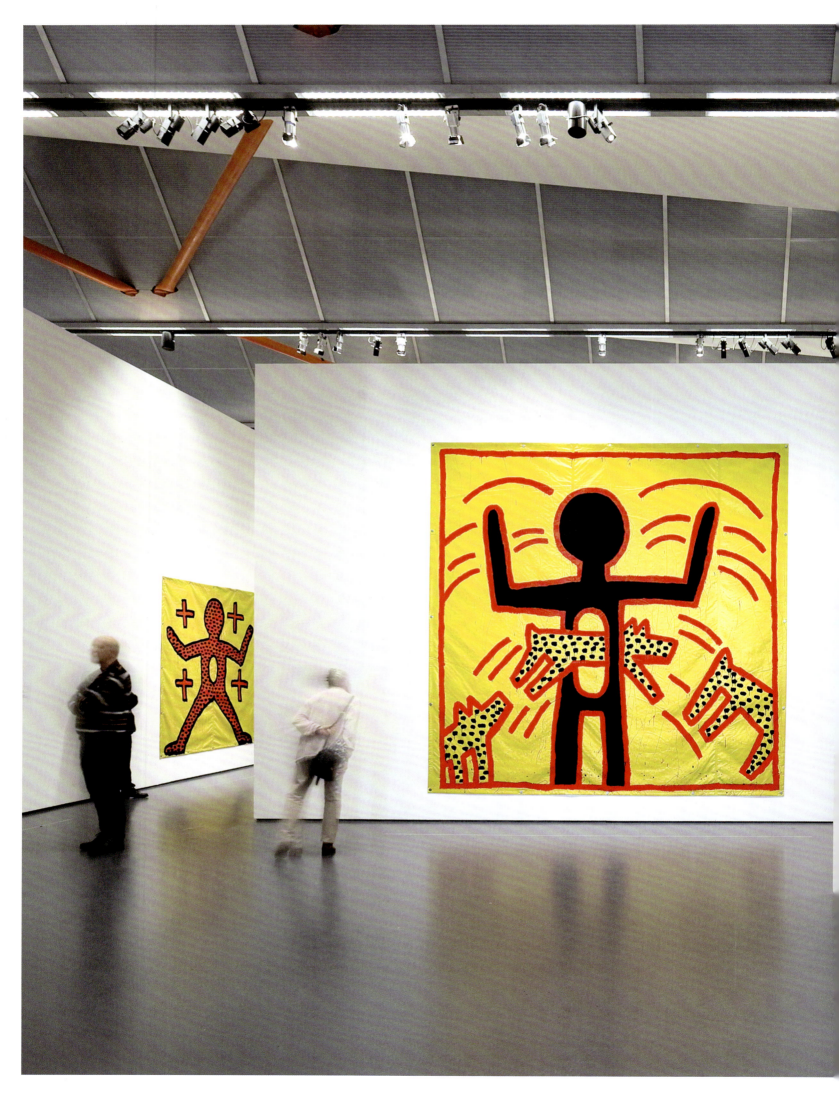

Kunsthal Art Shows

Rotterdam, the Netherlands

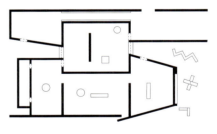

Discipline:

Interior

Typology:

Museum/Exhibition

Size: 1,400 m²
Design and Realization: 2015-2018
Client: Kunsthal Rotterdam
Design team: Mecanoo

Programme: 'Keith Haring: The Political Line', a 1,400 m² exhibition encompassing drawings, paintings, sculptures, and exhibition shop; 'Peter Lindbergh: A Different Vision on Fashion Photography', a 1,400 m² traveling exhibition presented in nine sections featuring photographic works and supplementary materials; and 'Calder Now', a 1,400 m² exhibition showcasing twenty sculptures and mobiles by Calder, in conjunction with works by ten renowned artists.

10

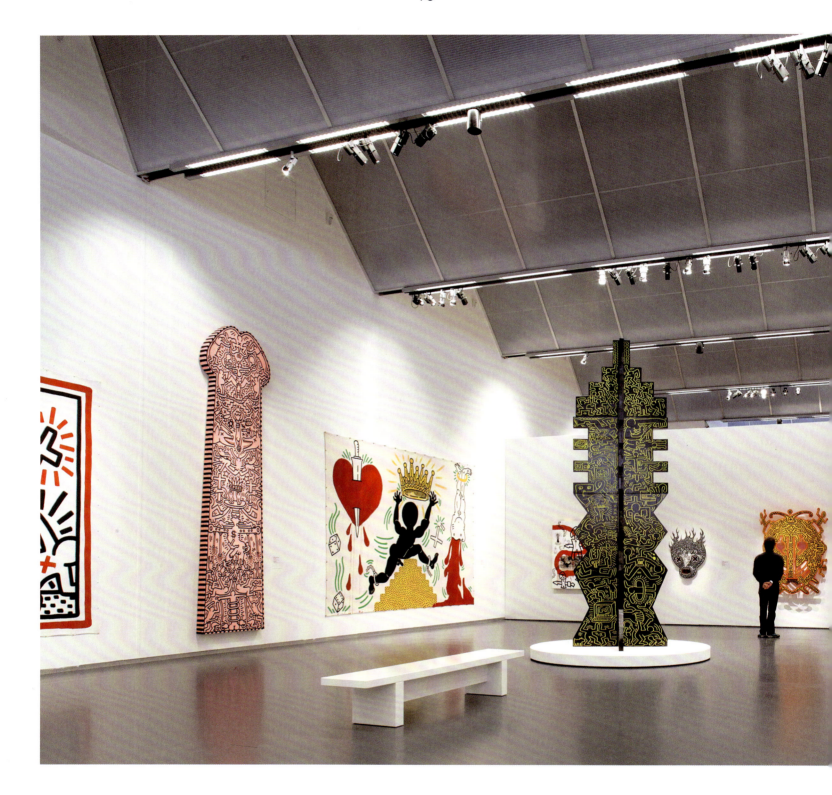

KEITH HARING

With his unique style Keith Haring (1958-1990) spawned a revolution in art during the 1980s

DEAR AUDIENCE

Keith Haring was inspired by graffiti, comic strips, music, dance, 'high' art and popular culture. The route including angled walls, and two walls with rectangular openings into the central gallery space, creates different perspectives on the artist's work.

Peter Lindbergh's (1944-2019) pure black-and-white photographs have determined the course of fashion photography since the 1980s

DEAR AUDIENCE

The black-and-white spaces of the exhibition emphatize Peter Lindbergh's photographs.

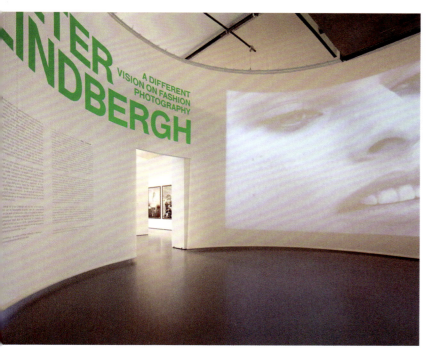

The exhibition features more than 220 photographs, including exclusive material varying from personal notes, storyboards, props, polaroids, contact sheets, films and monumental prints.

PETER LINDBERGH

2015-2018   Rotterdam, the Netherlands

The works of renowned artists such as Ernesto Neto's 'It happens when the body is anatomy of time', 2000 (bottom) and Žilvinas Kempinas 'Flaming Tape', 2021 (bottom right page) add a new perspective on the work of Calder.

Alexander Calder (1898-1976) was one of modern art's great innovators and a pioneer of kinetic art

CALDER NOW

DEAR AUDIENCE

Through a series of openings and windows, the visitors flow through the gallery spaces as Calder's gravity-defying installations and sculptures were given new context with pieces from the ten contemporary artists.

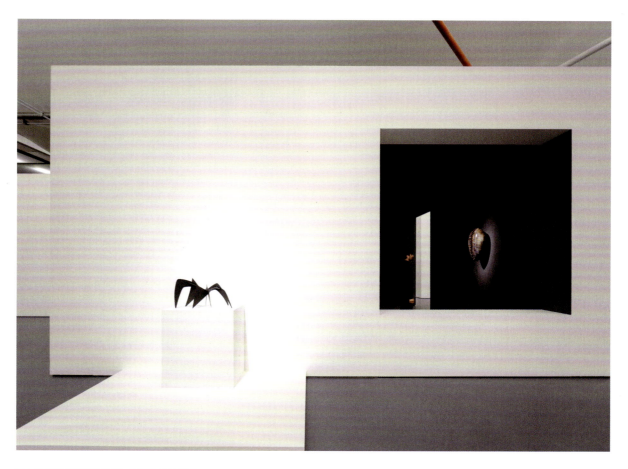

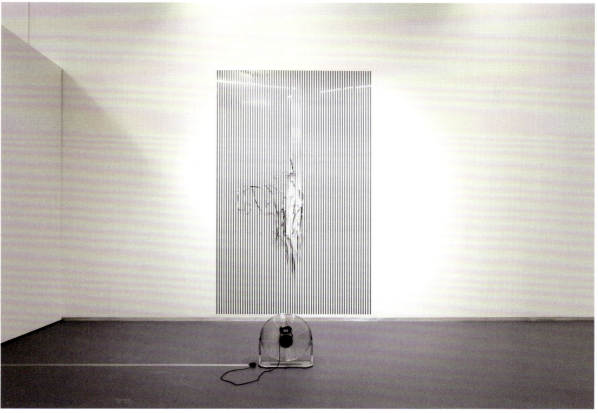

2015–2018   Rotterdam, the Netherlands

De Nieuwe Schuur

Herpt, the Netherlands

Discipline:

Architecture, Landscape, Interior

Typology:

Hotel/Leisure, Theatre/Concert Hall

Size: 622 m²
Design: 2018
Realization: 2019-2020
Client: Hans Andersson/De Nieuwe Schuur

Design team: Mecanoo

Programme: Mass timber, highly sustainable theatre of 622 m² including several rehearsal and meeting rooms, kitchen, jazz cellar, guest rooms, and including circular interior and biodiverse landscape design.

10

CULTURAL

The old barn was made of wood and had a sand floor.

Old barn transforms into a multi-functional cultural venue

The cross-laminated structure has a charred wooden cladding, a traditional technique originated by the Japanese in the eighteenth century.

De Nieuwe Schuur

DEAR AUDIENCE

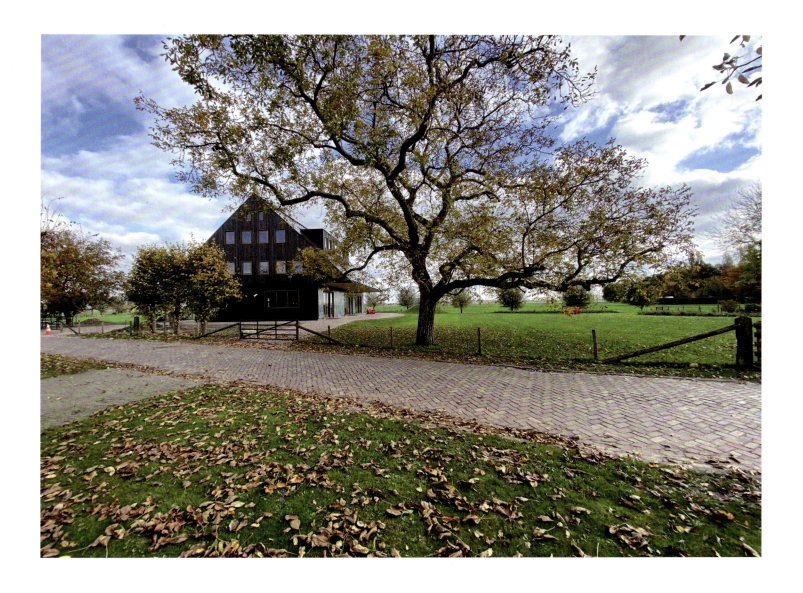

The facades are clad with glazed tiles made by Netherlands oldest ceramics company (1572), Royal Tichelaar.

The building's shape refers to the original barn and includes a multipurpose theatre for cultural try-outs and business retreats

BARN

2018-2020   Herpt, the Netherlands

The theatre floor is lined with wood, creating a warm and cosy atmospere.

The theatre hall can accommodate up to 100 people in theatre seating and is equipped with state-of-the-art theatre technology.

DEAR AUDIENCE

The wooden loft has all-round views over the vast landscape.

A place where performing artists can dream and create

In the upstairs rooms you can sleep in box beds.

Visitors may be captured by camera in the Blue Room.

11

Forward
to Basics!

What path are Mecanoo's designs taking to the future in a fast-changing world beset by challenges, not least the climate crisis, now declared a climate emergency. Its effects are more evident every year, and we have no Planet B. Mecanoo's approach is about People, Place, Purpose and Poetry. The biggest Place of all is the planet we share, and our ravenous exploitation of it needs to change. Nature has given us an amazing world which sustains us and it brings us wellbeing and joy. As Francine Houben says, 'nature has an irreplaceable value and beauty'. Going forward, she says: 'Mecanoo declares that Nature has equal priority with People in how we design.'

Collective Responsibility

The damage that we inflict on our planet has left a deep impression on Houben. 'I've been in the Amazon twenty years ago', she recalls. 'Everywhere was organized fire'. Coming from the Netherlands, the existential threat of environmental catastrophe is a constant — one third of the country is below sea level, and now the seas are rising. For the Dutch, 'it's a collective responsibility, otherwise we all drown', she says. 'That's also what we must do with this world.' She has long asserted that there must be a collective responsibility for sustainability, because it 'relates to the survival of us all'.

Climate change (and all the intricately interconnected, related issues such as biodiversity loss and industrial farming) is not the only challenge to our survival. There is also resource depletion, social and economic inequality, demographic trends and even the inexorable rise of the automated, digital world. That doesn't mean we should panic. Professionals evaluate an emergency situation and draw on the basics of their training, skills and experience to find a way through it. Francine Houben used the expression 'forward to basics' back in 2012, when she advocated planning that reconnects city and country. But the words apply to everything architecture, design and planning should do. Building on the basics of architectural practice, common sense and the humanistic approach to make people's lives better is not complacency, but a rational approach. And Houben's philosophy has always seen a 'love of nature' as a basic.

Analysis and Intuition

Environmental sustainability is at the heart of mitigating our onslaught on nature and the planet, but it has become a contemporary mantra. In architecture it has led to a regime defined by official targets and regulations and a plethora of what Houben calls 'technocratic solutions'. It is something that every project must proclaim, inevitably leading to a rise of corporate greenwashing. But Mecanoo designs don't shout sustainability — rather, it is integrated as a basic, even passive ingredient in the design mix, along with other ingredients such as concern for the user, the aesthetics, and so on. Hasn't sustainability been built into Mecanoo's DNA from the start? 'Yes,' Houben says, 'and now it's becoming more and more important.' Mecanoo has long invested in sustainable research and development projects, such as EWICON, a device designed together with the Delft University of Technology in 2010 that harvests wind energy without moving parts (see p. 508). We can expect many more sustainable solutions to emerge from Mecanoo. New ideas emerge from the combination of analysis and intuition, which Houben says are 'a source of energy and resilience within architectural practice'. Mecanoo is a team with diverse skills in its individual members, and of course, it works with others beyond the team. Houben says 'the future is very much about collaboration, bringing different disciplines together'.

Architecture cannot directly force the need to finish forever our deadly addiction to fossil fuels, but it can do something about CO_2 emissions. The carbon footprint of buildings, both in construction and when in use, is huge — in Europe, for example, they account for a third of fossil fuel consumption. Extending the life of an existing building instead of replacing it is intrinsically sustainable, because the structure itself is a resource not to be wasted, and it saves the materials and construction energy that new build would demand.

Circular

We have seen (in the Wisdom and Wizardry chapter) how Mecanoo are remaking three iconic American libraries to take them deep into the new century. Mecanoo are now taking on three great old buildings in their homeland. The Boijmans Van Beuningen Museum (see p. 52), home to a vast, world-class collection of art, is to be restored and reconnected to the park and the city of Rotterdam around it. In Zaanstad, near Amsterdam, the industrial heritage of a giant flour mill complex called Meneba will become an entire residential neighbourhood, Zaankwartier, with one third social housing (see p. 515). There are many more outstanding Mecanoo re-use projects, such as LocHal (see p. 148), and Westergasfabriek (see p. 318), and they stretch back to 1996, when a church was converted into a theatre called Trust (see p. 436) in Amsterdam. Now, in the same city, the De Nederlandsche Bank (DNB – see p. 44) will soon be completely refashioned within its original towering headquarters. Of course, new materials are still needed in any retrofit, including concrete with its notoriously large carbon footprint. The DNB project is a world first for carbon-neutral concrete, which is made from recycled material injected with CO_2. It's a landmark step for the circular economy, in which nothing we use, from food wrapping and clothing to entire buildings, is thrown away, but recycled or re-used. Mecanoo are turning this ideal into a reality.

CO_2 is the most dangerous of greenhouse gasses, but they are far from the only emissions from our activity that pollute the planet. Consider nitrogen pollution, which includes NOx, toxic to humans, and NH_3 (ammonia) which damages ecosystems. The Nonohouse is an initiative with partners including Delft University of Technology to address the nitrogen pollution that results from farming. It aims to take NOx and ammonia out of the air, and the first experimental building, incorporating algae into its construction, was showcased in Delft in 2019 (see p. 514).

Mobility

Mobility is another area where we need to take action to save the planet. According to the International Energy Agency, transport accounts for a shocking 37 per cent of global CO_2 emissions in 2021. As well as addressing shipping and road haulage, we need to shift rapidly from car culture to public transport, and revive low- or no-emission transport modes — which include cycling and walking. In the chapter On The Move we saw that Houben has a particular interest in mobility, and Mecanoo projects such as Kaohsiung Station (see p. 416) or the Rotterdam South vision (see p. 110) thread multiple modes of sustainable mobility together. They also fundamentally re-invent their locations, and that brings us back to the one of the four key P's driving Mecanoo's design philosophy: Place.

Place

Mecanoo is passionate about Place. It is clear in all the projects we have looked at. Place provides the context for the project, so that its landscape, history, culture and vernacular architecture are factors woven into the design. Deprived or isolated communities in Places that have known better times are re-energized and connected. Place-making creates new Places for social and economic activity. But what about Nature?

Nature

We can see and touch Nature in different ways in Mecanoo projects. Housing that integrates with a green environment has been developing since projects such as Nieuw Terbregge — a neighbourhood shaped as an island in a water landscape — in Rotterdam in 2002 (see p. 506). Biodiversity can bring the buzz of birds and pollinating insects in roof gardens into the heart of the city, such as at the Library of Birmingham (see p. 158) or the Martin Luther King Jr. Memorial Library (see p. 178) in Washington DC, or in landscaped public space in grounds hitherto barren of plant life, such as those around the Manchester Engineering Campus Development (see p. 272). They bring the living planet into the 'concrete jungle'. There are many other Mecanoo examples. Maybe soon, any architectural project where nothing visibly grows will be the exception, not the norm.

People

Mecanoo is devoted to People. The humanistic concern for those who will use and animate all its designs comes from a recognition of the value of every individual, underlined by the other great sustainability — social sustainability. 'Our public projects have always been something for all, they are inclusive,' says Houben. A decade of projects encountering people all around the world has revealed to her that everyone everywhere wants 'the very simple things, that you care for children and want to give them a future'. To that, we now add that people everywhere gain better health, mental wellbeing and even a sense of wonder and connection to the planet simply by being with Nature. It touches all the senses and has a transformative effect on People. A project such as the Nelson Mandela Park (see p. 312) delivers Nature to the doorstep of disadvantaged neighbourhoods, while the Nieuw Land National Park (see p. 128) uses the key of mobility to unlock nature for city folk, with its railway 'nature-station' where you can rent a bike to cycle through the vast, diverse natural landscape.

Purpose

Mecanoo is imaginative and innovative about Purpose. We have seen that delivering the function of a commissioned project — office, home, school, cultural centre, and so on — must simultaneously enhance the life of the project's users and make them want to be there. Now, we can see that there is a whole new level of Purpose — our own survival. Perhaps we should add another P to Mecanoo's drivers, the Planet. But the Earth permeates all our P's. It is the largest Place, it is home to us, the People, and now its future survival adds Purpose.

Poetry

You may wonder what relevance the fourth 'P' in the title of this book may have to facing the future. Actually, Poetry is crucial. In the early nineteenth century, British philosopher and reformer Jeremy Bentham argued that 'the measure of right and wrong' is how much it creates the 'greatest happiness of the greatest number'. For the first time since then, there is an awareness that instead of economic growth, happiness should be the goal for societies to strive for. Design alone cannot change the global economic system, nor instantly cancel the threats to the planet, or rewild it with Nature. But it can build, step by step, a world that is happier. The emotional magic of a building contributes to that happiness, and as Houben says, 'the right to beauty is extremely important'. Poetry, too, must be a basic in whatever the future brings.

'The world is in flux — swept up in climate change, ceaseless urbanization, the digitization of systems, knowledge and life, and global shifts in power, population, and wealth. We believe that our architecture can contribute to a better world, and we are passionate about solving complex challenges to create inspiring places for people.'

Francine Houben

BEGINNINGS

A Name

In 1981, students Henk Döll, Francine Houben and Roelf Steenhuis won an architectural competition to design a housing block. At the time, they hadn't even finished their studies at the Delft University of Technology. The competition site was at Kruisplein (see p. 503), just a city block from Rotterdam Central Station. Almost obliterated by Second World War bombing, the city centre was rebuilt with modernist style and ideas, but by the 1980s it was time for some different thinking. Houben and her partners applied that not just to their design, but also to their working name. In 1984, they became 'Mecanoo', inspired by three words. The first is Meccano, the popular British amateur construction kit that encouraged children and adults to apply logic and turn their imagination into real structures. Coincidentally, it resonates with the aesthetics of the high-tech architecture, then challenging the paradigms of modernism. Secondly, in the 1920s, Dutch artist Theo van Doesburg, linked to the De Stijl and Bauhaus design movements, created a magazine called Mécano in the crazy, free-thinking but meticulously formatted style of the Dadaists. Free-thinking but meticulous design would be Mecanoo characteristics too. Finally, 'Ozoo' was the motto of their competition submittal referring to the Kruisplein site where once the Rotterdam Zoo was located. The lane beside Mecanoo's building is still called Diergaardesingel, meaning Zoo Avenue.

A Leap into the Blue

One key Mecanoo character is the diver who is part of Mecanoo's logo, represented in Mecanoo blue. Where did this diver spring from? The answer is: from Delft's local market, not far from the Mecanoo office. A small wooden printing block found in 1980 has since been lost, but the flying diver it portrayed now makes many, many more impressions online than it ever did as a physical stamp! The graphic diver is freeze-framed with arms outstretched just after leaping into the air. All the emotions the diver feels — exhilaration, freedom, focus — are conveyed in this modest graphic. It is a fantastic, and poetic, metaphor for Mecanoo's design approach. The diver tells us of the empowering joy in People. The character's act of leaping into flight has a firmly-focused Purpose, and a precisely-targeted Place to land. Moreover, the diver literally conveys that each project is a leap into the future.

Diver, 1980 and 2008.

A Canal-side Campus

The old centre of Delft is an idyllic network of canals, bridges, alleys, market squares and historic structures. There, Mecanoo set up office in 1983 in a single room in a stately canal-side house at Oude Delft 203. They have remained at the original address ever since. It is less than a hundred metres from the fourteenth-century Oude Kerk, a church with a fantastic, 75-metre-high gothic tower that leans dramatically from the vertical, because one side began to sink as it was partly built over a filled-in canal. It's a reminder that in the Netherlands, there is a constant battle against water.

The history of the building dates back to 1536 when the wooden buildings along the Oude Delft canal burned down. Two stone houses separated by a narrow alley were built where the Mecanoo building now stands. In 1750 the two houses were joined together, and became home to prominent Delft citizens. Vernacular Dutch town houses are slim and their facades often have a distinctive symmetric roofline reaching upwards, but Oude Delft 203 has a square facade and flat roof eave. Influenced by Italian Renaissance architecture, some Dutch houses had begun to acquire a more palace-like grandeur by de-emphasizing the vertical and incorporating a bel-étage and refined plaster work, while maintaining an overall Dutch austerity. Oude Delft 203 has three steps to what is almost a bel-étage, but is above street level because it was built over ancient stone cellars that survived the 1536 fire. The entrance opens into a distinguished 40m-long corridor, with baroque plasterwork in the style associated with Louis XIV, the 'Sun King'. This is the work of Joseph Bollina, an Italian architect who lived in Delft. In 1886, it was sold and soon after, a charitable Catholic order of nuns started caring for victims of a cholera epidemic here. With the next-door house at 205, they established the St Hippolytus Hospital, which subsequently expanded into 207. In 1970, architects OD205 took over the complex. Mecanoo first took a room at the corridor's far end, facing a garden. As they expanded into all the buildings and created extensions, the complex became a campus.

Mecanoo's model workshop is beside the garden. Inside the listed building complex, a host of original features are retained. Noisiest is the great wooden staircase on one side of the central corridor. It creaks loudly as you climb it, almost paraphrasing Houben's words about the Stephen A. Schwarzman Building in New York (see p. 192) about 'listening to the logic of the building'. The staircase is saying 'listen to the history, structure and materiality of our building'!

Nowadays, Mecanoo have offices in New York, Kaohsiung, Abu Dhabi and London, but no setting is as poetic as Oude Delft 203's.

LEADERSHIP

Mecanoo is led by Francine Houben, Dick van Gameren, Nuno Fontarra, Rick Splinter, Arne Lijbers, Floris Overheul and Armand Paardekooper Overman. The Mecanoo team is made up of a multidisciplinary staff of over 130 creative professionals from 25 countries, including architects, interior designers, urban planners, landscape and restoration architects, as well as architectural technicians and support staff. Francine envisions this diverse team as a vibrant international 'symphony orchestra,' which is crucial to the success of Mecanoo's projects.

Francine M.J. Houben
FOUNDING PARTNER & CREATIVE DIRECTOR

Architecture must appeal to all the senses. Architecture is never a purely intellectual, conceptual, or visual game alone. Architecture is about combining all the individual elements into a single concept. What counts in the end is the arrangement of form and emotion.

Since 1984, Francine Houben is Founding Partner and Creative Director of Mecanoo and has led the firm to success in the Netherlands and abroad, amassing a wide-range portfolio of award-winning work, inspired by global challenges and a view on a sustainable society. Also referred to as the 'Library Whisperer', Francine has become internationally recognized for realizing world-class libraries such as the Martin Luther King Jr. Memorial Library in Washington DC and The New York Public Library. She has received numerous awards including the Prins Bernhard Cultuurfonds Prize 2015 for her lifetime achievement as a leading international architect by Queen Máxima of the Netherlands. As curator of the First International Architecture Biennale Rotterdam (2003), she brought the theme of the aesthetics of mobility to the forefront of international design consciousness. Francine lectures all over the world and was (visiting) professor at renowned universities such as Delft University of Technology, Harvard Graduate School of Design, US, Yale School of Architecture, US, and Accademia d'Archittettura in Mendrisio, Switzerland.

Dick van Gameren
PARTNER/DESIGN & RESEARCH DIRECTOR

A building that is not linked to its immediate surroundings and wider context is an obstacle. Designing a building means creating space for all, inside and outside, and connecting past, present and future.

Dick joined Mecanoo in 1988 and established his own office in 1991. Since 2013, he has been a Partner at Mecanoo, and in 2019, he became Dean of the Faculty of Architecture and the Built Environment at Delft University of Technology. Here, he leads an international education and research network focused on affordable housing in growing African and Asian cities. His innovative designs address issues such as densification, privacy, and mobility. He received the Aga Khan Award 2007 for the design of the Netherlands Embassy in Addis Ababa, Ethiopia. Dick continues to foster a critical approach to design by teaching and lecturing. As a visiting professor he has contributed his expertise at the KRVIA Mumbai, India and the Harvard Graduate School of Design, US. Dick consistently publishes influential works in the field of architecture and housing, exemplified by his book *Dutch Dwellings* and effectively applies his research to tangible contributions as a partner at Mecanoo, where he spearheads design initiatives.

Nuno Fontarra
PARTNER/ARCHITECT

The true beauty of architecture lies in the unspoken experiences it invokes, where words fall short, and emotions and sensations come to life.

Nuno joined Mecanoo in 2002. His pivotal role at Mecanoo extends beyond his design and creative contributions. For more than twenty years, he has been involved in Mecanoo's international portfolio of work including standout projects such as La Llotja de Lleida in Spain, the National Kaohsiung Center for the Arts in Taiwan, and the prestigious Natural History Museum in Abu Dhabi. By firmly relating each project to the landscape, he aims to enhance the context of each intervention. Maintaining an active role in academia, Nuno has taught at the Delft University of Technology and the Piet Zwart Institute in Rotterdam, and at a design studio at Soongsil University in Seoul.

Rick Splinter
PARTNER/ARCHITECT

In a successful design, we carefully compose a coherent, solid and attractive proposal using location-specific information. As architects, we take into consideration the time span over which people will use and experience our buildings and therefore dedicate maximum effort into the relatively short time designing them.

Rick joined Mecanoo in 2003. His residential and masterplan projects are distinguished by a diverse array of sustainable developments that carefully blend public spaces with existing structures, breathing new life into them and forging unique schemes. Over the course of the last twenty years, Rick has brought to life numerous distinctive neighbourhoods, both in the Netherlands and in the United Kingdom, including Villa Industria in Hilversum and Kampus in Manchester. His particular interest lies in exploring innovative and forward-thinking approaches to harmonize the concerns and goals of diverse stakeholders, while maintaining a pragmatic and coherent approach.

Arne Lijbers
PARTNER/ARCHITECT

Architecture is about more than just buildings, it is about creating your own environment. I believe that architecture can bring more quality to life in all its aspects, it can help us grow, create and excel.

Arne joined Mecanoo in 2012. Since then, he has advanced his design skills with a distinctive energy, a clear reflection of his vibrant personality. From a project's outset, working across all scales, from mobility, urban planning to interior, Arne establishes

Armand Paardekooper Overman, Nuno Fontarra, Arne Lijbers, Francine Houben, Dick van Gameren, Floris Overheul and Rick Splinter.

creative and user-based designs. Examples include the Unilever Benelux Headquarters in Rotterdam, the residential Brink Tower in Amsterdam and the International Quarter in London. His multidisciplinary, analytical and sensory-driven design approach ensures the seamless integration of complex information and procedures, leading to flexible as well as specific outcomes. From the very first dream, through the sketching and conceptual phase, Arne's hands-on approach is evident all the way to the delivery of state-of-the-art buildings.

Floris Overheul

PARTNER/FINANCIAL DIRECTOR

The most important asset of Mecanoo is our highly motivated team with creative professionals from more than 25 countries.

Floris joined Mecanoo in 2019. With his extensive international background and problem-solving character, he oversees the firm's Finance, Business Development, People & Organisation, ICT and Quality Management departments. He is responsible for the day-to-day management and, in coordination with the partners, for determining Mecanoo's overall strategy and direction. Since 2023, he is a board member at the Royal Institute of Dutch Architects (BNA), where he represents the interests of the architecture industry and its workforce.

Armand Paardekooper Overman

ASSOCIATE PARTNER/ARCHITECT

Our cities are a reflection of our human potential: to be social, well-connected, responsible, innovative, beautiful, in harmony with nature and to be human. This goes beyond what design can do, it's a responsibility.

Armand joined Mecanoo in 2018. His approach in architecture and urbanism is to understand and use the potential of the challenges we are facing today, the complex nature of our cities and processes. Armand enjoys the beauty of working from a collective intelligence with universities, start-ups, economists, politicians, entrepreneurs, and residents. This results in buildings, cities and landscapes that are inspiring, innovative, socially responsible — and widely appreciated — and contribute to a better future. Armand's portfolio of work includes the masterplan for the Railway Zone in Dordrecht, Nieuw Land National Park, the Co-Creation Centre & Nonohouse at the Delft University of Technology and housing project Habitat Royale in Amsterdam.

Mecanoo — the year rings of a tree

november 2023
Francine Houben

(spiral of project names, from innermost outward:)

- TU Delft
- Kruisplein
- UNESCO podium
- Stipendium
- Toneelstad Amsterdam
- Hillekop
- House and Studio
- Stedelijk Internationale Woonselling
- "Ruimte voor ruimte"
- Tent Theatre
- Chapel St. Mary of the Angels Rotterdam
- Boston urban renewal
- Alvaro Siza collaboration
- Mecanoo Blue exhibition
- Groningen Masterplan
- Boat exhibition
- Soeterijn theatre
- Arnhem
- Composition Contrast Complexity
- Netherlands Open Air Museum Rotterdam
- Montevideo highrise
- Palace of Justice, Córdoba
- Whistling Rock Korea
- golf clubhouse with a view
- Hilton Hotel, Schiphol
- Library of Birmingham
- Zaans Medisch Centrum
- Kaohsiung Social Housing
- Museum Boijmans van Beuningen
- Lochal Tilburg
- Martin Luther King Memorial Library Washington DC
- Natuurhistorisch museum
- Palace of Justice
- Jacobs Pillow
- Hester City Hall and Municipal offices
- London International Quarter Stratford
- National Park Nieuw Land
- Tekstmuseum Tilburg
- New York Public Library
- Villa 4
- Europan
- Cambridge University Housing
- Texel Museum Kaap Skil
- Fifty Two Degrees Nijmegen
- Kerkenhof — Cartesius Utrecht
- Waterspuitbank Park Amsterdam
- Mandela Engineering Campus
- Performing Arts Centre, Kaohsiung Taiwan
- Bijlmerpark Amsterdam
- Campus TU Delft, Mekelpark
- Vondelpark housing Utrecht
- AFF Maliebaan 16 Utrecht
- Faculty of Economy Maastricht
- Professor TU Delft
- Library Technical University Delft
- La Llotja de Lleida, theatre, Spain
- 7 International Architecture Biennale: Mobility a room with a view
- Station & Municipal offices, Delft
- Beurs WTC renovatie Rotterdam
- European Investment Bank Luxembourg
- Architecture & Aesthetics of Mobility
- Toneelschuur Haarlem
- Kaohsiung Station
- St. Gerlach pavilion
- Boston, Bruce C Bolling Building
- Shenzhen, cultural buildings and a bookmall
- Kampus Manchester
- Natural History Museum Abu Dhabi
- Unilever Benelux HQ
- Taiwan Library
- Nederlandsche Bank
- De Nieuwe Schuur
- A new perspective for Trinity College, Toronto
- Rotterdam South Railway zone Dordrecht
- Delfland Water Authority

FOUR DECADES OF MECANOO

1980

Students of the Delft University of Technology Roelf Steenhuis, Henk Döll and Francine Houben participate in the Kruisplein Flexible Youth Housing competition in 1980-1981. Their submittal OZOO wins!

Döll-Houben-Steenhuis is established.

In front of the Kruisplein site

Kruisplein, Rotterdam (collage: photo of the model glued onto a photo of the site)

Kruisplein Competition Book

'The idea competition for flexible youth housing on Kruisplein square in Rotterdam was noteworthy for two reasons. First, it was a turning point in Dutch social housing which was then mainly oriented towards family units. Second, it marked the creation of Mecanoo by the winning entrants, three students at the Delft University of Technology.'
Netherlands Architecture Institute, Rotterdam

1984

Francine, Henk and Roelf graduate from Delft University of Technology, and Kruisplein is realized.

Architectengroep Mecanoo is officially founded
Döll-Houben-Steenhuis becomes Architectengroep Mecanoo in 1984, made up of (from left to right) Erick van Egeraat, Chris de Weijer, Francine Houben, Roelf Steenhuis and Henk Döll.

Mentor Professor Max Risselada introduces Francine and Erick to the work of Charles and Ray Eames. They visit Ray many times and are inspired by their free and multidisciplinary way of working.

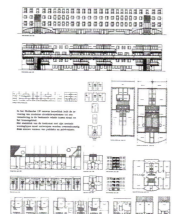

← Tommorow's Habitat, UNESCO (1984)
UNESCO launches a worldwide competition open to students and architects under the age of 35. The challenge of Tomorrow's Habitat is to develop ideas exploring the best ways to build homes for the new millennium. The prize is an excursion to Japan. Francine and Erick win first prize in the Netherlands.

→ Housing, Bospolder-Tussendijken, Rotterdam (1984-1987)
On the day Francine, Henk and Roelf graduate, they get the commission for seven sites in Bospolder-Tussendijken, Rotterdam.

Ted Schutten (1951-1999), educated at Delft University of Technology, is of great importance as a mentor on construction processes to the then inexperienced office. As a contractor, he realizes over a thousand Mecanoo houses, including Bospolder-Tussendijken, Dedemsvaartweg, Groothandelsmarkt, and Tanthof Urban Villas.

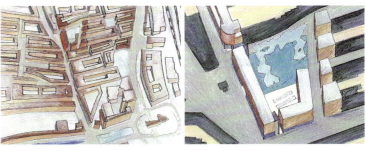

Affordable Housing Tiendplein, Rotterdam (1984-1989): urban renewal commission close to the Kruisplein site

1985

Francine and Erick receive a stipend and travel through Japan for three months in 1985. They meet architects such as Toyo Ito, Itsuko Hasegawa and Tadao Ando. They are impressed by the traditional Japanese architecture and landscaping.
Photo: Francine sitting on the right of Kazuyo Sejima, who worked for Toyo Ito.

In the 1980s Mecanoo acts as the local architect for Portuguese architect Álvaro Siza on Van der Vennepark in The Hague.

WORKING WITH SIZA TAUGHT US HOW TO DESIGN WITH RENEWED FREEDOM; IT LIBERATED US FROM THE MODERNIST WAY OF THINKING

1987

→ Mecanoo are awarded The Maaskant Prize for Young Architects
Jury report: 'Mecanoo's architecture proves that it is indeed possible to reach a high quality in affordable housing despite a limited budget.'

← Werkgroep 5x5 (1986–1989)
Five disciplines – politicians, housing corporations, architects, activists and publicists – address the focus on quantity in affordable housing and urban renewal of that time. Werkgroep 5x5 writes a manifesto about the need for quality. Members are: Adri Duivesteijn, Ypke Gietema, John Wevers, Jan Tromp and Francine Houben.

1989

Ruimte voor Ruimte masterplan, (Space for Space) Groningen (1989-1991)
Mecanoo create a cohesive design for the public space of Groningen city centre. It becomes an example for many cities in the Netherlands.

Collage on paper

1989: Roelf Steenhuis starts Steenhuis Bukman Architecten.

MECANOO'S ADDITION TO WAGENINGEN UNIVERSITY IS THE FIRST OF MANY EDUCATIONAL PROJECTS THAT ARE FLEXIBLE, SUSTAINABLE AND CAREFULLY INTEGRATED IN THEIR CONTEXT

Botanical Lab and Library, Wageningen University

Isala College, Silvolde

Faculty of Economics and Management, Utrecht: zen patio

The Mecanoo team in the garden of Oude Delft 203 headquarters

Hillekop, Rotterdam

DURING THE 1990S MECANOO BUILD A STRONG PORTFOLIO OF RESIDENTIAL SCHEMES, ALWAYS INCORPORATING GENEROUS PUBLIC SPACE

House with Studio, Rotterdam

Herdenkingsplein, Maastricht

Internationale Gartenbau Ausstellung, Stuttgart, Germany

← Ringvaartplasbuurt Oost, Prinsenland, Rotterdam
An important client is Peter van der Gugten of housing corporation Volkswoningen Rotterdam: Kruisplein, Tiendplein, Ringvaartplasbuurt Oost. And later as a developer working for Proper-Stok: Nieuw Terbregge, Vondelparc, Zilverreiger, Zwaluwpark and Villa Industria.

1993

Mecanoo win the competition for the Delft University of Technology Library. This iconic building becomes one of their most publicized projects.

Library Delft University of Technology: collage on paper of the winning design

1995

A Mecanoo monograph is published in the book series 'Monographs of Dutch Architects'. This series, published by Uitgeverij 010 Publishers in collaboration with the Netherlands Architecture Institute, documents the work of Mecanoo during their first decade, including projects such as Kruisplein, the Hillekop tower, Park Hotel, and the Ringvaartplasbuurt Oost and Herdenkingsplein neighbourhoods.

1995: Erick van Egeraat starts Erick van Egeraat Architecten.

Library Delft University of Technology

'Mecanoo Blue', originally a stage paint, is used for the Library Delft University of Technology and becomes a common thread connecting Mecanoo projects worldwide. Mecanoo first used theatre paint, specifically red and gold, at the Trust Theater.

CREATING UNFORGETTABLE, ICONIC INTERIORS BECOMES A TRADEMARK OF MECANOO IN THE 1990S AND INTO THE NEW MILLENNIUM

St. Mary of the Angels Chapel, Rotterdam

Trust Theater, Amsterdam

1997-2000: Francine is a member of the VROM council, advising the Dutch government on planning and mobility.

1999

The Minister of Transport invites Francine to lecture about 'The Art of Integral Engineering and the Aesthetics of Mobility'. It is an absolute eye-opener for political administrators, engineers, urbanists, and architects, and marks the start of several studies on mobility in the Netherlands, and later on, worldwide.

MOBILITY IS NOT ONLY ABOUT ASPHALT AND RAILWAY TRACKS. WHAT IF WE CONSIDER MOBILITY AS 'A ROOM WITH A VIEW'?

One of the mobility studies is **Holland Avenue**, which explores the roads of the future from the perspective of road users. Four cameras installed in a car capture everything along the Randstad circuit. The images are converted into maps and diagrams.

1999: Chris de Weijer starts DP6.

4a International Architecture Biennale São Paulo (20 November 1999 - 25 January 2000)
Max Risselada curates the Dutch submission 'Past Modernism, Three Moments of Post-War Dutch Architecture' with Aldo and Hannie van Eyck, Herman Hertzberger and Mecanoo. Humanism is a very strong link among the three.

← In Brazil Francine is impressed by the work of architect Lina Bo Bardi, known for her emphasis on social modernism and expressive use of materials, such as SESC Pompeía in São Paulo.

2000

Netherlands Open Air Museum, Arnhem
The museum is designed in close collaboration with museum director Jan Vaessen and is opened by Queen Beatrix of the Netherlands. Francine's three children present the Queen with a bouquet of flowers.

Together with landscape architect Kathryn Gustafson, Mecanoo win the competition to masterplan the Cultural Park Westergasfabriek, Amsterdam

Office Villa Maliebaan 16, Utrecht
Winner Best Undergrond Building Award 2001.

INTEGRATING LANDSCAPE AND GENEROUS PUBLIC SPACE BECOMES A MORE PROMINENT THEME

Nieuw Terbregge, Rotterdam
Mecanoo introduce a new typology for housing, 'the double-decker', stacking two layers of public space.

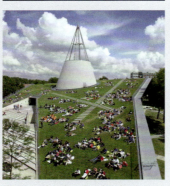

Library Delft University of Technology
A building that is also a landscape.

2000-2008: Francine is appointed Professor Architecture and the Aesthetics of Mobility at the Delft University of Technology.

2001

In 2001 Francine publishes her manifesto on architecture: *Composition, Contrast, Complexity*. It illustrates Mecanoo's approach to architecture, urbanism, landscape and interior architecture, and includes her 'Ten Statements'. The book, designed by Rick Vermeulen, wins the 2001 Best Dutch Book Design Award.

2001/2002: Francine is made honorary fellow of the RIBA and AIA.

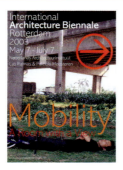

Between 2001 and 2003, Francine is director and curator of the first International Architecture Biennale in Rotterdam with 'Mobility - A Room with a View' as a theme. The book *Mobility* presents the research of universities all over the world.

Francine is appointed City Architect of Almere (2002-2006)
With Mecanoo, Francine develops visions for high-rise buildings, mobility and the coastline of Almere.

Coastline study

On 9 March 2007, the new pavilion of architecture centre CASLa in Almere opens its doors. The first exhibition is 'Dutch Mountains', dedicated to Francine as Almere's City Architect and the work of Mecanoo.

2003

A few years after winning the Cultural Park Westergasfabriek project, Mecanoo design another park in Amsterdam. Nelson Mandela Park is part of the revitalization strategy for the Bijlmer area and integrates nature, sports facilities and housing.

2003: Henk Döll starts Döllab.

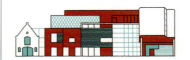

Toneelschuur Theatre, Haarlem (1998-2003)
Mecanoo works closely with theatre director Frans Lommerse and graphic designer/cartoonist Joost Swarte to develop Joost's ideas into a theatre complex with two theatre halls, cinemas and a café in the historic inner city of Haarlem.

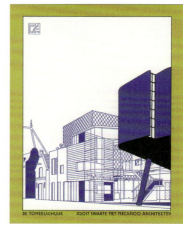

2005

In 2005 Francine receives the Culture Award of the Province of South Holland and together with film maker Ireen van Ditshuyzen, makes the documentary *Focussed Insight* (2006). The film shows what it's like to be an architect working in the Netherlands and Albania. At that time, Francine works on a masterplan for Tirana by invitation from Mayor Edi Rama.

Montevideo, Rotterdam (1999-2005)
Montevideo is the first high-rise tower designed by Mecanoo, together with structural engineer Walter Spangenberg of ABT, a long-standing collaborator on many of Mecanoo's projects.
At its opening in 2005, Montevideo is the tallest residential tower in the Netherlands.

In Spring 2005, Mecanoo win the international competition for the theatre and conference centre La Llotja de Lleida in Lleida, Spain

SINCE 2005, MECANOO GO INTERNATIONAL AND START WINNING INTERNATIONAL COMPETITIONS

Winning competition design for Palace of Justice, Córdoba, Spain (2006)

National Kaohsiung Center for the Arts in Taiwan
An exciting milestone is winning the competition for a 141,000 m² theatre complex in Taiwan in 2007.

Library of Birmingham integrated with the REP Theatre, United Kingdom
Another milestone is winning the European tender for the Library of Birmingham in 2008. It opens up the UK market for Mecanoo.

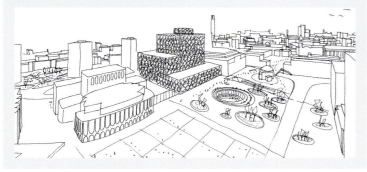

2006

Mecanoo wins the competition for the City Hall and Railway Station in their hometown Delft. The interior draws inspiration from Delft Blue ceramics and the city's rich history.

2006-2007: Francine is appointed Professor at Harvard University, Cambridge MA, US.

What's in a name

[Dutch newspaper column by Francine Houben]

Between 2006 and 2013 Francine is a columnist for *Het Financieele Dagblad* in which she shares her opinion on many topics concerning her profession.

2007

The official closing of Mekelweg road on 1 February by Francine, Alderman Anne Koning and Chairman of the Board of Delft University of Technology, Dirk Jan van den Berg, is a huge step forward in creating a car-free, green campus where students and staff can meet.

Mekel Park, Delft University of Technology

2007: Francine becomes honorary fellow RAIC (Royal Architectural Institute of Canada).

3 June 2007: fire at the Mecanoo Headquarters in Delft
The fire caused considerable damage, but was quickly under control thanks to the fire brigade's alert response. After the fire, the monumental building was restored to its former glory and modernized.

2007: Aart Fransen and Francesco Veenstra both become Partner.

Philips Business Innovation Centre FiftyTwoDegrees, Nijmegen (2004-2007)
The 86-metre high office and lab building for chip producer Philips Semiconductors (later NXP) is realized.

2008

Mecanoo is featured in the Images 'Master Architect Series', 2008, with the St. Mary of the Angels Chapel on the cover.

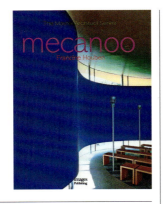

2008: Francine receives Prix Veuve Clicquot Business Woman of the Year.

2008: Ellen van der Wal becomes Partner.

Whistling Rock Golf Clubhouse, Chuncheon, Korea
A linear 'room with a view' contrasting with the undulating landscape.

Kaap Skil, Maritime and Beachcombers Museum, Texel
The museum, with a facade made of glass and reclaimed wooden slats, has a roofscape that fits into the historical maritime village.

THE CONTEXT OF EACH PROJECT FORMS AN IMPORTANT INSPIRATION

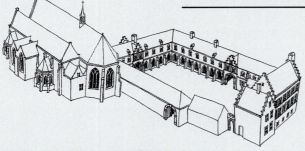

Het Hof van Nederland Museum, Dordrecht
A collection of thirteenth-century monuments are restored and internally connected around its historic public square. Here, in 1572, the foundation was laid for the independent Dutch Republic, precursor to the current Kingdom of the Netherlands.

Winning competition design National Historic Museum, Arnhem
Mecanoo's most published unbuilt project is the National Historic Museum, which exhibits the 'Canon of Dutch History'. Many years later, after much political debate, the Canon exhibition is integrated into Mecanoo's Netherlands Open Air Museum.

Sustainability is in the DNA of Mecanoo. On several projects, Mecanoo collaborate with Wubbo Ockels (1946-2014), former astronaut and Professor of Sustainable Engineering and Technology at Delft University of Technology (on the bike). One of the projects is the Stadstimmerhuis 010 competition.

2009

In the competition design for Stadstimmerhuis 010, a mixed use project for municipal offices, exhibition spaces and residences, the electrostatic wind converter EWI-CON is integrated into the rooftop signage celebrating Rotterdam's nickname '010'.

← EWI-CON (2010-2013)
Collaboration with Delft University of Technology and Wageningen University on EWI-CON (Electrostatic Windenergy Convertor). A prototype was showcased on the Delft University of Technology Campus.

2010

Francine explains the design of La Llotja de Lleida to King Juan Carlos and Queen Sofia of Spain at its grand opening on 23 March 2010.

2010: Francine becomes a member of Akademie der Künste, Berlin, Germany.

2011

Dutch Mountains showcases eight projects from five countries. The concept of the book was created by Judith Baas, who didn't want to showcase traditional, glamorous architecture photography. Photographer Harry Cock travels with Francine through the Netherlands, UK, Spain, South Korea, and Taiwan, documenting the progress of several projects on site. Jan Tromp narrates this journey.

2011: Paul Ketelaars becomes Partner.

Rabobank Advice Centre, Sittard is 'a bank that doesn't want to look like a bank', an inspiring working environment for both employees and customers

OVER THE YEARS, LEARNING AND WORKING CONCEPTS HAVE CHANGED

The inspiration for Amsterdam University College was to create an attic atmosphere for its Liberal Arts and Sciences students

Fontys School of Sport Studies, Eindhoven: a transparent, sports-inspired learning environment

2013

National Kaohsiung Center for the Arts, Taiwan
Dutch and local shipbuilders collaborate to meet the challenge of constructing the giant building's Banyan Plaza's double-curved skin.

2013: Dick van Gameren (Professor of Architecture and Dwelling at Delft University of Technology since 2006) becomes Partner.

2013-2019: Peter Haasbroek Financial Director.

Mecanoo partners and directors – with a staff of around 100 people – in 2013: (from left to right) Aart Fransen, Paul Ketelaars, Peter Haasbroek, Ellen van der Wal, Francesco Veenstra, Francine Houben and Dick van Gameren.

The Library of Birmingham is opened by Nobel Prize laureate Malala Yousafzai on 3 September 2013
After winning the RIBA National Award, the Library of Birmingham is shortlisted for the RIBA Stirling Prize for Architecture, and wins the vote for 'Most Popular Building' in the UK.

Winning design for the renovation of the Martin Luther King Jr. Memorial Library, Washington DC, US (originally designed by Mies van der Rohe), 2014

THE LIBRARY IS THE CATHEDRAL OF OUR TIME, A PLACE TO MEET, TO LEARN, TO STAY CONNECTED; IT IS ITS PEOPLE, ITS PLACE, AND ITS PURPOSE

Tainan Public Library, Taiwan, winning design 2016

Winning vision for The New York Public Library Midtown Campus Renovation, US, 2015

2014

Exhibition 'A People's Palace' at the Aedes Gallery of Kristin Feireiss and Hans-Jürgen Commerell in Berlin, Germany.

2014: Francine awarded 'Architect's Journal's Woman Architect of the Year'.

2014: Francine becomes a member of the Akademie van Kunsten, KNAW, the Netherlands.

Over the years, Mecanoo has welcomed many architects who have been a source of inspiration to the Delft office.

Max Risselada together with Kengo Kuma from Japan, June 2014

Charles Correa (1930-2015) from India, June 2014

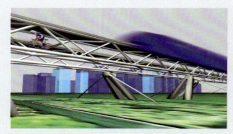

Future of mobility: Magnetic Suspension Track study

Future of Learning study

Mecanoo's inhouse research team MEC-LAB researches topics such as the future of mobility, the future of learning, the history of monumental buildings and sustainability, often in collaboration with third parties.

→ World Trade Centre, Rotterdam
Mecanoo is house architect for the ongoing renovation from 2002-2014 of this modernist monument designed by Dutch architect J.F. Staal.

← European Investment Bank, Luxembourg
Winning scheme by Mecanoo together with Buro Happold for the competition of the European Investment Bank.

Filming becomes an integral part of Mecanoo's way of working. Explore this by visiting Mecanoo's YouTube channel.

Mecanoo's interior design team redesigns the interior of several hotels for the Hotel Royal Group in Taiwan: Hotel Royal Hot Spring & Health Centre Beitou (2011-2014), The Place Tainan (2011-2014), The Place Taipei (2014-2019), The Place Yilan (2016-2017).

↑ Hotel The Place Taipei, Nangang, Taiwan (2014-2019)

↑↓ Hotel The Place Tainan, Taiwan (2011-2014)

← Zaans Medical Centre, Zaandam
The first Dutch hospital based on Lean Design principals.

MECANOO CREATES HEALING ENVIRONMENTS ON A HUMAN SCALE

↑ Leo Kanner College, Leiden
A secondary school for pupils with autism.

← Zinzia Psychiatric Care Centre Oranje Nassau's Oord, Wageningen
For elderly residents with dementia.

2015

Celebrating three decades of Mecanoo with the book *People Place Purpose*. The first copy is presented to Queen Máxima of the Netherlands.

the world according to mecanoo

Francine receives Prins Bernhard Cultuurfonds Prize
Francine is awarded this prestigious prize for her lifetime achievements as a leading international architect. The prize is presented by Queen Máxima of the Netherlands.

Bruce C. Bolling Municipal Building, Boston, MA, US (2011-2015)
Mecanoo's first US project. The building wins prestigious awards such as the Harleston Parker Medal.

← Mayor Tomas M. Menino and the neighbourhood of Roxbury are very much involved

Life Sciences Incubator Utrecht University, Utrecht (2013-2015)
A business centre for start-ups and more established companies in the bioscience field with both laboratories and offices.

 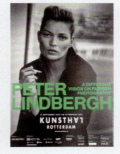

Dick van Gameren designs (traveling) exhibitions for the Kunsthal, Rotterdam: 'Caldic Collection of Joop Caldenborgh' (2011), 'Keith Haring, The Political Line' (2015-2016), 'Peter Lindbergh' (2016-2017), 'Action <–> Reaction' (2018) and 'Calder Now' (2021).

Delft City Hall and Railway Station
28 February 2015, the first train runs through the new Delft Station.

↓→ **Hilton Amsterdam Airport Schiphol (2009-2015)**
Schiphol Airport now has an iconic addition with curves and diagonal patterns.

The restaurant and hotel rooms feature artwork by artist Israel Páez, who was, at that time, an architect at Mecanoo.

↑ **Bloomberg Offices, Amsterdam (2015-2016)**
For the interior design of Bloomberg's two-level office, Mecanoo collaborates with paper-cut artist Hesje Andersson.

Mecanoo and Gispen collaborate on the award-winning HUBB furniture series (2014-2016). HUBB offers endless combinations for learning environments and was awarded the ARC17 Award and the Red Dot Award in 2017. HUBB is highly sustainable, future-proof, and adheres to Circular Economy principles.

← HUBB at Fontys University of Applied Sciences, Tilburg

2016

HOME Arts Centre, Manchester, UK
Manchester's place-to-be for theatre, film and visual art is named winner of the National Award 2016 by the Royal Institute of British Architects.

2016: Francine receives a Honorary Doctorate from Utrecht University.

A legacy of Mies and King
In this documentary by Nienke Andersson, Francine explores archives, meets contemporaries of Mies van der Rohe and Dr. King, and interviews library visitors in the design process for the Martin Luther King Jr. Memorial Library. Available on the Mecanoo YouTube channel.

Het geheim van Montevideo (**The secret of Montevideo**)
Mecanoo's Montevideo tower is the topic of a thrilling children's book. The book is written by Hanneke Hollander and illustrated by Jelle Post.

  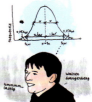

The Mecanoo team of 130 during the annual Mecanoo weekend in Herpt, 2016

Interior redesign Library Delft University of Technology
Together with the librarians, Mecanoo continue to adapt the interior of this iconic library to new ways of learning (2008-2011/2015-2016).

2017

Francine leads an Advanced Design Studio at Yale School of Architecture. The students research branch libraries in New York and Amsterdam, focusing on their evolving role for local communities.

OBA Mercatorplein Branch Library, Amsterdam (2019-2020)

2017: Francine receives a Honorary Doctorate of Université de Mons.

2017: Francesco Veenstra, Ellen van der Wal and Paul Ketelaars start Vakwerk Architecten.

BREATHING NEW LIFE INTO LISTED BUILDINGS

↑ **Delfland Water Authority, Delft**
Unifying and upgrading a collection of listed buildings from the sixteenth, seventeenth and twentieth century.

Perth Museum, UK
The former city hall transforms into a museum housing treasures from Scotland and beyond.

↓ **St. Gerlach Pavilion & Manor Farm, Valkenburg Aan De Geul**
Renovation of a listed Manor Farm and adding a new conference and event facility to a rural seventeenth-century chateau for client Camille Oostwegel.

Shenzhen North Station Urban Design
Winning scheme of twelve staggering skyscrapers, an elevated pedestrian network, transportation nodes on subterranean levels and a beautiful green urban park.

As part of Mecanoo's popular 'Render vs Reality' series posted on social media, the team regularly showcases how closely renderings can reflect the built reality of their work. Renderings are essential tools that are both promises to clients and the general public, as well as representations of a shared vision.

Heungkuk Tower Namdaemun, Seoul, South Korea (render 2014, photo 2017)

Eurojust, The Hague (2011-2017)
The new headquarters for Eurojust, located in the International Zone of The Hague and with stringent security measures carefully integrated into the building and landscape design, is realized.

Mecanoo: Inspiration and Process in Architecture
Mecanoo is featured in a series of monographs on key figures in modern and contemporary architecture. Mecanoo's Brand Manager Eliano Felício, who edited the book, wanted to show the value of freehand drawing as part of the creative process.

2017: Aart Fransen leaves Mecanoo.

2018

On 12 July the four-part documentary by Ivo Niehe *Francine Houben, een Hollandse architect met wereldsucces* (a Dutch architect with world success) premieres. The series gives behind-the-scenes insight into Mecanoo's projects, including the design process of the New York Public Library and the construction of the National Kaohsiung Center for the Arts, Taiwan.

Opening ceremony on 13 October 2018 at the National Kaohsiung Center for the Arts in Taiwan

After 12 years of working together on the design, the core team celebrates the opening: (from left to right) Nuno Fontarra, Francine Houben, Friso van der Steen, Albert Xu and Louis Janssen.

← Kaohsiung Station, Taiwan
14 October 2018: the first train runs through the new tunnel and the first phase of the canopy is completed.

→ Villa Industria, Hilversum (2004-2018)
Under the leadership of Rick Splinter, Mecanoo masterplans and designs a new neighbourhood on the site of a former gasworks.

→ Model maker Henk Bouwer joined Mecanoo in 1984. Henk brought his craft and artistry and shaped what would become one of the most inspiring spaces in the Mecanoo office – the Model Room. In his wood workshop, Henk made most of Mecanoo's wooden models that excel in exquisite detailing.

MODELS HELP TO EXPERIENCE A DESIGN'S PROPORTIONS AND SCALE IN AN INTUITIVE WAY

The workshop has been extended for a new generation of modelmakers led by Mattia Cavaglieri, working with new technologies and materials.

Francine is awarded the BNA Kubus
This oeuvre award is presented on 1 November 2018 to Francine Houben. In his speech, architect Hubert-Jan Henket suggests adding Poetry to Mecanoo's philosophy of People, Place, Purpose.

→ Kaap Skil, Maritime and Beachcombers Museum, Oudeschild, Texel
The museum's facade is composed of sawn hardwood sheet piling reclaimed from the Noord-Hollands Canal.

↑ LocHal Library, Tilburg
In LocHal, a former locomotive shed, old train chassis get a second life as movable tables.

THE URGENCY TO MAKE THE TRANSITION TO A CIRCULAR ECONOMY IS GREATER THAN EVER

→ De Nederlandsche Bank, Amsterdam
The bank sets an example for circularity as well as sustainability. Its cylindrical tower is structurally dismantled to be reused as care pavilions.

Dutch Design Week showcases 'NS Vision Interior Train of the Future', a modular train interior in collaboration with Dutch interior design brand Gispen. 'NS Journey of the Future' focuses on the passenger's door-to-door journey.

→ Sarah Schiffer of Gispen, Joost van der Made of NS, Arne Lijbers and Francine Houben

2019

A New Perspective for Rotterdam South (study, 2016-2021)
Francine initiates a comprehensive exploration of Rotterdam South and concludes that South needs an integrated urban vision for future development. This vision is presented at the City Makers Congress in Rotterdam.

↑ Cartesius, Utrecht
This sustainable and green neighbourhood is inspired by the Blue Zones in the world where people live longer and healthier.

← Key Worker Housing University of Cambridge, UK
The housing complies with the Code for Sustainability Homes level 5, the highest sustainability code for housing in the UK.

COMMITMENT TO CREATING A GREENER, MORE SUSTAINABLE FUTURE

←↓ Co-Creation Centre & Nonohouse, The Green Village, Delft
Sustainable living lab at Delft University of Technology where researchers, students, and companies collaborate on sustainable innovations.

↑ The Co-Creation Centre is a testbed for innovative solutions across disciplines.

→ Nonohouse is designed to absorb more nitrogen than it produces.

Lawson Centre for Sustainability, Toronto, Canada
A LEED Platinum and CaGBC Zero Carbon building with a rooftop urban farm and community kitchen.

Longgang Cultural Centre, Shenzhen, China (2012-2019)
The Longgang Cultural Centre opens: an art museum, a youth centre, a science centre and a book mall.

Machteld Schoep, photographer (1962-2019)
Machteld joined Mecanoo in 2003 as desktop publisher and developed into Mecanoo's in-house photographer. She photographed the Mecanoo team depicting their hobby or passion.

MACHTELD WAS DRIVEN, ENTHUSIASTIC AND CREATIVE. HER PHOTOS DO NOT ONLY SHOW A BUILDING, THEY TELL A STORY

← Four times Machteld in the life-size model of NS Vision Interior for the Future

2019: Dick van Gameren is appointed Dean of the Delft University of Technology Faculty of Architecture and the Built Environment.

2019: Francine receives the International Prize, Prix des Femmes Architectes in Paris.

Nieuw Land National Park, Flevoland (2018-2019)
With its 29,000 hectares, the largest man-made national park in the world.

← Francine hiking with family and friends in Yosemite National Park, US
'the Netherlands should have more and larger national parks because they add spatial quality to our densely populated country.' Francine Houben, newspaper Het Financieele Dagblad, 2007.

← Villa Vught
The Villa in the Dutch countryside near Vught gives a contemporary twist to the local farmstead typology.

REINTERPRETING THE VILLA TYPOLOGY

↑ Glass Villa on the Lake, Lechlade, UK
The house is designed from inside out, creating uninterrupted views to the surrounding nature while providing shelter and intimacy.

← Villa BW, Schoorl
The building volume is characterized by a double-curved roof coupled with a custom ceramic tile wrapping the entire building.

2020

The winning competition entry for the renovation and modernization of Museum Boijmans Van Beuningen in Rotterdam.

Under the leadership of Arne Lijbers, offices and office lobbies are being revitalized into lively places to work and meet.

Unilever Benelux Headquarters, Rotterdam (2019-2020)

World Port Centre, Rotterdam (2020-2021)

Blaak555, Rotterdam (2018-2020)

Following Dutch Government's advice on preventing the spread of Covid-19, coronavirus, Mecanoo worked in a hybrid way (safely) from the office and from home to serve our clients, partners and suppliers. In 2020, the annual Christmas party took place virtually.

Natural History Museum Abu Dhabi, United Arab Emirates
Winning competition entry for the Natural History Museum Abu Dhabi. The design under the leadership of Nuno Fontarra is inspired by natural rock formations and features hanging gardens.

Zaankwartier, Wormerveer
Transforming the Meneba flour factory complex into a mixed-use residential area.

EXPLORING A VISIONARY APPROACH TO URBAN LANDSCAPES

↑ The Hague Central Station Urban Plan
Arriving in a vibrant, raised city park.

← Amstel Design District, Amsterdam
A flexible framework for a living and working community.

2020: Francine Delft University of Technology Alumnus of the Year.

2021

The year of the Mecanoo Libraries
A unique year in which three major libraries opened. Due to Covid, Mecanoo was unable to attend the festivities.

↑ Tainan Public Library, Taiwan
Opening on 2 January 2021.

↑ Martin Luther King Jr. Memorial Library, Washington, US
Limited opening on 24 September 2020.
Grand opening on 25 September 2021.

→ Stavros Niarchos Foundation Library, New York, US
Opening on 1 June 2021.

2021: Francine is awarded the Female Frontier Award - Architect of the Year.

Macau Central Library, China
Mecanoo's competition-winning design for the new Macau Central Library blends seamlessly with the historic UNESCO World Heritage Site. The facade cleverly manages light and indoor climate, while the building revitalizes the square and inspires visitors to engage with this new public space.

Taichung Green Corridor, Taichung, Taiwan (2017-2021)
A 1.7 km existing dyke and former railway track is transformed into a linear park with herb gardens, street fitness, sitting steps, playground, viewpoint and waterpark.

Nuno Fontarra, Rick Splinter and Arne Lijbers all become Partners
Nuno started at Mecanoo in 2002 and has propelled the designs of many innovative and sculptural projects. Rick, who joined Mecanoo in 2003, excels in designing sustainable housing with carefully integrated public spaces creating distinct identities. Arne joined Mecanoo in 2012 and excels in highly innovative living, working and educational environments.

Jacob's Pillow, Beckett, MA, US
Jacob's Pillow, a global leader and innovator in dance for nearly 100 years, located in the woodlands of the Berkshires, selects Mecanoo to reimagine the new Doris Duke Theatre, which was lost to a fire in November 2020. The entirely wooden new Doris Duke Theatre, inspired by indigenous values, will open its doors during the annual dance festival in 2025.

Dick and Francine receive Mecanoo's 2021 European Prize for Architecture in Athens, Greece

KAMPUS, Manchester, UK (2016-2021)
Under the leadership of Rick Splinter, Kampus is finalized. For this cherished urban area, Mecanoo designed the masterplan and two buildings, as well as the public realm and gardens.

ICOON Residential Tower, Frankfurt, Germany
A business area transforms into a neighbourhood for living and working.

Kaohsiung Social Housing, Taiwan
The first social housing project of Kaohsiung.

PIONEERING HIGHRISE BUILDINGS

Hart 010, Rotterdam
A mixed-use programme on a public transport node.

Brink Tower, Amsterdam
An energy-positive residential tower.

Mecanoo weekend, Herpt, an annual tradition
The Mecanoo team celebrates a yearly weekend together in an old barn. The event in 2021 was a special one. Following the pandemic, the joy of coming together in the New Barn (De Nieuwe Schuur), designed by Mecanoo, felt extra festive.

2022

Manchester Engineering Campus Development (2014-2024)
The new 81,000 m² home of four engineering schools and two research institutes with a wide range of laboratories including high-voltage labs, opens its doors in 2022.

2023

Dick van Gameren publishes *Dutch Dwellings*. Throughout his entire career, he has been deeply involved in housing design, complemented by his dedicated research and teaching tenure at Delft University of Technology.

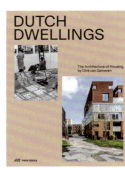

ENVISIONING THE FUTURE IN AMBITIOUS MASTERPLANS

→ **Regional Vision Drechtsteden**
Strategy for seven municipalities, 25,000 new homes and 30,000 new jobs while strengthening identity and cohesion.

Railway Zone Dordrecht
A barrier in the city becomes a place to stay, of connectivity, and for new developments.

2023: Financial Director Floris Overheul becomes Partner.

← **Natural History Museum Abu Dhabi**
Team visit to the site in Abu Dhabi. The museum will be completed end of 2025: (left to right) Fedele Canosa, Francine Houben, Carmen Pereira, Pieter Hoen, Nuno Fontarra, and Paulo Borralho.

→ **Ede-Wageningen Railway Station**
January 2023, construction starts of the Ede-Wageningen Railway Station. The wood-and-glass roof covers the platforms and provides shelter while letting diffused daylight enter freely.

← **De Nederlandsche Bank, Amsterdam**
The renovation of the 1968 building is well underway. The re-opening is expected end of 2024.

Heerlen City Hall and Municipal Offices (2017-2023)
25 August 2023, Heerlen City Hall and Municipal Offices is officially opened. The design makes clever use of the level differences in the South Limburg landscape and is connected to the well-known and landmarked 1942 City Hall designed by architect Frits Peutz.

International Quarter London, UK
Masterplan for six towers on one of the last remaining sites of the London Olympic Legacy area for Hadley Property Group. The site wil be a connector for communities within the Stratford neighbourhood and beyond.

Shenzhen Guangming Scientist Valley, Liantang, China
Mecanoo and Meng Architects, with LOLA Landscape Architects win the international competition for an international science and technology innovation centre.

TextielMuseum, Tilburg
Mecanoo together with engineering firm ABT are chosen to envision the redevelopment of the TextielMuseum and its surroundings. The museum will be renovated, made more sustainable, offering improved functionality and will include new textile-related functions.

Quantum Science Building, Princeton University, US
Francine Houben, Coco van Egeraat and Polina Strukova are exploring Princeton University the Dutch way – by bike – to design the new Quantum Science Building for which Mecanoo, in partnership with HGA, have been selected.

Mecanoo Partners 2023: Floris Overheul, Rick Splinter, Nuno Fontarra, Francine Houben, Arne Lijbers, Armand Paardekooper Overman and Dick van Gameren.

PROJECT DATA

2 Fitting In

Museum Kaap Skil
Texel, the Netherlands
Programme: Museum building of 1,200 m², exhibition galleries, café and offices.
Design: 2007-2009
Realization: 2010-2011
Client: Maritiem & Juttersmuseum
Design team: Mecanoo
Exhibition design: Kossmanndejong
Structural engineer: Pieters Bouwtechniek
M&E engineer: Peter Prins
Project management: ABC Management Groep
Main contractor: De Geus Bouw & Duin Bouwbedrijf

Whistling Rock Golf Clubhouse
Chuncheon, Republic of Korea
Programme: 11,400 m² golf clubhouse on a 27-hole golf course including a start house, three tea houses, restaurants, pro shop, wine cellar, banquet rooms, bathing areas, multiple lobbies, and a parking garage.
Design: 2007-2009
Realization: 2010-2012
Client: Dong Lim Development Co.
Design team: Mecanoo (lead architect), Gansam Architects & Partners (local architect) and Pinnacle Landscape Company (landscape architect).
Main contractor: Dong Lim Engineering & Construction Co.

Taekwang Country Club Café
Gyeonggi-do, Republic of Korea
Programme: 300 m² pavilion on a 36-hole golf course including café, kitchen, and service areas.
Design: 2014
Realization: 2015
Client: Taekwang Leisure Development
Design team: Mecanoo

Eurojust
The Hague, the Netherlands
Programme: 18,500 m² high security office building for the agency of the European Union dealing with judicial co-operation in criminal matters among agencies of the EU member states, including office and conference facilities, restaurant, underground parking for 272 cars, and integrated landscape design, BREEAM-NL Very Good.
Design: 2011-2014
Realization: 2014-2017
Client: Rijksgebouwendienst (Central Government Real Estate Agency) and Ministry of Security and Justice.
Design team: Mecanoo and DS landschapsarchitecten (landscape design).
Engineering: Royal HaskoningDHV
Fire safety consultant: SVBB
Main contractor: Heijmans

Palace of Justice
Córdoba, Spain
Programme: 48,000 m² courthouse including 26 courtrooms, wedding room, Forensic Institute, offices, café, archive, jail cells and parking garage.
Design: 2006
Realization: 2014-2017
Client: Junta de Andalucía
Design Team: Mecanoo (lead architect) and Ayesa (engineering and local architect).
Main contractor: Ute Isolux Corsán-Copcisa

De Nederlandsche Bank
Amsterdam, the Netherlands
Programme: 67,000 m² renovation and transformation of the 1968 building of the central bank of the Netherlands in the historic city centre of Amsterdam, including new entrance area, information, exhibition and education spaces, lobby, auditorium, reception areas, staff restaurant, staff fitness room, work space environment, new atrium of 400 m² with stairs, three zones of security from public to high security zones, and landscape design park, patios and roof gardens, BREEAM Outstanding and WELL Platinum.
Design: 2018-2020
Realization: 2020-2025
Client: De Nederlandsche Bank
Design team: Mecanoo
Construction: Pieters Bouwtechniek
M&E engineer: Valstar Simonis
Building physics and fire safety consultant: DGMR
Lighting design: Frans van Hooijdonk
Project management: Stevens Van Dijck Bouwmanagers en Adviseurs
Cost consultant: IGG Bouweconomie
Main contractor: SPIE

Museum Boijmans Van Beuningen
Rotterdam, the Netherlands
Programme: Winning competition design for the restoration and transformation of an approx. 25,000 m² partly listed museum building and associated outdoor space, including a new entrance area with museum shop, exhibition spaces, flow of people and goods, educational spaces, café, event space, logistics centre, depots, offices, workshops, facility spaces, and landscape design.
Design: 2019-2024
Realization: 2024-2029, expected
Client: Municipality of Rotterdam
Design team: Mecanoo (lead architect) and BBM architecten (restoration architect).
Structural engineer: Pieters Bouwtechniek
M&E engineer, fire safety and sustainability consultant: Arup
Building physics consultant: Deerns and ZRi
Lighting consultant: Deerns
Cost consultant: Bremen Bouwadviseurs

Natural History Museum Abu Dhabi
Abu Dhabi, United Arab Emirates
Programme: 35,000 m² iconic museum on a 82,000 m² site, including plaza, gardens and waterfront, galleries, display areas, café, education centre, laboratories, logistics and operations, public spaces, research and administrative facilities, V.I.P. areas, multipurpose and event space and parking (206 spaces).
Design: 2020-2022
Realization: 2022-2025
Client: Department of Culture and Tourism, Abu Dhabi (DCT Abu Dhabi) in partnership with Miral.
Concept design team: Mecanoo (architecture, interior and landscape design), Aurecon (architect of record), Ralph Appelbaum (exhibition design), Arcadis (engineering), Theateradvies (theatre consultant), Trinity Design (landscape consultant), Plan A (design management).

3 Home Sweet Home

Kampus
Manchester, United Kingdom
Programme: Urban plan for a garden neighbourhood in the city centre, next to Manchester Piccadilly Station, for 533 apartments and leisure/retail spaces across five buildings of which two grade II listed warehouses, transformation of an existing office tower (1964) and two new buildings, totalling 44,000 m², and landscape design for gardens and public realm; architectural design for the two new apartment buildings including 352 apartments and the building transformation with 123 apartments, BREEAM Very Good.
Design: 2016
Realization: 2017-2022
Client/Property Developer: Capital & Centric and Henry Boot Developments.
Design team: Mecanoo (urban plan including landscape design, lead architect new buildings and transformation tower), Shed KM (architect listed canal warehouses), Exterior Architecture (delivery landscape architect), Chapman Taylor (delivery architect new buildings and transformation tower).
Structural and civil engineer: Buro Happold
Mechanical and electrical engineer: Hannan Associates
Fire safety consultant: Omega Fire
Main contractor: Mount Anvil Ltd

Villa Industria
Hilversum, the Netherlands
Programme: Urban plan and design of 357 dwellings, 400 m² small-scale businesses, and 4,000 m² swimming pool and sports facilities, totalling 74,000 m².
Design: 2004-2015
Realization: 2007-2018
Client: Heijmans; De Alliantie
Design team: Mecanoo (architect, landscape, urban planning)
Structural engineer: ABT; Goudstikker de Vries
M&E engineer: Viac Installatieadviseurs
Building physics and fire safety consultant: Nex2us
Artist: Berend Strik
Main contractor: Heijmans

Key Worker Housing, University of Cambridge
Cambridge, United Kingdom
Programme: 232 sustainable dwellings for researchers and key university employees, totalling 19,500 m², 3,100 m² parking and 5,100 m² public realm design, Code For Sustainable Homes Level 5.
Design: 2012-2014
Realization: 2014-2018
Client: North West Cambridge Development, University of Cambridge
Design team: Mecanoo (architect, landscape)
Engineering: URS
Project management: Aecom
Cost consultant: Gardiner & Theobald
Main contractor: BAM Construct UK

Lawson Center for Sustainability, Trinity College
Toronto, Canada
Programme: 14,450 m² student residence and academic building, a mass timber facility including full-service cafeteria, academic offices, meeting rooms, lecture hall, seminar rooms, community kitchen, event pavilion, 343 bed dormitory, student lounges, study spaces, and rooftop farm, LEED Platinum and CaGBC Zero Carbon.
Design: 2019-2022
Realization: 2022-2025
Client: Trinity College in the University of Toronto
Design team: Mecanoo (design architect and landscape architect), RDHA (architect of record), NAK (delivery landscape architect).
Structural engineer: Blackwell
M&E engineer: Smith + Andersen
Acoustic and fire safety consultant: Aercoustics
Cost consultant: Turner and Townsend
Contractor: Graham Construction

Glass Villa on the Lake
Lechlade, United Kingdom
Programme: Three-storey house of 600 m² with one level below water with screening room, games/bar area, wellness/spa area, 80 m² roof terrace and 176 m² ground floor terrace.
Design: 2015-2016
Realization: 2016-2018
Client: private
Design team: Mecanoo (concept design) and Arquitectura y Ordenación Urbana S.L. (executive architect.
Development: Boheme Development S.L.
Structural engineer: Fernando Sarria
M&E engineer: INARQ S.L.
Contractor: IZA Construction LTD

Villa Vught
Vught, the Netherlands
Programme: 683 m² mass timber, highly sustainable private villa complex with a separate professional cooking studio and a guest suite with extensive gardens.
Design: 2016-2018
Realization: 2018-2019
Client: private
Design team: Mecanoo (design architect) and Anne Laansma (landscape architect).
Structural engineer: Bartels Ingenieursbureau
Mechanical engineer: Heluto
Electrical engineer: Welvaarts
Building physics and acoustic consultant: Mobius
Contractor: Van den Bouwhuijsen

4 The Big Picture

A New Perspective for Rotterdam South
Rotterdam, the Netherlands
Programme: An integral vision for better connections between Rotterdam South, the port area and Central Rotterdam with, amongst other interventions, an education strip, a cultural campus, new forms of living, working and mobility interconnected by an adaptive 10-kilometre dyke park.
Design: 2016-2021, ongoing.
Initiative: Francine Houben, Manifesto Group Rotterdam South.
Clients: Municipality of Rotterdam; Bernard van Leer Foundation.
Design team: Mecanoo

Dordrecht Railway Zone
Dordrecht, the Netherlands
Programme: Urban masterplan for the railway zone in Dordrecht including five development areas: Maasterras, Spuiboulevard, Central Station area, Learning Park and Health Park with 6000 homes, commercial functions, community amenities, parks and stations.
Design: 2020-2021
Client: Municipality of Dordrecht
Design team: Mecanoo

Nieuw Land National Park
Flevoland, the Netherlands
Programme: Masterplan vision for a 29,000-ha national park bringing together four core nature reserves: the Oostvaardersplassen, the Lepelaarplassen, Marker Wadden and Trintelzand.
Design: 2018-2019
Clients: Province of Flevoland, Municipality of Almere, Municipality of Lelystad, Staatsbosbeheer and Natuurmonumenten, Stichting Flevo-landschap, Rijkswaterstaat, Waterschap Zuiderzeeland.
Design team: Mecanoo

5 Wisdom and Wizardry

Library Delft University of Technology
Delft, the Netherlands
Programme: University library of 15,000 m² with reading rooms and study spaces, trésor for historical books, archive, offices, university publisher, book binder and bookshop; ongoing interior upgrades learning environment, café, and new media centre.
Design: Library 1993-1995, learning and working environment upgrades 2008-ongoing.
Realization: Library 1996-1997, learning and working environment upgrades 2010-ongoing.
Client: ING Real Estate; Delft University of Technology.
Design team: Mecanoo (architecture, interior, landscape)
Structural engineer: ABT
Mechanical engineer: Ketel
Electrical engineer: Deerns
Main contractor: Van Oorschot Versloot Bouw; Boele van Eesteren.

LocHal Library
Tilburg, the Netherlands
Programme: 7,000 m² interior design for the Midden-Brabant public library and two cultural institutions, Kunstloc Brabant and Brabant C, in a former locomotive hall of the Dutch National Railways including 1,300 m² of offices.
Design: 2016-2018, ongoing.
Realization: 2018, ongoing.
Client: Bibliotheek Midden-Brabant and Kunstloc Brabant.
Design team: Mecanoo (interior design), CIVIC (architecture), Braaksma & Roos (restoration), Inside Outside and TextielMuseum (interior concept and textiles).
Engineering and lighting consultant: Arup
Interior construction: Coors
Main contractor: Binx Smartility

Library of Birmingham
Birmingham, United Kingdom
Programme: Central library of 31,000 m² with adult and children's library, study spaces, music library, multimedia, city archives, integration of the historical Shakespeare Memorial Room, offices, exhibition gallery,

resources for health and wellbeing, cafés and lounge space, three roof terraces, 300-seat auditorium (shared with the REP Theatre); 4,000 m² renovation and extension of the REP Theatre including new back of house, rehearsal spaces and stage building workshops; urban plan for Centenary Square, BREEAM Excellent.
Design: 2008-2009
Realization: 2010-2013
Client: Birmingham City Council
Design team: Mecanoo (architecture, interior, landscape, urban planning)
Engineering: Buro Happold
Theatre consultant: Theateradvies
Design manager: AECOM
Main contractor: Carillion Building

Tainan Public Library
Tainan, Taiwan
Programme: 37,000 m² central library with areas for the children's, teenagers' and general collections, exhibition spaces for the modern art and heritage collection, 24/7 study room (130 seats), multimedia library, café, theatre (324 seats), conference hall (123 seats), offices, multipurpose rooms, maker space, bookshop, archive, parking garage, four patios, roof gardens and a square.
Design: 2016-2017
Realization: 2018-2020
Client: Cultural Affairs Bureau, Tainan City Government
Design team: Mecanoo (lead architect) and MAYU Architects (architect of record).
Artist: Paul Cocksedge
Structural engineer: Envision Engineering
M&E engineer: Frontier Tech Institute of Engineering Design & Consultant
Wayfinding: Path & Landforms
Main contractor: Fu Tsu Construction; Shing Tai Hydro-Power Engineering.

Martin Luther King Jr. Memorial Library
Washington DC, United States of America
Programme: 39,600 m² central library renovation (1972, Mies van der Rohe) including children's library, teen's space, digital commons, main reading room, DC Welcome Center, Conference Center, Special Collections archives, exhibition and performance spaces, fabrication lab, creative lab, auditorium (291 seats), event spaces, café, and roof garden, LEED Silver certified.
Design: 2014-2016
Realization: 2017-2020
Client: District of Columbia Public Library, Washington DC
Design team: Mecanoo (lead architect) and OTJ Architects (executive architect).
Artist: Xenobia Bailey
Structural engineer: Silman
M&E engineer: Collaborative Engineering
Acoustic consultant: Jaffe Holden
Building physics consultant: Wiss
Fire safety consultant: Engenium
Main contractor: Smoot Gilbane

The New York Public Library,
Stephen A. Schwarzman Building
New York, United States of America
Programme: Central research library, part of the Midtown Campus masterplan, including app. 23,000 m² interior restoration and transformation, a new entrance on 40th Street, new stairs and elevators, Visitor Center, welcoming desks, Library Shop and Café, the 'Polonsky Treasures Exhibition' in Gottesman Hall, photo gallery, Center for Research in the Humanities, Center for Education, reading and study rooms, staff spaces, back of house logistic improvements, public and staff restrooms.
Design: 2015-2018, ongoing.
Realization: 2017-2023, ongoing.
Client: The New York Public Library
Design team: Mecanoo and Beyer Blinder Belle Architects & Planners.
Exhibition design: Pure+Applied
Structural engineer: Silman
M&E engineer: Kohler Ronan
Costs consultant: Stuart-Lynn Company
Fire safety consultant: Code Consultants International
Main contractor: Turner Construction Company

The New York Public Library,
Stavros Niarchos Foundation Library
New York, United States of America
Programme: 16,722 m² renovation and transformation of the central circulating library (former Mid-Manhattan Library) including circulating library, 400,000 books, children's library, teens library, business library, adult learning centre, general reading and study spaces, multipurpose space for events and lectures, café and rooftop terrace and garden, LEED Gold certified.
Design: 2015-2018
Realization: 2017-2021
Client: The New York Public Library
Design team: Mecanoo (lead architect) and Beyer Blinder Belle Architects & Planners (architect of record, historic preservation and wayfinding).
Artists: Hayal Pozanti, Melinda Beck
Chair design: Thos. Moser in collaboration with Mecanoo.
Structural engineer: Silman
M&E engineer: Kohler Ronan
Acoustic consultant: Shen Milsom & Wilke
Costs consultant: Stuart Lynn
Fire safety consultant: Code Consultants International
Sustainability consultant: Atelier Ten
Main contractor: Tishman Construction Corporation

6 Come Together

Longgang Cultural Centre
Shenzhen, China
Programme: Cultural complex of 95,000 m² with 13,500 m² public art museum, 10,000 m² science museum, 8,000 m² youth centre, 7,000 m² retail and a 35,000 m² book mall with cafés and restaurants, 21,500 m² of underground parking and a 3.8-ha public square.
Design: 2012-2016
Realization: 2015-2019
Client: Longgang Government, Vanke and SPDG.
Design team: Mecanoo (lead architect) and CCDI (local architect).
Engineering: CCDI
Project management: Jiuzhou Real Estate Company

Heerlen City Hall and Municipal Offices
Heerlen, the Netherlands
Programme: Renovation of the existing landmark City Hall of 6,900 m² and new Municipal Offices of 9,100 m² with public lobby, call centre, offices, meeting centre, entrepreneurs house, co-working space and council chamber including landscape design, totalling 16,000 m².
Design: 2017-2018
Realization: 2019-2023
Client: Municipality of Heerlen; Aannemersbedrijf Jongen BV.
Design team: Aannemersbedrijf Jongen B.V. (contractor), Mecanoo (architect, interior and landscape), ABT (structural and M&E engineer, acoustic, building physics and fire safety consultant) and Dijkoraad (landmark consultant).
Signage and graphic design: Ritzen-Design-Consult
Main contractor: Aannemersbedrijf Jongen BV

Unilever Benelux Headquarters
Rotterdam, the Netherlands
Programme: Interior design for the new Unilever Benelux headquarters on the fourth to ninth floors of a mid-century modern building, including an entrance on the ground floor, a variety of activity-based workplaces, staff restaurant and bars, auditorium, brand hubs, kitchens for development of Unilever brands and displays for Unilever products, totalling 8,400 m².
Design: 2019
Realization: 2019-2020
Client: Unilever Nederland
Design team: Mecanoo
Graphic design: Silo Creative Agency
Structural engineer: Strijbos Constructie Advies
M&E engineer, building physics and fire safety consultant: Royal HaskoningDHV
Project management: Arcadis
Main contractor: Verwol Interieurrealisatie

Amsterdam University College
Amsterdam, the Netherlands
Programme: 5,800 m² liberal arts and sciences college, a compact, sustainable building with class rooms, library, restaurant, living room, project rooms, conference rooms and workstations.
Design: 2008-2010
Realization: 2010-2012
Client: University of Amsterdam; VU University Amsterdam.
Design team: Mecanoo (architect, interior)
Structural engineer: ABT
M&E engineer: Linssen
Building physics, sustainability, acoustic and fire safety consultant: DGMR
Cost consultant: Basalt Bouwadvies
Project management: Arohnsohn
Main contractor: Bouwbedrijf M.J. de Nijs

Manchester Engineering Campus Development
Manchester, United Kingdom
Programme: Technical University of 81,000 m² integrating four engineering faculties (Chemical, Material, Electrical and Mechanical engineering) and two research institutes merged into six buildings, including 76,000 m² of new construction and 4,300 m² renovation. The six buildings include a state-of-the-art new learning environment MEC Hall of 59,000 m², four lecture halls (600, 450, 250 and 150 seats), a wide range of laboratories (1,161 m² laser labs, 8,784 m² dry labs, 2,412 m² chemical labs, 630 m² biochemical labs, 1,141 m² laboratory for electron microscopy and cleanrooms), meeting and conference rooms, workshops, offices, student facilities, café, restaurant, and storage areas, BREEAM Excellent.
Design: 2014-2016
Realization: 2017-2024
Client: University of Manchester
Design team: Mecanoo (lead architect, interior concept, landscape), Penoyre & Prasad (refurbishment and extension of Odd Fellows Hall), BDP (delivery architect).
Engineering: Arup
Environmental sustainability advisor: Buro Happold
Acoustic consultant: Hoare Lea
Cost consultant: Arcadis
Project management: Buro4
Main contractor: Balfour Beatty

7 Touch Me, Feel Me

Netherlands Open Air Museum
Arnhem, the Netherlands
Programme: Project 1: 3,185 m² museum and panoramic theatre with 'HollandRama', including landscape design. Project 2: Museum extension with integration of the permanent national exhibition 'Canon of Dutch History', new entrance pavilion for ticketing and information, update of restaurant and museum shop, including landscape design, totalling 3,300 m².
Design project 1: 1995-1998, project 2: 2015-2016
Realization project 1: 1999-2000, project 2: 2016-2017
Client: Nederlands Openluchtmuseum
Design team: Mecanoo (architecture, interior, landscape)
Project 1:
Structural engineer: Goudstikker-de Vries / ACN
M&E engineer: Technical Management
Project management: ARBA Minch projectmanagement
Cost consultant: Basalt Bouwadvies
Main contractor: Strukton Bouwprojekten
Project 2:
Exhibition design: Kossmanndejong
Structural engineer and building physics consultant: ABT
M&E engineer: Valstar Simonis
Fire safety consultant: Sweco
Main contractor: KuiperArnhem Bouw en Ontwikkeling

Bruce C. Bolling Municipal Building
Boston, United States of America
Programme: 16,700 m² office and community building for the Boston Public Schools Department with community spaces and retail, integrating three listed historical buildings, LEED Gold certified.
Design: 2011-2012
Realization: 2012-2014
Client: City of Boston, MA
Design team: Mecanoo and Sasaki Associates.
Historic preservation consultant: Building Conservation Associates
Engineering: Arup
Lighting consultant: LAM Partners
Construction manager: Shawmut Design and Construction

St. Gerlach Pavilion & Manor Farm
Valkenburg, the Netherlands
Programme: 1,300 m² conference and event pavilion with three multifunctional meeting rooms, lobby, and catering kitchen; 500 m² renovation of the historical Manor Farm, a listed building from 1668, and landscape design of surrounding gardens.
Design 2013-2015
Realization 2015-2017
Client: Landgoed Corneli II, Camille Oostwegel
Design team: Mecanoo (architecture, interior, landscape) and HVN architecten (restoration).
Structural engineer: Palte
M&E engineer, building physics and fire safety consultant: Huygen
Acoustic consultant: LievenseCSO
Main contractor: Coppes/van de Ven

Nelson Mandela Park
Amsterdam, the Netherlands
Programme: Urban masterplan with 700 dwellings and landscape design for a 32-ha urban and nature park and 8-ha sports programme, including gates and bridges.
Design: 2003-2004
Realization: 2009-2011
Client: District Amsterdam Zuidoost
Design team: Mecanoo
Design fence sports park: Dutch Design House Demakersvan
Design game park and playing elements: Carve
Project management: Projectmanagementbureau Amsterdam
Main contractor: Ballast Nedam
Contractor bridges: Haasnoot

Westergasfabriek Terrain
Amsterdam, the Netherlands
Programme: Transformation of the former 13.5-ha Westergasfabriek gasworks in a cultural park, with re-development of 8,000 m² historical industrial buildings and 3,500 m² new development.
Design: 1997-2000
Realization: 2000-2001
Client: Stadsdeel Westerpark, Amsterdam; Projectgroep Westergasfabriek; MAB.
Design team: Mecanoo and Gustafson Porter + Bowman.
Management consultant: MAB
Structural engineer: ABT
M&E engineer: Techniplan adviseurs

Keukenhof
Lisse, the Netherlands
Programme: 3,200 m² entrance building of the world-famous Keukenhof flower gardens, including ticketing, restaurant, retail, visitor facilities and offices, and 1.35-ha landscape design including entrance square with two plazas and combined landscaping and furniture elements.
Design: 2013-2015
Realization: 2015-2016
Client: Stichting Internationale Bloemententoonstelling Keukenhof
Design team: Mecanoo
Structural engineer: IMD

M&E engineer: DWA,
Project management: Frans de Brabander
Main contractor: Van Wijnen

Mekel Park, Delft University of Technology
Delft, the Netherlands
Programme: Masterplan and landscape design for the 10-ha university campus preparing it for the future, pedestrians-, cyclists- and community-focused, adding biodiversity and water management, and integration of bus and tram lines.
Design: 2004-2006
Realization: 2007-2009
Client: TU Delft Vastgoed
Design team: Mecanoo (masterplan, landscape)
Main contractor: Arcadis

Delfland Water Authority
Delft, the Netherlands
Programme: 8,800 m² renovation and restoration of a partly fifteenth-century listed building complex, including a variety of workplaces, restaurant, conference rooms, archive and landscape design of the patios and garden.
Design: 2014-2015
Realization: 2016-2017
Client: Hoogheemraadschap van Delfland
Design team: Mecanoo (architecture, interior, landscape)
Spatial branding and textile: SILO Creative Agency in collaboration with TextielMuseum.
Project management: Heuvel-op
Structural engineer: Zonneveld
M&E engineer: Nelissen Ingenieursbureau
Acoustic, building physics and fire safety consultant: Peutz
Cost consultant: Basalt bouwadvies
Consultant: Draaijer & Partners
Main contractor: Koninklijke Woudenberg

8 Things are Looking Up

Montevideo
Rotterdam, the Netherlands
Programme: 152 metres mixed-use high-rise tower of 57,500 m², including 192 apartments (37,000 m²), 900 m² pool, fitness and service spaces, 6,000 m² offices, 1,600 m² retail and a 8,400 m² parking garage.
Design: 1999-2002
Realization: 2003-2005
Client: ING Real Estate
Design team: Mecanoo (architecture, interior)
Artists: Ineke Hauer; Rick Vermeulen
Structural engineer: ABT
M&E engineer: Schreuder Groep
Acoustic and building physics consultant: Peutz
Cost consultant: Basalt Bouwadvies
Main contractor: BESIX

Icoon
Frankfurt, Germany
Programme: Mixed-use complex totalling 58,000 m², with 55,000 m² residential programme of which 16,500 m² social housing, two underground garage levels, 1,300 m² kindergarten and 1,700 m² commercial functions, 1st prize competition.
Design: 2018-2019
Realization: to be planned
Client: Groß & Partner; Phoenix Real Estate Development
Design team: Mecanoo

Kaohsiung Social Housing
Kaohsiung, Taiwan
Programme: Two residential towers, 45-metre and 42-metre-high, totalling 15,840 m² with 245 units, 870 m² of commercial spaces, 4,050 m² of shared facilities (gym, shared kitchen, reading room and outdoor spaces), kindergarten, parking garage for 130 cars and 280 scooters, and roof gardens and public square.
Design: 2016

Realization: 2018-2023
Client: Urban Development Bureau, Kaohsiung City Government
Design team: Mecanoo (lead architect) and C.M. Chao Architect & Planners (executive architect)
Structural engineer: Supertech

Brink Tower
Amsterdam, the Netherlands
Programme: 90-metre-high, energy-positive residential tower of 30,184 m² including 408 homes (266 rental homes in the middle segment, 120 at affordable rent), a residential care facility, community centre, a communal roof, inner garden, and commercial functions including co-working, a bowling centre with restaurant, and various retail and catering venues.
Design: 2019-2020
Realization: 2022-2025
Client: Xior Student Housing; DubbeLL-Neighbourhood Developers.
Design team: Mecanoo
Structural engineer: Van Rossum
Sustainability consultant: Merosch
M&E engineer, fire safety, building physics consultant: Nelissen
Main contractor: Cordeel

Heungkuk Tower Namdaemun
Seoul, South Korea
Programme: 14-floor building of 5,900 m² with offices and retail.
Design: 2014-2015
Realization: 2015-2017
Client: Heungkuk Life Insurance Co.
Design team: Mecanoo (lead architect) and Hanlim Architecture Group (architect of record)
Facade consultant: Excfirm
Main contractor: TSIS/Donglim E&C

Heungkuk Tower Busan
Busan, South Korea
Programme: 20,000 m² office tower.
Design: 2016
Realization: 2017-2021
Client: Heungkuk Life Insurance
Design team: Mecanoo (lead architect) and DA Group (executive architect).
Facade consultant: Excfirm
Main contractor: TSIS/Donglim E&C

Shenzhen North Station Urban Design
Shenzhen, China
Programme: Urban masterplan for 1.36 million m² development with offices, retail, apartments and hotel, underground parking, connection to public transport hub, design public space, 1st prize competition.
Design: 2017
Client: Government of Longhua District / Urban Planning, Land & Resources Commission of Shenzhen Municipality
Design team: Mecanoo (lead architect) and HSA Architects (local architect).
Facade consultant: VS-A Korea, VS-A Hong Kong

9 On the Move

St. Mary of the Angels Chapel
Rotterdam, the Netherlands
Programme: Chapel of 120 m² on a cemetery.
Design: 1998-1999
Realization: 2000-2001
Client: Roman Catholic Cemetery St. Laurentius
Design team: Mecanoo
Artist: Mark Deconink
Structural engineer: ABT
Cost consultant: Basalt Bouwkostenadvies
Main contractor: H&B Bouw

Hilton Amsterdam Airport Schiphol
Schiphol, the Netherlands
Programme: Hilton hotel with 433 rooms, 4,100 m² meeting and conference centre with 23 meeting rooms,

restaurants, health club, swimming pool, company rooms, lounge areas, a banquet hall for 600 guests and a parking garage for 135 cars, totalling 40,150 m².
Design: 2009-2012
Realization: 2013-2015
Client: Schiphol Real Estate
Design team: Mecanoo (lead architect), Hirsch Bedner and Merx+Girod (interior design lobby, restaurants, meeting centre, health club and guest rooms).
Artist: Israel Paez
Project management: Schiphol Real Estate/CPO
Structural engineer: ABT
Mechanical and electrical engineer, acoustic consultant: Deerns
Sustainability, building physics and fire safety: DGMR
Lighting consultant: dpa lighting
Cost consultant: BBN Adviseurs
Main contractor: Heddes Bouw / Ballast Nedam Bouw & Ontwikkeling Noord.

Delft Railway Station and City Hall
Delft, the Netherlands
Programme: 28,320 m² railway station and city hall, including a 3,550 m² station hall with 850 m² retail spaces; 19,430 m² municipal offices and a 2,230 m² public hall with counters on the ground floor; an archive and loading dock.
Design: 2006-2010
Realization: 2012-2016
Client: Ontwikkelingsbedrijf Spoorzone
Design team: Mecanoo
Ceiling graphics: Geerdes Ontwerpen
Structural engineer: ABT
M&E engineer and acoustic consultant: Deerns
Building physics: LBPSight
Risk analysis: Aboma Keboma
Cost consultant: Basalt Bouwadvies
Main contractor: BAM Utiliteitsbouw

Kaohsiung Station
Kaohsiung, Taiwan
Programme: Site of 8.5 ha with sunken station plaza (13,000 m²), green canopy (35,000 m²), multi-layered bicycle path, landscape (60,000 m²), hotel (22,000 m²), commercial buildings (52,000 m²), local and intercity bus terminal, restoration of colonial Japanese station building, and masterplanning for future developments.
Design: 2014-2016
Realization: 2014-2025
Client: Taiwan Railway Reconstruction Bureau
Design team: Mecanoo (lead design) and PECL, Pacific Engineers & Constructors (local architect).
M&E engineer: PECL, Pacific Engineers & Constructors
Structural engineer: Supertech
Project management: Sinotech, Taipei, Taiwan
Contractor: RSEA Engineering Corporation

Taichung Green Corridor
Taichung, Taiwan
Programme: Transformation of the 1.7 km existing dyke and former railway track into a linear park with herb gardens, street fitness, stepped seating, playground, viewpoint and waterpark.
Design: 2017
Realization: 2018-2020
Client: Taichung City Government
Design team: Mecanoo, S.D Atelier and ARIA architect & planners.

10 Dear Audience

Trust Theater
Amsterdam, the Netherlands
Programme: Transformation and restoration of a listed former Lutheran church (1793) into a 2,700 m² theatre.
Design: 1995
Realization: 1996
Client: Trusttheater
Design team: Mecanoo
Structural engineer: ABT
Mechanical engineer: Ketel
Building physics: Peutz
Project management: J. van Rijs
Main contractor: Konst en van Polen

National Kaohsiung Center for the Arts
Kaohsiung, Taiwan
Programme: Theatre complex of 141,000 m² in the Wei-Wu-Ying Metropolitan Park with a total capacity of 5,861 seats (Concert Hall 1,981 seats, Opera House 2,236 seats, Playhouse 1,210 seats, Recital Hall 434 seats), exhibition space of 800 m², 1,000 m² of rehearsal/education halls for music and dance, two conference halls with 100 and 200 seats and stage building workshops, lobbies and restaurants, the grand covered public space Banyan Plaza, and 7-ha landscape design.
Design: 2007-2009
Realization: 2010-2018
Client: Preparatory Office of The Wei-Wu-Ying Center for the Arts of the Council for Cultural Affairs
Design team: Mecanoo (lead architect) and Archasia Design Group (architect of record).
Acoustic consultant: Xu-Acoustique
Theatre consultant: Theateradvies; Yi Tai
Organ consultant: Oliver Latry
Structural engineer: Supertech
Mechanical engineer: Yuan Tai
Electrical engineer: Heng Kai
Lighting consultant: CMA lighting
Fire safety consultant: Ju Jiang
Roof and facade consultant: CWI
3D consultant: Lead Dao
Traffic consultant: Su International
Main contractor: Chien Kuo Construction

HOME Arts Centre
Manchester, United Kingdom
Programme: Art house of 7,600 m² with two theatre halls (500 and 150 seats), five cinemas (250, 150, 60, 40 and 40 seats), a restaurant, café, roof terrace, gallery, three foyers, bookshop, sponsor's room, offices, rehearsal room, work places, educational spaces, dressing rooms, expedition rooms and a public square, BREEAM Very Good.
Design: 2011-2012
Realization: 2013-2015
Client: Manchester City Council
Design team: Mecanoo (architecture, interior) and Concrete (interior consultant).
Theatre consultant: Theateradvies; Charcoalblue.
Engineering: Buro Happold
Design management, cost consultant: AECOM
Main contractor: Wates Construction

La Llotja de Lleida
Lérida, Spain
Programme: Multifunctional theatre and conference centre of 37,500 m² with a 1,000-seat theatre/conference hall, two conference halls (400 and 200 seats), a multifunctional exhibition hall, two foyers, a lounge, roof terraces, Mercolleida office, 2,600 m² of retail, 9,500 m² of parking, and a public square of 15,000 m².
Design: 2004-2006
Realization: 2006-2010
Client: Centre de Negocis i de Convencions S.A.
Design team: Mecanoo (lead architect) and Labb arquitectura (executive architect).
Structural engineer: BOMA (realization), ABT (competition).
Acoustic consultant: Higini Arau (realization), Peutz (competition).
Mechanical and electrical engineer: Einesa Ingenieria (realization), Deerns (competition).
Security and fire safety consultant: Einesa Ingenieria
Technical architect: J/T Ardèvol i Associats
Cost consultant: J/T Ardèvol i Associats (realization), Basalt Bouwkostenadvies (competition).
Project management: Eptiza S.A. Direcció Integrada
Main contractor: UTE Dragados + Obrum

Kunsthal Art Shows
Rotterdam, the Netherlands
Programme: 'Keith Haring: The Political Line', a 1,400 m² exhibition encompassing drawings, paintings, sculptures, and exhibition shop; 'Peter Lindbergh: A Different Vision on Fashion Photography', a 1,400 m² traveling exhibition presented in nine sections featuring photographic works and supplementary materials; and 'Calder Now', a 1,400 m² exhibition showcasing twenty sculptures and mobiles by Calder, in conjunction with works by ten renowned artists.
Design and realization: 2015-2018
Client: Kunsthal Rotterdam
Design team: Mecanoo

De Nieuwe Schuur
Herpt, the Netherlands
Programme: Mass timber, highly sustainable theatre of 622 m² including several rehearsal and meeting rooms, kitchen, jazz cellar, guest rooms and including circular interior and biodiverse landscape design.
Design: 2018
Realization: 2019-2020
Client: Hans Andersson
Design team: Mecanoo (architecture, interior, landscape)
Structural engineer: Constructie Adviesbureau Geuijen
Mechanical and electrical engineer: Ketelaars-Vroman
Acoustic consultant: Peutz
Building physics and fire safety consultant: ABT
Main contractor: Mecanoo and Derix, Niederkrüchten, Germany

AWARDS

2023

- PROVADA Middle Rent Award 2023 for Brink Tower, Amsterdam, the Netherlands.
- ARCHITECT Light & Architecture Design Awards, Merit Award, Interior Lighting for Martin Luther King Jr. Memorial Library, Washington DC, USA.
- AIA Awards, Interior Architecture Award for Martin Luther King Jr. Memorial Library, Washington DC, USA.

2022

- WAN Awards, Bronze Award, Residential category for KAMPUS, Manchester, United Kingdom.
- AIA Virginia Design Awards, Interior Design Award of Honor for Martin Luther King Jr. Memorial Library, Washington DC, USA.
- Docomomo Modernism in America Awards, Civic/Institutional Design Citation of Merit for Martin Luther King Jr. Memorial Library, Washington DC, USA.
- International Architecture Awards, Library category for Stavros Niarchos Foundation Library, New York, USA.
- FIABCI Taiwan, Real Estate Excellence Awards, Golden Award on Best in Placing and Design for Kaohsiung Social Housing, Taiwan.
- FIABCI Taiwan, Real Estate Excellence Awards, Special Mention on Best of Social Housing for Kaohsiung Social Housing, Taiwan.
- Structural Engineers Association of New York (SEAoNY), Excellence in Structural Engineering Awards, Winner Renovation/Retrofit/Rehabilitation for Stavros Niarchos Foundation Library, New York, USA.
- Architectuurprijs Nijmegen, Jury Prize for Het Rijks Vocational School & Jorismavo, Nijmegen, the Netherlands.
- ALA/IIDA Library Interior Design Award, Public Libraries - over 30,000 sq. ft. category for Stavros Niarchos Foundation Library, New York, USA.
- SARA|NY Design Awards, Special Award for Innovation in Civic Architecture for Stavros Niarchos Foundation Library, New York, USA.
- Architizer A+Awards Jury Winner in the Best in Europe category.
- Architizer A+Awards Finalist in the Best Large Firm category.
- Architizer A+Awards Finalist in the Institutional - Library category for Martin Luther King Jr. Memorial Library, Washington DC, USA.
- WLA Awards - World Landscape Architecture - Award of Excellence in the Built Urban Design category for Taichung Green Corridor, Taichung, Taiwan.
- ICE North West Awards, Large Project of the Year Award for Manchester Engineering Campus Development, Manchester, United Kingdom.
- AIA/ALA Library Building Award for Martin Luther King Jr. Memorial Library, Washington DC, USA.
- Insider North West Residential Property Awards, Apartment Development of the Year (more than 300 homes), HBD and Capital & Centric for Kampus, Manchester, United Kingdom.
- IIDA Mid-Atlantic Chapter Awards, Award of Merit in the Education category and the Pinnacle Award for Martin Luther King Jr. Memorial Library, Washington DC, USA.
- European Union Prize for Contemporary Architecture – Mies van der Rohe Award 2022, shortlisted project for LocHal Library, Tilburg, the Netherlands.

2021

- IDA Design Awards, Silver in Architecture/Institutional for Stavros Niarchos Foundation Library, New York, USA.
- World-Architects winner of the public vote for US Building of the Year for Martin Luther King Jr. Memorial Library, Washington DC, USA.
- Architect's Newspaper, Best of Design Awards, Institutional - Libraries category for Stavros Niarchos Foundation Library, New York, USA.
- Herengracht Industrie Prijs winner for LocHal Library, Tilburg, the Netherlands.
- Richard H. Driehaus Foundation National Preservation Award, Historic Preservation for Martin Luther King Jr. Memorial Library, Washington DC, USA.
- ENR MidAtlantic Excellence in Sustainability, Award of Merit Renovation/Restoration for Martin Luther King Jr. Memorial Library, Washington DC, USA.
- THE PLAN Award, Honorable Mention, Urban Planning/Future category for Railway Zone Dordrecht, the Netherlands.
- The Municipal Art Society of New York, MASterworks Award, Best Adaptive Reuse for Stavros Niarchos Foundation Library, New York, USA.
- European Prize for Architecture by The European Centre for Architecture Art Design and Urban Studies and The Chicago Athenaeum: Museum of Architecture and Design
- AZ Awards, Urban Design Visions, Award of Merit for Railway Zone Dordrecht, the Netherlands.
- Yuan Ye Award, Architecture and Landscape for Tainan Public Library, Taiwan.
- Fast Company's World Changing Ideas Awards 2021, category Transportation, Finalist for RET Metro Interior.
- Female Frontier Award by World Architecture News, Winner Architect of the Year 2021 for Francine Houben.
- Cambridge Design and Construction Awards, commendation best new large building for Key Worker Housing, University of Cambridge, United Kingdom.
- Architizer A+Firm Awards Winner in the Architecture - Cultural category.
- Architizer A+Firm Awards Finalist in the Architecture - Institutional category.
- Architizer A+Firm Awards Finalist in the Best in Europe category.

2020

- Luxury Lifestyle Awards, category Best Luxury Architect Studio in the Netherlands.
- AIT-Award 2020, Best in Interior and Architecture, 2nd prize, category Public Buildings/Culture, LocHal Library, Tilburg, the Netherlands.
- ABB LEAF Awards 2020/21 Lifetime Achievement Winner for Francine Houben.
- Beste Bibliotheek van Nederland Award for LocHal Library, Tilburg, the Netherlands.
- IES Illumination Awards, Award of Merit to National Kaohsiung Center for the Arts, Kaohsiung, Taiwan.
- THE PLAN Award, Honorable Mention, Villa category for Villa Vught, Vught, the Netherlands.
- Chicago Athenaeum, International Architecture Awards, Museums and Cultural Buildings category for National Kaohsiung Center for the Arts, Kaohsiung, Taiwan.
- Architizer A+Awards, Special Mention, Private House (XL >5000 sq ft) category for Villa Vught, the Netherlands.
- TU Delft Alumnus of the Year 2020 for Francine Houben.
- Médaille d'Architecture Fondation Le Soufaché for Francine Houben.
- BUILD's Design & Build Awards, Recognised Leaders in Urbanism and Landscape Design, 2020 - the Netherlands.

2019

- China Construction Engineering Luban Prize for Longgang Cultural Centre, Shenzhen, China.
- International Prize, Prix des Femmes Architectes for Francine Houben.
- INSIDE - World Festival of Interiors Award, Creative Re-use category for LocHal Library, Tilburg, the Netherlands.
- Taiwan Architecture Award, Honorable mention for National Kaohsiung Center for the Arts, Kaohsiung, Taiwan.
- WIN - World Interiors News Awards, Gold Winner, Learning category for LocHal Library, Tilburg, the Netherlands.
- London Design Awards, Silver in the Residential category for Glass Villa on the lake, Lechlade, United Kingdom.
- Dezeen Awards, shortlisted for Architect of the Year in the category Studios.
- Dezeen Awards, Rebirth project of the year for LocHal Library, Tilburg, the Netherlands.
- MIPIM Asia, Silver Award, Best Infrastructure Development for National Kaohsiung Center for the Arts, Kaohsiung, Taiwan.
- MIPIM Asia, Special Jury Award for National Kaohsiung Center for the Arts, Kaohsiung, Taiwan.
- Fast Company's Innovation by Design Awards, category Spaces, Place, and Cities, Honorable Mention for National Kaohsiung Center for the Arts, Kaohsiung, Taiwan.
- DFA Design for Asia Awards, Silver Award for National Kaohsiung Center for the Arts, Kaohsiung, Taiwan.
- Architizer A+Awards, Special Honoree Award for National Kaohsiung Center for the Arts, Kaohsiung, Taiwan.
- Architizer A+Awards, Popular Choice Winner in the Cultural - Hall / Theater category for National Kaohsiung Center for the Arts, Kaohsiung, Taiwan.
- Architizer A+Awards, Jury Winner in the Cultural Hall / Theater category for National Kaohsiung Center for the Arts, Kaohsiung, Taiwan.
- AZ Awards, Adaptive Re-Use, Award of Merit for LocHal Library, Tilburg, the Netherlands.
- NRP Gulden Feniks Award, Category S for LocHal Library, Tilburg, the Netherlands.
- Dutch Design Awards, Habitat category for LocHal Library, Tilburg, the Netherlands.
- BNA Building of the Year'19, Liveability & Social Cohesion Award for LocHal Library, Tilburg, the Netherlands.
- BNA Building of the Year'19, Public Vote Award for LocHal Library, Tilburg, the Netherlands.
- THE PLAN Award, Interior category for LocHal Library, Tilburg, the Netherlands.
- THE PLAN Award, Villa category for Glass Villa on the lake, Lechlade, United Kingdom.
- THE PLAN Award, Honorable Mention in the Culture category for National Kaohsiung Center for the Arts, Kaohsiung, Taiwan.
- Dutch Creativity Awards, Architecture Award for National Kaohsiung Center for the Arts, Kaohsiung, Taiwan.
- European Union Prize for Contemporary Architecture – Mies van der Rohe Award 2019, nomination for Palace of Justice, Córdoba, Spain.

2018

- SDA Design Award, Best Architecture and Spatial Planning, for National Kaohsiung Center for the Arts, Kaohsiung, Taiwan.
- Silver in the New York Design Awards, Architecture - Public & Institutional, for National Kaohsiung Center for the Arts, Kaohsiung, Taiwan.
- BNA Kubus Award for Francine Houben.
- Architizer A+Award, Popular Choice in the category Government & Municipal Buildings for Palace of Justice, Córdoba, Spain.
- MIPIM/Architectural Review, Future Project Award 2018 Commendation, Big Urban Projects for Kaohsiung Station, Taiwan.
- Frame Awards People's Vote, Healthcare Centre of the Year for Zaans Medical Centre, Zaandam, the Netherlands.
- Transportation Concept Award at the RTF Sustainability Awards 2017 for Kaohsiung Station, Taiwan.
- Best Meeting Location of the Year at the Meetings Award 2017 for St. Gerlach Pavilion & Manor Farm, Valkenburg Aan De Geul, the Netherlands.
- Honor Award for Design Excellence at the BSA Design Awards for Bruce C. Bolling Municipal Building, Boston, USA.

2017

- Université de Mons, Belgium, Honorary Doctorate for Francine Houben.
- Digital prize at Idea-Tops Awards for National Kaohsiung Center for the Arts, Kaohsiung, Taiwan.
- De Architect, ARCH17 Award in the category of furniture for HUBB - Learning Environments, the Netherlands.
- RAP Leiden Award, Jury Prize for Langebrug Student Housing, Leiden, the Netherlands.
- Regeneration Award at the Housing Design Awards for Southmere, South Thamesmead, United Kingdom.
- Dedalo Minosse Special Prize, Stanislao Nievo Special Prize for collaboration with Birmingham City Council on the Library of Birmingham, United Kingdom.
- Architizer A+Award, Jury Prize and the popular choice in the category Contract Furniture for HUBB – Learning Environments, the Netherlands.
- Red Dot Award Product Design for HUBB – Learning Environments, the Netherlands.
- Civic Trust Selwyn Goldsmith Award for Universal Design for HOME Arts Centre, United Kingdom.
- Harleston Parker Medal for Bruce C. Bolling Municipal Building, Boston, USA.

2016

- RIBA North West Award for HOME Arts Centre, United Kingdom.
- RIBA National Award for HOME Arts Centre, United Kingdom.
- THE PLAN Award in the office category for Bruce C. Bolling Municipal Building, Boston, USA.
- Boston Preservation Alliance, Preservation Achievement Award for Bruce C. Bolling Municipal Building, Boston, USA.
- Utrecht University, Honorary Doctorate for Francine Houben.
- The Architectural Review, AR MIPIM Future Projects Award, Cultural Regeneration for Longang Cultural Centre, Shenzhen, China.
- Rietveldprijs Foundation Utrecht, Rietveld Prize, special mention for Anne Frankschool, the Netherlands.
- Architects' Journal, Architecture Tomorrow, Highly Commended for Manchester Engineering Campus Development, United Kingdom.
- European Hotel Design Awards, Architecture Award for Hilton Amsterdam Airport Schiphol, the Netherlands.

2015

- Prins Bernhard Cultuurfonds Prize for Francine Houben.
- BAC Craft Award from the International Union of Bricklayers and Allied Craftworkers for most innovative use of masonry for the Bruce C. Bolling Municipal Building, Boston, USA.
- The International Architecture Award from The Chicago Athenaeum Museum of Architecture and Design for the Library of Birmingham, United Kingdom.
- Schueco Excellence Award in the cultural category for the Library of Birmingham, United Kingdom.
- Civic Trust Awards, Selwyn Goldsmith Universal Design Award for Library of Birmingham, United Kingdom.
- Architizer, A+ Award in the category of Architecture + Workplace for Rabobank Westelijke Mijnstreek Advice Centre, Sittard, the Netherlands.
- Architizer, A+ Award in the category of Architecture + Ceiling for the Delft Railway Station Hall, the Netherlands.

2014

- Special Commendation at the annual European competition of the Luigi Micheletti Foundation for Kaap Skil, Texel, the Netherlands.
- RIBA National Award for Library of Birmingham, United Kingdom.
- RIBA West Midlands Building of the Year for Library of Birmingham, United Kingdom.
- RIBA Stirling Prize Nomination for Library of Birmingham, United Kingdom.
- RIBA West Midlands Emerging Architect of the Year for Patrick Arends, Mecanoo.
- Architects' Journal UK Woman Architect of the Year 2014 for Francine Houben.

2013

- Architects' Journal Building of the Year for Library of Birmingham, United Kingdom.
- Korea Color Design Award, Grand Prix for Whistling Rock Golf Club, Chuncheon, South Korea.
- Lieven de Key Medal for Architecture of the City of Haarlem for Sterren College, Haarlem, the Netherlands.
- School Building Innovation Award of the Dutch Ministry for Education, Culture and Science for Sterren College, Haarlem, the Netherlands.
- Property Award, Jury's Special Project for Library of Birmingham, United Kingdom.
- World Architecture Festival Award, Schools Category for Fontys School of Sports, Eindhoven, the Netherlands.
- Amsterdam Architecture Prize 2013 (Golden A.A.P.), Amsterdam University College, the Netherlands.
- Architizer A+ Award, Kaap Skil, Texel, the Netherlands.

2012

- Wood Architecture Award, 2nd prize for Kaap Skil, Texel, the Netherlands.
- Daylight Award 2012, Living Daylights Foundation for Kaap Skil, Texel, the Netherlands.
- International Design Award, second prize cat. other architectural designs for La Llotja de Lleida, Lérida, Spain.

2011

- Dedalo Minosse International Prize, special Commendation for collaboration with Centre de Negocis i de Convencions on La Llotja de Lleida, Lérida Spain.
- Chicago Athenaeum Europe International Architecture Award 2011, La Llotja de Lleida, Lérida Spain.
- Chicago Athenaeum Europe International Architecture Award 2009 for Amphion Theatre, Doetinchem, the Netherlands.
- Royal Town Planning Institute, Commendation for significant contribution to Town Planning in the West Midlands for Library of Birmingham, United Kingdom.

2010

- Chicago Athenaeum Europe Green GOOD DESIGN Award 2010 for design Municipal Offices and Railway Station, Delft, the Netherlands.

2009

- Chicago Athenaeum Europe International Architecture Award 2009 for FiftyTwoDegrees, Nijmegen, the Netherlands.
- Chicago Athenaeum Europe International Architecture Award 2009, National Kaohsiung Center for the Arts, Kaohsiung, Taiwan.
- International Design Award 2009, 1st prize cat. commercial buildings, of IDA, Los Angeles for FiftyTwoDegrees, Nijmegen, the Netherlands.
- International Design Award 2009, 3rd prize cat. Landscape/urban planning, of IDA, Los Angeles for National Kaohsiung Center for the Arts, Kaohsiung, Taiwan.

2008

- Cityscape Architectural Award 2008 of Cityscape Dubai for National Kaohsiung Center for the Arts, Kaohsiung, Taiwan.
- Dedalo Minosse Special Eurotherm Prize for Sustainability2007/2008 for FiftyTwoDegrees, Nijmegen, the Netherlands.
- Veuve Clicquot Business Woman of the Year Award 2008 for Francine Houben.

2007

- Brick Development Association Brick Award for Swimming Pool and Sports Centre Het Marnix in Amsterdam, the Netherlands.
- Honorary fellowships for Francine Houben of the American Institute of Architects and the Royal Architectural Institute of Canada.

2006

- International Highrise Award 2006 for Montevideo, Rotterdam, the Netherlands.
- International Prize Dedalo Minosse 2005/2006 for Montevideo, Rotterdam, the Netherlands.
- National Steel Construction Prize 2006 Nomination for Montevideo, Rotterdam, the Netherlands.
- City of Rotterdam Building Quality Prize 2006 for Montevideo, Rotterdam, the Netherlands.

2005

- Province of South Holland Culture Award for Francine Houben.
- Real Estate Society of Nieuwe Maas in Rotterdam Golden Boulder 2005 Prize for Montevideo, Rotterdam, the Netherlands.

2004

- Ministry of Education, Culture and Science Best School Building Prize 2004 for primary school Het Braambos, Hoofddorp, the Netherlands (design Mecanoo i.c.w. N2 architecten).

2003

- Dutch Building Prize Foundation Dutch Building Prize 2003 for the National Heritage Museum, Arnhem, the Netherlands.
- Foundation Het Zeeuwse Gezicht Zeeuwse Architecture Prize 2003 Second prize for Psychiatric Hospital, Goes, the Netehrlands.
- 5 Dutch Ministries Egg of Columbus prize for innovation and sustainability for the Glass House as Energy Source.

2002

- Association Stadswerk Nederland Extraordinary Idea 2002 Second prize for The Glass Village, Zuidplaspolder, the Netherlands.
- Foundation of Attention to Architecture for the city of Arnhem Heuvelink Public Prize 2002 for residential area The Bastion, Rijkerswoerd, Arnhem, the Netherlands.
- City of Hilversum Architecture Prize 2002, Public Prize Nomination for Oude Torenstraat, Hilversum, the Netherlands.

2001

- Honorary fellowship for Francine Houben of the Royal Institute of British Architecture, United Kingdom.
- Wood Centre, Almere Wood Prize Nomination for National Heritage Museum, Arnhem, the Netherlands.
- The A.M. Schreuders Foundation A.M. Schreuders Prize 2001 for best underground building for Office Villa Maliebaan 16, Utrecht, the Netherlands.

2000

- Fundaçao Bienal de São Paulo, Brazil 4a Bienal Internacional de Arquitectura's Award for the exhibition Mecanoo Blue – Composition, Contrast, Complexity.
- Corus Construction Award for the Millennium for the Library Delft University of Technology, the Netherlands.
- KM Europa Metal Aktiengesellschaft Osnabrück, Germany 'TECU' Architecture Award 2000 for the National Heritage Museum, Arnhem, the Netherlands.
- City of Rotterdam Building Quality Award 2000 for residential area Nieuw Terbregge, Rotterdam, the Netherlands.

1998

- Dutch Steel Building Institute National Steel Construction Prize 1998 for the Library Delft University of Technology, the Netherlands.

1997

- Achterhoek Promotion Prize for Isala College, Silvolde, the Netherlands.

1996

- Ministry of Education, Culture and Science Best School Building Prize 1996 for Isala College, Silvolde, the Netherlands.
- Prize for Public Space Nomination for residential area Herdenkingsplein, Maastricht, the Netherlands.
- Mies van der Rohe Pavilion Award for European Architecture 1996 Nomination for Faculty of Economics and Management, Utrecht, the Netherlands.

1995

- Design Prize Rotterdam 1995 Nomination for Nationale Nederlanden Headquarters and ING-bank in Budapest, Hungary.

1994

- Prize for Public Space Nomination for residential area Ringvaartplasbuurt East, Rotterdam, the Netherlands.
- City of Maastricht Jhr. Victor de Stuerspenning Prize for residential area Herdenkingsplein, Maastricht, the Netherlands.
- Bund Deutscher Architekten Experimental Housing Hugo Häring Prize B.D.A. for Internationale Gartenbau Ausstellung, Stuttgart, Germany.
- Ministry of Education, Culture and Science Best School Building Prize 1994 Nomination for school 'de Brug', Leiden, the Netherlands.
- Ministry of Housing, Regional Development and Environment Bronzen Bever Prize for Building and Housing 1994 Nomination for residential area Park Haagseweg, Amsterdam, the Netherlands.

1993

- Bund Deutscher Architekten for Experimental Housing Auszeichnung Guter Bauten Prize B.D.A. 1993 for Internationale Gartenbau Ausstellung, Stuttgart, Germany.
- City of The Hague Berlagevlag Prize for the offices for Gravura Lithographers, The Hague, the Netherlands.

1987

- City of Rotterdam Rotterdam Maaskant Prize for Young Architects.

FOUR DECADES, 1500 PEOPLE

Aagje Roelofs, Aart Fransen, Acelya Öcalan, Ada Fekete, Ada Petrela, Adam Peavoy, Adrienne Groeneveld, Aernoud van 't Hof, Agnès Mandeville, Agnes van Ommen, Agnieszka Batkiewicz, Agnieszka Radziszewska, Aisrel Magloire-Isidora, Alberto Carbonell, Alberto Favero, Alberto Seller Robles, Alejandra Garcia Hooghuis, Alejandra Martinez, Alejandro Vega Tajada, Aleksandra Danilos, Aleksandra Milanowska, Alenca Mulder, Alessandro Fontanella, Alessandro Luporino, Alessandro Miti, Aletta van Manen, Alex Maas, Alex Pritchett, Alex van Eekelen, Alexander Krol, Alexander Sikkens, Alexandra Berdan, Alexandra Boeva, Alexandra Cosma, Alexandra Häsler, Alexandre Lamboley, Alfa Hügelmann, Alice Soranidi, Alicia Martinez Velazquez, Alijd van Doorn, Allard Assies, Allart Joffers, Allegra Tombolini, Ally Hyun, Alvaro Laanen Baca, Alvaro Viera Rodriguez, Amber van Schaick, Ambra Migliorisi, Amos Gyasi Acheampong Konadu, Ana Fontainhas Carneiro De Azevedo, Ana Rocha, Ana Sofia Pereira Saraiva, Anahita Asgharpour, Analu Almeida Brandao, Andrea Claassen, Andrea Guazzieri, Andrea Klerks, Andrea Möhn, Andreas Buijs, Andres Ambauen, Andrew Hollands, Angela Loman-van der Zee, Angela Moragues Gregori, Angelika Bisseling, Angelique Wisse, Angelos Palaskas, Anja Lübke, Anke van Sluijs, Anna Rusinowska, Anne Busker, Anne Hoekstra, Anne Marie van der Weide, Anne Soutendijk, Annelies Keus-Daeleman, Annelies van der Stoep, Annelies van Eenennaam, Ann-Elise Hampton, Annemarie van der Meer, Annemiek Segeren, Annemieke Diekman, Annemieke Punter, Annemieke van Houte, Annenies Kraaij, Annette Pasveer, Anouk Geutjes, Ans van Reeuwijk, Anthony Barzen, Anthony Hoete, Antje Rohr, Antonio Paoletti, Antonio Sanna, Aoife Rath-Cullimore, Ard Buijsen, Arianna Balboni, Arianna Fornasiero, Arif Bagcivan, Arjan Siebelink, Arjan van der Bliek, Arjan van Toorenburg, Armand Paardekooper Overman, Arne Lijbers, Arno Ottevanger, Arno Smedinga, Arthur Hilgersom, Arthur Kleinjan, Artin Mahmoudi Rodbahne, Arzu Ayikgezmez, Ascen Barranco Martin, Ashleigh Watkins, Ashti Tahir, Aslı Soytürk, Assaf Barnea, Astrid Cornelissen, Astrid Huwald, Astrid Spaink, Astrid van Vliet, Audric Menu, Axel de Stampa, Axel Koschany, Aydan Suleymanli, Ayla Ryan, Barbara Costantino, Barbara van Boxtel, Barbara van de Broek, Barbara Wieland, Bart Brugmans, Bart Koevoet, Bart Rijper, Bart Telleman, Bart Van Den Broek, Bart van der Linden, Bart van der Meer, Bart van Jole, Bart Wolbert, Bartek Winnicki, BartJan van der Gaag, Bas Streppel, Bas van Dijk, Bas Verhagen, Bas Vijn, Bas Weststrate, Bastiaan Jongerius, Begona Garcia Giner, Ben Vincent, Benedetta Lenci, Benjamin Dobbin, Benjamin Kagenaar, Berenike van Manen, Bernhard Vester, Berthe Jongejan, Bianca Breumelhof, Bianca Calzolari, Bianca Wennekes, Birgit de Bruin, Birgit Jürgenhake, Birgit Verburgt, Birgitte Vergouw, Birgitte Wolf-Földesi, Bjarne Buijs, Bjarne Mastenbroek, Bjorn Andreassen, Björn Bleumink, Bob Ronday, Bob Zwinkels, Bob-Willem van Hooft, Bohui Li, Borja Fernandez Goni, Boy de Groot, Boyd Heeres, Branco Giebels, Brenda Bello, Brendan Cormier, Brett Albert, Brigitte Vergouw, Bryan Lelieveld, Busra Coban, Carlo Bevers, Carlos Andrés López Galvis, Carlos De Liniers Martinez, Carlos Espejel, Carmen Da Silva Pereira, Carmen Engelbertink, Cecilia Bottaro, Cecilia Chiappini, Celine Becker, Celio Vrolijk, Cesc Massanas, Charlot Maas, Chess Parera, Ching Mou Hou, Chi-Yi Liao, Chorech Jegoebi, Chris de Weijer, Chris Falla, Chris Luth, Chris Perry, Christa de Bruin, Christian Gafner, Christian Müller, Christian Quesada van Beresteijn, Christina Fernandez, Christina Gestra, Christopher Borges Malheiros, Christopher Falla, Cindy Wouters, Cirella Jongste, Claire Dycha, Claire Oude Aarninkhof, Claire Teurlings, Clara Velez Perez, Claudia Amann, Claudia Ruitenberg, Claudia Schmidt, Claudia Weidhaas, Clemens Nuyens, Cock Peterse, Coco van Egeraat, Coen Ooijevaar, Conny Zingler, Constanza Profumo, Conxa Gene Garcia, Coos van Ginkel, Coosje Tuijtel, Cort Widlowski, Cris Mitry, Cristina Fernandez, Cristina Genovese, Cushla Frances Whiting, Daan Hartman, Daan ter Avest, Daan van der Vlist, Daan Zandbergen, Daisy Maat, Dane Minords, Daniel Behro, Daniele Delgrosso, Daniëlle Buzalko, Daniëlle Huls, Danique Landburg, Danny do Livramento, Danny Lai, Danny van Grieken, Daria Dobrodeeva, Dave van Goch, David Ferreira da Silva, David Vuong, David Willems, Dayo Oladunjoye, Dean Cassano , Debbie Bosch, Defne Bozkurt, Denise Heidema, Dennis Honders, Dennis Krol, Dennis Verdam, Derk Poortvliet, Diana Meinster, Diana Uson, Diana Went, Dianne Anyika, Dick Donhuysen, Dick van Gameren, Dietmar Haupt, Dimitrios Andrinopoulos, Dion Ammerlaan, Dirk Durrer, Dirk Kriesten, Dirk van den Berg, Dolf Schulte, Dorine Vos, Dorthe Kristensen, Douglas Ardern, Douwe de Haan, Ebami Tom, Edith de Jong, Edoardo Nobili, Eduardo Callejo Canal, Eduardo Garcia Diaz, Edwin Tukker, Eefje Hendriks, Efe Gozen, Eirini Trachana, Ekaterina Andrusenko, Elad Eisenstein, Elena Verzella, Elger Secker, Elia Fontani, Eliano Dias Felicio, Elife Koc-Koctas, Elisa Gallazzi, Ella Gerstenkorn, Ellen Burghoorn, Ellen Droogers, Ellen Koring, Ellen Muntinga, Ellen Schindler, Ellen van de Laar, Ellen van der Wal, Ellen van Eck, Els Frankemolen, Els Hazelhof, Els Molenaar, Elvira van der Reijken-van Erven, Emanuel Kiriaty, Emanuele Faccini, Emeline Debackere, Emilie Meaud, Emma Lomas Escribano, Emma van der Staaij, Emma van Eijkeren, Emma Winkler Prins, Emmett Scanlon, Emmy Sterenberg-Weeber, Enes Sever, Enrico Cerasi, Erfan Farahmand, Ergün Erkoçu, Eric de Leeuw, Eric Drieënhuizen, Eric Mesman, Eric van den Berg, Erica Bol, Erich Renner, Erick van Egeraat, Erin Kremers, Ernst ter Horst, Esmee van der Leeden, Eunkyu Hong, Eve Robidoux, Eveline Schildmeijer, Fabio Buondonno, Fabrizio Maiorano, Faisal Samim, Farah Haidar, Fatih Sarikaya, Fay Verplancke, Fedele Canosa, Federica Fogazzi, Federico Biancullo, Federico Fiorino, Federico Nannini, Fedrico Babina, Fernando Silva Gutierrez, Fevzi Köstüre, Filip John, Fleur de Meijer, Floor de Voogt, Floor Hoogenboezem, Floor Moorman, Floris Overheul, Fouad Addou, Francesca Guerrieri, Francesco Garofalo, Francesco Nardacci, Francesco Pasquale, Francesco Veenstra, Francine Houben, Franck Del-Zotto, Frank Huibers, Frank Kühne, Frank Rocks, Frank Segaar, Frank van Gameren, Frederico Nunes Francisco, Frederique van Andel, Freek Lindeman, Friedemann Römhild, Friso van der Steen, Gabriel Kozlowski Maia, Gareth Williams, Geer Klijn, Geerte Baars, Geert-Jan van Damme, Gemma Biesheuvel, Gemma Tico Mananich, George Orfanopoulos, George Taran, Georgia Katsi, Gerben Jan van Harten, Gerben Modderman, Gerrit Bras, Gerrit Schilder, Gert Jan van der Harst, Gert Wiebing, Gertjan Bestebreurtje, Gido Murk, Gijs Sluijter, Giorgio Larcher, Giovanni Gentili, Giovanni Mortilli, Giusseppina Borri, Gonzalo J. Lopez Garrido, Gonzalo Zylberman, Graciëlla Torre Sidawy, Greg Davey, Gretha Kuurstra, Gualtiero Rulli, Guido van Veghel, Gulce Onganer, Guus Peters, Guy Scott, Gwenda Westhoven, Hadi Boudouch, Haneen Al Hafadhi, Hank van 't Wout, Hanna Euro, Hannah Elenbaas, Hanne Kjeldsen, Hanneke Hollander, Hanneke van der Heijden, Hanneke van Etten, Hannes Krimpelstätler, Hans Berger, Hans Goverde, Hans Hidskes, Hans Schepman, Hans van der Heijden, Hans van der Horst, Hao Wu, Harald Kurzhals, Harry Boxelaar, Haw-Wei Liou, Heikki Viiri, Heleen Bothof, Helga van Wijk, Henk Bouwer, Henk Döll, Henny Pries, Herng Tzou, Hieke Bakker, Holger Wirthwein, Hratc Hovanisian, Hugo Schut, Huib de Jong, Huw Wiliams, Ibrahim Vural, Ida van den Hoogen, Iemke Bakker, Igor Freire De Vetyemy, Ilonis Bairamidis, Iman Nasre Esfahani, Immanuel Tashiro, Ineke Dubbeldam, Ineke Meijer, Ines De Almeida Lourenco, Ines Ferreira, Ines Quinteiro Antolin, Inez Spaargaren, Inga Hilburg, Ingo Hörig, Ingrid Oron, Inma Fernandez Puíg, Irgen Salianji, Irina Niculescu, Iris Mastenbroek, Isabel Potworowski, Isabella Banfi, Israel Paez Lopez Bravo, Iulia Cruceru, Iulian Pînzaru-Stănescu, Ivan Nevzgodine, Ivo de Bruin, Ivo de Nooijer, Izabela Boinska, Jaap de Vries, Jaap Duenk, Jacky Choi, James Bayless, James Harper, James Murray, James Taylor-Foster, Jan Bekkering, Jan Kees Dibbets, Jan Kooi, Jan Kudlicka, Jan Maarten van Hemert, Jan van der Lans, Jan van Spanje, Jana Schultz, Jana Zuntychova, Janica Sipulova, Janneke Nijs, Janos Tiba, Jarno Koenen, Jarno van Iwaarden, Jasmijn Kok, Jason Torres, Jasper Griep, Jasper Kaarsemaker, Jasper Tonk, Javier Briasco Garcia, Javier Sancho Andrés, Jayden Baltus, Jaytee van Veen, Jean Pierre Droge, Jeanne Lev, Jeannette de Jong, Jeffrey Reule, Jennifer Schrage, Jeroen Dollé, Jeroen Ekama, Jeroen Hamers, Jeroen Harmsen, Jeroen Luykx, Jeroen Nanne, Jeroen Schipper, Jeroen Schröder, Jeroen Snellens, Jeroen van Zutphent, Jesse van Keeken, Jessica Cullen, Jevgeni Shirokov, Jie Wang, Jill Vogels, Jim Njoo, Jiyun Lee, Jo Edwards, Joan Alomar Mateu, Joana de Castro Ribeira Pereira Cancela, Joanna Cleary, Joanna Dendewicz, Joanna van Vreeswijk-Hoevers, Job van Eldijk, Job van Stralen, Jochen Eggert, Joëll Thepen, Johan Hanegraaf, Johan Kralt, Johan Selbing, Johan van der Esch, Johanna Clearly, Johanna Irander, John Brown, John Buijs, John Kraak, Johnathan Dall, Johnno Peters, Joke Klumper, Joke Nowee, Jonathan Connerney, Joost Laméris, Joost van Bree, Joost van der Graaf, Joost Verlaan, Joost Vlot, Joost Woertman, Jop van Beek, Jordy Vos, Jorren Verheesen, José Albuquerque de Sousa, Jose Ingles, Josephine van den Born, Joyce van der Knaap, Judith de Jongste, Judith Egberink, Judith Gieseler, Judith Hopfengärtner, Judith Siegeler, Julia Hogervorst, Julia Luger, Julia van Gent, Julia van Oosterhout, Julian Hooijmans, Julie Bonder, Julien Merle, Juliette Brouwer, Julin Ang, Juraj Palovic, Jurre van Kuijk, Just Popp, Jutta Rentsch, Kaan Kalak, Kai den Hollander, Karien Hofhuis, Karin Uittenbogaart, Karin van Viegen, Karina Sultan, Karlijn Borremans, Karoline Poorter, Karsten Buchholz, Kasia Orzechowska, Kasper Zoet, Katharina Sander, Kathrin Siebert, Kathrin Weiss, Katinka Buters, Katja van Dalen, Katrien Donneux, Kedi Zhou, Kerem Masaraci, Keren Zhang, Kerstin Hahn,

Keshia Groenendaal, Ketty Voltat, Kika Notten, Kimberly van Dijk, Kirsten Reekers, Knut J. Wentink, Koen Heslenfeld, Kolja Preuss, Konstantina Georgoula, Kotaro Horiuchi, Kristel Aalbers, Kristin Jensen, Kristin Schaefer, Kristina Schönwälder, Kristof Houben, Lada Hrsak, Laertis Vassiliou, Lantos Pin, Lars Spuybroek, Laura Alvarez Rodriguez, Laura Blauw, Laura Maria Jaime Fraga, Laurens Kistemaker, Laurens Schuitmaker, Laurens Veth, Laurie Neale, Leanne van de Erve, Leartis Vassiliou, Leen Kooman, Leen Temmink, Leo Oorschot, Leon Delhez, Leon van der Velden, Leonardo Zuccaro Marchi, Leonie Brinks, Lester Wilson, Leticia Balacek, Lex van Opstal, Lidwien Pikkemaat, Lieke Koen, Lies Spruit, Liesbeth van Brakel, Linda Chamorro, Linda den Hartog, Linda Kronmüller, Lisa Boer, Lisa Gerards, Lisette Magis, Lisette Plouvier, Liza Kormilets, Loes Oudenaarde, Loren Supp, Lorenzo de Vecchi, Lotte van der Zee, Louisa Hollander, Louise Bjork, Louise Rogier, Louiza Chafi, Lowie Swinkels, Luca Laponder, Luca Pozzati, Luca Sassi, Luca van Egeraat, Lucia Polito, Lucretia van Groningen, Lucy Knox-Knight, Luís Pires, Luisa Rainer, Lukas Drasnar, Lukas Kuncevicius, Lutz Mürau, Luuk Bijleveld, Luuk van de Berg, Luuk van den Elzen, Luuk van Wijlick, Luuk Verweij, Lyanne Oosterhof, Lydia Fraaije, Lydia Giokari, Maaike Bruins, Maarten Dickhoff, Maarten Hartman, Maarten Tenten, Maarten van Bremen, Maarten Wijsman, Maartje Lammers, Maartje van de Berg, Machiel Broeren, Machteld Schoep, Machthild Stuhlmacher, Maddalena Idili, Madeleine Deshaires, Madieke Reijn, Magdalena Curdova, Magdalena Stanescu, Magnus Weightman, Maksym Rokhmaniiko, Malou Speets, Manfredi Bozzi, Manfredi Valenti, Manon Schrage, Maor Vernik, Marc Fleer, Marc Kellerman, Marc Prins, Marc Prosman, Marc Roos, Marc Springer, Marcel Davidse, Marcel Kellner, Marcello Licitra, Marcia de Boer-Bennemeer, Márcia Lima Gonçalves Da Costa, Marcio Rodrigues, Marck Vrieling, Marco van Zal, Marcos Rodriguez, Maria Aller Rey, María Castrillo Carreira, Maria Dominguez Abreu, Maria Garcia, Maria Garcia Orille, Maria Hänsch, Maria Castillon Espert, Maria Vasiloglou, Mariagiulia Pistonese, Mariana Meneguetti, Marie-Anne Souloumiac, Marie-Fleur van der Valk, Marieke Pouw, Mariëlle Strampraad, Marielle Strampraad-Zonderop, Marije Hoornstra, Marije Kitselaar, Marijke Gantvoort, Marilisa Lino, Marina Kounavi, Mario Rudelli, Marion Gruber, Marja Stam, Marjolein Verbist, Marjolijn Adriaansche, Marjolijn Hoelen, Mark Adam, Mark Jongerius, Mark Kanters, Mark Peter, Markus Freigang, Marleen Klompenhouwer, Marlies Boterman, Marloes Dijkink, Maroš Belopotocký, Marta Roy Torrecilla, Marta Teixeira de Carvalho, Martijn Meester, Martijn Potters, Martin Stoop, Martin Zamazal, Martine Prokop, Marzena Staron, Mateo Kuypers, Mathis Meyer, Matilde Tavanti, Matt Morris, Matteo Gioacchini, Matteo Meschiari, Matteo Missaglia, Matthew Murphy, Matthew Nicholl, Matthew Strong, Matthijs de Stigter, Mattia Cavaglieri, Mauro Parravicini, Mauro Saenz de Cabezon Aguado, Max Fukkink, Maxe van Heeswijk, Maxime Heng, Mazlum Django, Mechtild Stuhlmacher, Mehmet Emin Yildiz, Meinou van der Kooi, Melina Sharp, Mendel Robbers, Mercedes Garcia Ballester, Merel Miedema, Merel Smit, Michael Dax, Michael Gore, Michael Seeling, Michael Thistle, Michael Woodford, Michal Czeszejko-Sochacki, Michel de Kok, Michel Parlevliet, Michel Tombal, Michelle Pals, Michelle Zwiers, Michiel Akkerman, Michiel Raats, Michiel Verkroost, Mieke Nagtegaal, Mike Mur, Mike Pennings, Mike van Rheenen, Mike Vink, Milad Besharat, Milda Liubinskaite, Milo Greuter, Miranda Nieboer, Miriam de Rover, Miriam Fitzmorris, Mirjam de Heer, Mirjam van Dam, Mitchel Ovens, Mohebullah Ehsan, Monica Adams, Monika Mullen, Monique Voogd, Mustapha Chatar, Myrtille Ferté Fogel, Nadia Pahladsingh, Najmus Chowdhry, Naomi Cheung San, Nasim Razavian, Natacha Chaves, Natalia Leszczynska, Natalia Nikolopoulou, Nathalia Vigaray, Nathalie de Vries, Nathalie Frankowski, Nathalie Jansen, Nathalie van Mullem, Nelleke van Gulik, Nestor Montenegro, Nick Marks, Nicky Sluis, Nicole Carstensen, Nicole Haustermann, Nicolet Bekker, Nicolo Lewanski, Nicolo Riva, Niek Nesheretov, Niek van de Calseijde, Niels Hoeve, Niels Onderstal, Nienke Andersson, Nienke Smits van Burgst, Nilvia Coffy, Nout Sterk, Nuno da Graça Ribeiro, Nuno Gomes Moura, Nuno Gonçalves Fontarra, Olga Banchikova, Olga Korstanje, Olga Pedryc, Oliver Boaler, Olivier Brouwez, Omar El Hassan, Ondrej Palencar, Oriol Peus, Oscar Benet Ramos, Ottavia Sarti, Otto Diesfeldt, Otto Driessen, Otto Fitzi, Pablo Baena Vega, Paddy Tomesen, Pamela Laloge, Paolo Rossetti, Paolo Turconi, Pascal Tetteroo, Patricia Tamayo Perez, Patricia van den Berge, Patrick Arends, Patrick Eichhorn, Patrick Koschuch, Patrick Longchamp, Patrycja Ogonowska, Paul Daly, Paul Dijkstra, Paul Ketelaars, Paul Meurs, Paul Numan, Paul Thornber, Paul van den Hof, Paula Nooteboom, Paul-Martin Lied, Paulo Vieira Borralho, Pavel Matyska, Pedro Campos da Costa, Peggy van der Wijck, Pepijn Holthuis, Perry Klootwijk, Peter Bakker, Peter Batenburg, Peter Bruijkers, Peter Claeys, Peter Donker, Peter Haasbroek, Peter Hong, Peter Jollie, Peter Plaisier, Peter van der Schans, Peter Vervoorn, Peter Williams, Petra Postler, Pia Fischer, Pieter Hoen, Pieter Klomps, Pieter Krog, Pieter Spoelstra, Pieter Voogt, Pim Köther, Pipa Voogd, Polina Strukova, Qian Li, Qian Ren, Qian Yang, Quijng Wu, Rachel Lin, Radu Matei, Rajiv Sewtahal, Ramiro Losada Amor, Ramon Wijsman, Ramona Verhoek, Rasa Gravite, Rashanie Ramautar, Raymond Duivesteijn, Rebecca Lopes Cardozo, Rebecca Weijand, Reem Saouma, Regien Kroeze, Remco Theunissen, Remko Eppink, Renate Gobius du Sart, René Bouman, Renee Nycolaas, Renée van Gennip, Reuske Groenewold, Richard Hagg, Richard Smit, Rick de Lange, Rick den Oudsten, Rick Splinter, Rik Boijmans, Rik Kuipers, Rik Verberk, Rikkert van Bellen, Rina Sanders, Rinie Mersel, Rinske van der Hout, Rixt Bouman, Roan van Marrewijk, Rob Koningen, Rob Lemaire, Robbert Guis, Robert Alewijnse, Robert Osinga, Robert Schoutsen, Robert Uijttewaal, Robert van Driel, Robert van Rij, Roberta Ciccarelli, Roberto Pavan, Robin Kerssens, Roderick Tong, Rodney Kastelan, Rodrigo Bandini dos Santos, Rodrigo dos Santos Louro Flor, Roel Bosch Reitz, Roel van der Sman, Roel Wijmans, Roel Wildervanck, Roelf Steenhuis, Roelof Heida, Rogier Coopmans, Rogier Laterveer, Rohan Varma, Rombout Loman, Rombout Reijnders, Ron van Logchem, Ronald Dumas, Roos van Duuren, Rosa van Hijfte, Rose Goehring, Rossella Donetti, Rozemarijn Frima, Rozemarijn Maleki-Tabrizi, Ruben Buno Heslinga, Ruben Pluimers, Ruben van der Plas, Rudi le Hane, Rui Didier, Rui Pedro Silva Alves Fernandes, Ruoxi Wang, Ruth Lorenz, Ruth Visser, Ryan Fat Leong, Ryan van Kanten, Sabrina Friedl, Safiye Janson, Salar Bagheri, Sam Austin, Sanda Lenzholzer, Sander Boer, Sander Malschaert, Sander Meert, Sander van der Drift, Sander van Santen, Sander Vijgen, Sandra Bouwman, Sandra d'Urzo, Sandra Hoogendijk, Sandra Sequeira, Sandra Sneekes-Pacqué, Sandra Vegter, Sanne Oehlers, Sanne van Bekkum, Sara Carbonera, Sara di Lallo, Sara Hammond, Sara Navrady, Saskia Fokkema, Saskia Groenendijk, Saskia Hebert, Saskia Heusmann, Sebas Veldhuisen, Sebastiaan Kaal, Sebastian Winkler, Seger Bekkers, Selin Gülsen, Sem Hartman, Sergio Martinez Gutierrez, Sergio Pinto, Sérgio Tavares Andrade, Shabnam Otaderian Mozaffarian, Shachar Zur, Shadan Amien, Shahir Malikzai, Shakar Musa, Shangjun Cai, Shannon Perdijk, Sharmila Nasheed, Shima van der Ster, Shin Sakuma, Siebold Nijenhuis, Sijtze Boonstra, Silvia Albers, Silvia de Nolf, Simon A. Kallionen, Simon Bush King, Simon Nuñez de Arenas Fraile, Simona Rossi, Simone Costa, Simone Creemers, Simone Drost, Simone Koch, Simone op den Kamp, Simone van der Linden, Simone Venditti, Sinéad O'Flanagan, Sjaak Janssen, Sjoerd Redel, Sjoukje van Heesch, Sofia Azevedo, Sofia Pereira, Sophie den Ouden, Sörel Chitoe, Sorin Bompa, Stanley Dynamus, Stef de Wit, Stefan te Vaarwerk, Stefan Werrer, Stefano Corbo, Stefano Sabatino, Stephan Collier, Stephan Mosler, Stephan Moylan, Stephan van Berkel, Stephanie Kol, Stephanie Tunka, Steven Anton, Steven van Kooten, Su Jeong Park, Sun Ming Lee, Sunmin Whang, Susan Konu, Susan Veldhuis, Susana Ayres, Susanna Horn Jardemark, Susanne Hendriks, Susanne Pietsch, Susanne Pisciella, Susanne Vijverberg, Suse Koch, Sven Ove Cordsen, Sylvia Albers, Sylvia Pijnenborg, Sylvie Beugels, Sylvie Bruyninckx, Ta Chi Ku, Taco Oost, Tamara Klassen, Tania Lemke, Tania Sanjurjo, Tanja Broekhuijsen, Tanja Eggert, Tanja Lebsanft, Tessa de Rijk, Theo Kupers, Thijs van Waveren, Thomas Drenth, Thomas Huacuja-Gallmann, Thomas Scheepens, Thomas Schonder, Thomas van Schaick, Thomas-Luuk Borest , Tijmen Sanderink, Tijn van de Wijdeven, Tijs den Uijl, Tim van Beurden, Tim Vogel, Tjalling Cohen Tervaert, Tjeerd Roelsma, Tjerk Webbers, Tobias Manzke, Tom Berkhout, Tom Bruins Slot, Tom Grootscholten, Tom Manwell, Tom van Kats, Tom Vanhaelen, Tomas Løvset, Tomasz Crompton, Ton Muller, Ton Salman, Toon de Wilde, Tristan Battistoni, Tsai-Ling Shih, Uda Visser, Ulf Schrader, Ursula Fritz, Valdeta Bajrami, Valentijn Yousif, Valjdeta Bajrami, Vanessa Lamounier de Assis, Vanessa Ramdas, Vanessa Wegner, Veerasu Sae-Tae, Verena Steiner, Veronika Mutalova. Victor Fuentes Del Valle, Victor Serbanescu, Ville Nurkka, Vincent Hector, Vincent Taapken, Vittorio Fragasso, Viviane Chan, Vladimir Konovalov, Wai H. Tsang, Wan Jen Lin, Wei Huang, Wei Zhou, Wendy Verhoef, Wendy Voorwinde, Wieke Villerius, Will Lindley, Willeke Joffers, Willeke Smit, Willem de Groot, Willem Jan Snel, William Richards, William Yu, Willmar Groenendijk, Wilson Lai, Wim van Zijl, Winod Bansie, Wiro Boomstra, Wouter Hesterman, Wouter Huynen, Wouter van de Bor, Xian Chen, Yan Shi, Yana Daynovich, Yentl Odinot, Yichun He, Yinan Yu, Yinxian Zhang, Ylber Kahuqi, Yolanda Dullaart, Yuanyuan Chen, Yuli Huang, Yun Dai, Yun Ying Chiu, Yura Markin, Yuri Sigmond, Zain Kiyani, Zarisheili Melendez Ortega, Zhiyu Li, Ziyang Xu, Zjhounathan Evans.

CREDITS

Editors:
Francine Houben, Hanneke Hollander, Eliano Felicio

Texts:
Herbert Wright

Copy editing:
Leo Reijnen, Taal & Teken

Design:
Jelle F. Post in collaboration with Eliano Felicio, Mecanoo Annemieke van Houte, Mecanoo: chapter 'Four Decades of Mecanoo'

Lithography: BFC, Bert F.C. van der Horst, Amersfoort
Printing and binding: Wilco, Amersfoort
Paper: 130 grams Galerie Art mat (insides)
Production: Marja Jager, nai010 publishers
Publisher: Eelco van Welie, nai010 publishers

© 2023 Mecanoo and nai010 publishers, Rotterdam. All rights reserved. No part of this publication may be reproduced, stored in a retrieval system, or transmitted in any form or by any means, electronic, mechanical, photocopying, recording or otherwise, without the prior written permission of the publisher.

For works of visual artists affiliated with a CISAC-organization the copyrights have been settled with Pictoright in Amsterdam.
© 2023, c/o Pictoright Amsterdam

Although every effort was made to find the copyright holders for the illustrations used, it has not been possible to trace them all. Interested parties are requested to contact nai010 publishers, Korte Hoogstraat 31, 3011 GK Rotterdam, the Netherlands.

nai010 publishers is an internationally orientated publisher specialized in developing, producing and distributing books in the fields of architecture, urbanism, art and design. www.nai010.com

nai010 books are available internationally at selected bookstores and from the following distribution partners:
North, Central and South America - Artbook | D.A.P., New York, USA, dap@dapinc.com

Rest of the world - Idea Books, Amsterdam, the Netherlands, idea@ideabooks.nl

For general questions, please contact nai010 publishers directly at sales@nai010.com or visit our website www.nai010.com for further information.

Printed and bound in the Netherlands.

ISBN 978-94-6208-560-2
NUR 648
BISAC ARC000000, ARC011000

MECANOO People, Place, Purpose, Poetry
is also available as e-book:
ISBN 978-94-6208-824-5 (e-book)

Photography and Illustrations (by page order):
Thijs Wolzak: p. 13, 16 (bottom), 17 (top and middle right), 294-295.
Christian Richters: p. 14, 15 (bottom right), 22 (top), 23 (middle left, bottom left and right), 162 (top left), 165 (top), 166-167, 264-265, 268-271, 290 (top right and bottom), 390-391, 394 (top), 396-397, 436-437, 438 (top), 439 (top and bottom left), 466-467, 469 (top), 470, 472 (bottom), 473.
Machteld Schoep/Mecanoo: p. 16 (top), 17 (middle left and bottom), 29, 30 (bottom), 31-33, 76-77, 80-81, 140-141, 158-159, 165 (bottom), 192-193, 198-199, 218-219 (top centre), 288-289, 291-293, 296-297, 300-302, 304-305, 306 (top), 307 (bottom), 308-311, 314 (middle and bottom left), 315, 317 (top), 323 (bottom right), 324 (top), 324-325 (bottom middle), 325 (top), 326-327, 328 (top), 329-330, 336 (top right and bottom), 337 (top), 340-341, 342 (top), 343, 344-345, 395 (bottom), 398-403, 404-405, 407 (bottom), 408, 410-413, 439 (bottom right), 460-461, 462 (bottom left), 463, 464 (top), 465, 474-475, 476-485.
Sijtze Boonstra: p. 19, 21, 22 (bottom), 23 (top and middle right), 444, 451, 457.
Harry Cock: p. 25-27, 142 (bottom), 147 (bottom), 161 (bottom left), 162 (top right, middle and bottom), 163-164, 246 (top), 314 (top and bottom right), 313 (bottom), 317 (bottom), 355, 395 (top), 442-443 (top middle), 442 (bottom), 468 (bottom), 471 (top).
Mecanoo: p. 30 (top), 45, 47, 48-53, 55-63, 70 (top and bottom left), 71 (bottom left), 78 (bottom left), 84, 88-91, 110-111, 114 (bottom left), 115, 116-119, 120-123 (top and bottom left), 124-127, 130 (top), 131-133, 160, 161 (top), 180 (bottom), 181 (middle and bottom), 195 (top right and bottom right), 196-197, 204 (bottom), 205 (middle and bottom), 206, 209 (bottom), 210 (bottom), 211 (bottom), 216 (top right), 217, 244 (bottom), 247 (bottom), 266-267, 274 (top and bottom right), 275 (bottom), 290 (top left), 299, 321, 335 (bottom), 337 (bottom), 338-339, 352 (top), 353 (top), 358-363, 370-373, 380-385, 418-419, 421, 424, 428 (bottom and middle), 442 (top left), 443 (top right), 446, 453, 488, 489 (top).
Fernando Alda: p. 35, 37-43.
Greg Holmes: p. 68-69, 71 (top and bottom right), 72-75, 82-83, 85-87, 144-145, 147 (top), 272-273, 275 (top), 276-283, 353 (bottom right), 462 (top).
Mariashot.photo: p. 92-93, 94 (bottom), 95.
Blue Sky Images: p. 94 (top), 96-97.
Ossip van Duivenbode: p. 98-105, 142 (top), 143, 146, 148-149, 151-157, 184 (top), 185-186, 187 (top, middle left and bottom), 213, 218 (top left and bottom), 220, 221 (top left and right, bottom right), 222, 224, 226, 228, 242-243, 246 (bottom), 247 (top), 248, 249 (top), 251 (bottom), 252-257, 258-259, 260 (top), 261-263, 324 (bottom left), 325 (bottom right), 332-333, 336 (top left and middle), 350-351, 353 (bottom left), 354, 356-357.
Ethan Lee: p. 168-169, 171-173, 174 (top), 175-176, 364-369, 416-417, 420, 422-423, 425, 426-427, 428 (top), 429-431, 449, 454.
Robert Benson: p. 178-179, 182 (top), 184 (bottom), 188, 190 (top).
Trent Bell: p. 182 (bottom), 182-183, 187 (middle right), 189, 190 (bottom), 191.
Max Touhey: p. 200-201, 223 (bottom), 225, 227 (bottom).
John Bartelstone: p. 202-203 (top and bottom right), 204 (top), 205 (top), 207 (top and bottom right), 208, 209 (top), 210 (top), 211 (top), 212, 214-215, 219 (bottom), 221 (middle and bottom left), 227 (top), 229.
Stijn Poelstra: p. 486-487, 489 (bottom), 490 (top and middle right), 491, 492-493.
Others: Joann Dost & David Michael: p. 23 (bottom right); Mateusz Plinta: p. 36 (bottom left); De Nederlandsche Bank: p. 46; Gert Eijkelboom: p. 47 (bottom); Museum Boijmans Van Beuningen: p. 54; Stadsarchief Rotterdam: p. 112-113; Eric Fecken: p. 114 (middle); Frank de Roo: p. 114 (top); Stadsarchief Dordrecht: p. 123 (bottom right); John Gundlach: p. 128-129; Adobe Stock: p. 130 (bottom); Collection Regionaal Archief Tilburg: p. 150 (top left and bottom); Melissa GirlEatWorld: p. 170 (bottom); Tainan Public Library: p. 174 (bottom); Yu-Chen Chao: p. 177; Time Life magazine collection/ Shutterstock: p. 180 (top left); Franz Jantzen: p. 181 (top); The New York Public Library: p. 194, 195 (top left), 203 (bottom left), 207 (bottom right), 216 (bottom left), Pierce Harrison: p. 221 (middle right); Thos. Moser: p. 223 (top); Zhang Chao: 234-241; Gemeente Heerlen: p. 244 (top left); Rijckheyt: p. 245 (top); Klaus Tummers: p. 245 (bottom), 249 (bottom), 251 (top); Philip Driessen: p. 250; Broekbakema: p. 274 (bottom left); Boston Archive: p. 298; Esto Photographics Inc: p. 303; Air-Vision Luchtfotografie: p. 306 (bottom); Etienne van Sloun: p. 307 (bottom); Aerophoto Stock: p. 312-313, 316 (top); Siebe Swart: p. 318-319, 322, 331, 335 (top); Gemeentearchief Amsterdam: p. 320 (top left); Thomas Schlijper: p. 323 (top and bottom left); Fotografische Dienst TU Delft: p. 334; Collection Stadsarchief Delft: p. 342 (bottom); Kyungsub Shin: p. 374-379; Scief Houben: p. 394 (bottom); Ronald Tilleman: p. 407 (top), Mauritshuis: p. 406 (top); Geerdes Ontwerpen: p. 409 (top); Jared Chulski: p. 414-415; Iwan Baan: p. 440-441, 450; Andrés Gallardo: p. 445, 456 (bottom), 458-459; Shawn Liu Studio: p. 447, 448; National Kaohsiung Center for the Arts (Weiwuying): p. 452, 455, 456 (top); Paul Karalius: p. 462 (bottom right), 464 (bottom); La Fotográfica: p. 469 (bottom), 471 (bottom), 472 (top); Tammy van Nerum_De Beeldunie: p. 490 (middle left and bottom).

Four Decades of Mecanoo:
p. 503: Charles and Ray Eames, by Eames Office, LCC. Álvaro Siza, by Teresa Siza.
p. 504: Space for Space, Botanical Lab and Library, Faculty of Economics and Management, House with Studio, Herdenkingsplein, by Christian Richters.
p. 505: Library Delft University of Technology, by Greg Holmes. St. Mary of the Angels Chapel, Trust Theater, 4a International Architecture Biennale São Paulo, by Christian Richters.
p. 506: Office Villa Maliebaan 16, by Christian Richters. Toneelschuur Theatre, by Joost Swarte.
p. 507: Montevideo, FiftyTwoDegrees, by Christian Richters. Mekel Park, by Siebe Zwart.
p. 508: Whistling Rock Golf Clubhouse, by Sytze Boonstra. La Llotja de Lleida, by Christian Richters.
p. 509: Rabobank Advice Centre, Amsterdam University College, Fontys School of Sport Studies, National Kaohsiung Center for the Arts (Banyan Plaza), by Christian Richters. National Kaohsiung Center for the Arts (bird view), by Kouzi Isita.
p. 510: Exhibition *A People's Palace*, by Adriaan van Dam. World Trade Centre, by Christian Richters. Hotel The Place Taipei, by Ethan Lee. Hotel The Place Tainan, by Harry Cock. Zinzia Psychiatric Care Centre, by Ossip van Duivenbode.
p. 511: Prins Bernhard Cultuurfonds Prize, by Robin Utrecht. Het geheim van Montevideo (design), by Jelle Post. Kunsthal Exhibitions, by Kunsthal Rotterdam. A legacy of Mies and King, by Time Life magazine collection/ Shutterstock.
p. 512: OBA Mercatorplein Branch Library, by Ossip van Duivenbode. Heungkuk Tower Namdaemun, by Kyungsub Shin.
p. 513: Opening ceremony of the National Kaohsiung Center for the Arts, Kaohsiung Station, by Shawn Liu Studio. Henk Bouwer, by Harry Cock. BNA Kubus, by Just Justa Fotografie. LocHal Library, by Ossip van Duivenbode. De Nederlandsche Bank, by Gert Eijkelboom. NS Vision Interior Train of the Future, by Maaike Poelen.
p. 514: Key Worker Housing University of Cambridge, by Greg Holmes. Co-Creation Centre & Nonohouse, by Ossip van Duivenbode. Longgang Cultural Centre, by Zhang Chao.
p. 515: Villa Vught, Villa BW, Unilever Benelux Headquarters, World Port Centre, Blaak555, by Ossip van Duivenbode. Glass Villa on the Lake, by Mariashot.photo. Tainan Public Library, by Ethan Lee. Martin Luther King Jr. Memorial Library, by Robert Benson. Stavros Niarchos Foundation Library, by John Bartelstone.
p. 516: Taichung Green Corridor, Kaohsiung Social Housing, by Ethan Lee. Kampus, Manchester Engineering Campus Development, by Greg Holmes.
p. 517: Heerlen City Hall and Municipal Offices, by Ossip van Duivenbode.

All remaining images are copyrighted by Mecanoo.

In remembrance of Machteld Schoep (1962-2019). As Mecanoo's in-house photographer, Machteld captured many of Mecanoo's projects in a way that allowed one to immerse oneself.